The MILITARY and DEMOCRACY in ASIA and the PACIFIC

The MILITARY and DEMOCRACY in ASIA and the PACIFIC

R.J. May & Viberto Selochan
Editors

ANU
THE AUSTRALIAN NATIONAL UNIVERSITY
E PRESS

ANU

E PRESS

Published by ANU E Press
The Australian National University
Canberra ACT 0200, Australia
Email: anuepress@anu.edu.au
Web: http://epress.anu.edu.au
Previously published by Crawford House Publishing Pty Ltd
Bathurst 2795 New South Wales, Australia

National Library of Australia Cataloguing-in-Publication entry

The military and democracy in Asia and the Pacific.

Includes index.
ISBN 1 9209420 1 7
ISBN 1 9209420 0 9 (Online document)

Civil supremacy over the military – Asia. 2. Civil supremacy over the
military Pacific Area. 3. Militarism – Asia. 4. Militarism – Pacific
Area. 5. Democracy – Asia. 6. Democracy – Pacific Area. 7. Asia –
Politics and government. 8. Pacific Area – Politics and government.
I. May, R. J. (Ronald James), 1939– . II. Selochan, Viberto, 1957– .

322.5

All electronic versions prepared by UIN, Melbourne
Cover design by Michael Birch with a photo by
George Gittoes, courtesy of the Australian War Memorial, Canberra

CONTENTS

PREFACE

Over the past decade the military in a number of countries has played an important role both in bringing about changes of political regime and in resisting pressures for change. This volume, whose compilation was undertaken within the context of the Regime Change and Regime Maintenance in Asia and the Pacific project of the Australian National University's Department of Political and Social Change, Research School of Pacific and Asian Studies, brings together a number of prominent regional specialists to take a fresh look at the military's changing role in selected countries of Asia and the island Pacific, with particular regard to their performance against criteria of democratic government. The book provides a sequel to Selochan's earlier collection, *The Military, the State, and Development in Asia and the Pacific* (Westview, 1991).

Claire Smith, Bev Fraser and Allison Ley again provided expert midwifery in bringing the book into being and our colleagues Harold Crouch and Bob Lowry made helpful comments on the manuscript. As always it has been difficult to avoid being overtaken by events and we are grateful to our co-contributors for their forbearance in providing updates and waiting out the (mostly) inevitable delays in finalising the volume.

V.S. and R.J.M.
Canberra

PREFACE TO THE ANU E PRESS PUBLICATION

We are fortunate to be able to produce this title six years after the initial publication of *The Military and Democracy in Asia and the Pacific*. It forms part of an ANU E Press series that is intended to make critical research done at The Australian National University available to a wider readership.

The original edition of *The Military and Democracy in Asia and the Pacific* was undertaken within the context of the Regime Change and Regime Maintenance in Asia and the Pacific project of The Australian National University's Department of Political and Social Change, Research School of Pacific and Asian Studies, bringing together a number of prominent regional specialists to look at the military's changing role in selected countries of Asia and the Pacific.

As the original edition sold out, we hope that this new publication will reach an even wider audience who can reflect on the issues raised in this volume and watch with interest the developments within the region.

CONTRIBUTORS

Emajuddin Ahamed is professor and chairman of the Department of Political Science at the University of Dhaka, Bangladesh, and former pro vice chancellor of that university. His numerous publications include *Military Rule and Myth of Democracy* (1988) and *Society and Politics in Bangladesh* (1989).

Suchit Bunbongkarn is professor and head of the Department of Government at the Political Science Faculty, Chulalongkorn University, Bangkok, Thailand. He was an adviser to former Prime Minister Prem Tinsulanoud from 1981 to 1987. His many publications on Thai politics include *The Thai Military in Politics 1981-1986* (1987).

Stephanie Lawson is a fellow in the Department of International Relations, Research School of Pacific and Asian Studies at the Australian National University. Her doctoral thesis from the University of New England, Australia, on *The Failure of Democratic Politics in Fiji*, was published by Oxford University Press in 1991 and she has recently completed a book on *Tradition and Democracy in the South Pacific*.

Ronald J. May is senior fellow in the Department of Political and Social Change, Research School of Pacific and Asian Studies at the Australian National University, and former director of the Papua New Guinea Institute of Applied Social and Economic Research (now National Research Institute). He is a graduate of Sydney and Oxford universities and has published extensively on the politics of Papua New Guinea and the Philippines, including *The Changing Role of the Military in Papua New Guinea* (1993).

Yung Myung Kim is a graduate of Seoul National University and the State University of New York at Buffalo and currently associate professor in Political Science at Hallym University, Chunchon, Kangwon-do, Korea. He has written on various aspects of Korean politics, including civil-military relations.

Hasan Askari Rizvi is professor and chairman of the department of Political Science at the University of the Punjab, Lahore, Pakistan. He holds a doctorate from the University of Pennsylvania. Dr Rizvi's many publications include *The Military and Politics in Pakistan* (1986) and *Pakistan and the Geostrategic Environment* (1993).

Viberto Selochan is a graduate of the Australian National University and former research fellow at the Centre for the Study of Australia-Asia Relations at Griffith University, Australia, currently working with the Australian Department of Foreign Affairs and Trade. He is the author of *Could the Military Govern the Philippines?* and editor of *The Military, the State, and Development in Asia and the Pacific* (1991). His PhD thesis on 'Professionalisation and Politicisation of the Armed Forces of the Philippines' is being prepared for publication.

Josef Silverstein has recently retired as professor and chairman of the Department of Political Science at Rutgers University, USA. He is a leading authority on Burma, whose extensive publications include *The Political Legacy of Aung San* (1972), *Burma: Military Rule and the Politics of Stagnation* (1977), and *Burmese Politics: The Dilemma of National Unity* (1980).

Michael Vatikiotis is a graduate of the London School of Oriental and African Studies who has spent a number of years in Southeast Asia working for the BBC and as bureau chief and ASEAN correspondent for the *Far Eastern Economic Review*. His book on *Indonesian Politics Under Suharto* was published in 1993.

1

INTRODUCTION: DEMOCRACY AND THE MILITARY
IN COMPARATIVE PERSPECTIVE

R.J. May, Stephanie Lawson and Viberto Selochan

From the processes of decolonisation which dominated the political history of Africa, Asia and the island Pacific in the mid twentieth century, most post-colonial states emerged with constitutional structures inherited from, or at least heavily influenced by, the Western democratic models of former colonial powers. Among the principal general features of such constitutions were: separation of the legislature, executive and judiciary; popularly-elected legislatures in which competitive political party systems were expected to provide the basis for a division between government and opposition; and the subservience of the military (whose primary role was generally seen to lie in defending the country against external aggression) to the civil authorities.

In the early stages of decolonisation it was expected that indigenous armies, following the models set by the metropolitan powers which created them, would refrain from direct involvement in politics. Nevertheless, even in those newly independent states in which the military did not gain a political inheritance by virtue of its role in the winning of independence, rather than imbuing the armed forces with a military professionalism which required absolute obedience to the civil authority, colonial rule left behind armed forces more often oriented towards maintaining internal order than to external defence, and therefore implicitly attuned to domestic politics. This was particularly evident in states marked by strong ethnic cleavages, where colonial policies often involved the recruitment of military personnel from those ethnic groups which appeared most compliant (see below).

In fact, shifts from parliamentary democracy to one-party or military-dominated regimes were not long in coming. Africa had its first military coup in 1958 and there were coups in Burma, Thailand and Pakistan in the same year. A torrent of military interventions followed during the 1960s and 1970s. Between 1945 and 1976, Nordlinger (1977:xi) estimated, more than two thirds of the countries of Latin America, Asia, Africa and the Middle East had experienced varying levels of military intervention. A study of sub-Saharan Africa between 1960 and 1982 alone recorded 90 plots to overthrow governments, 60 attempted coups, and 50 successful coups (Orkand Corporation quoted in Seitz 1991:65). In 1977 La Palombara commented: 'Military coups are now so frequent and widespread they must be considered as significant as elections' ('Foreword' in Nordlinger 1977:x); even earlier, Janowitz (1971:306) wrote:

> The intervention of the military in the domestic politics [of non-Western states] is the norm; persistent patterns of civil supremacy are the deviant cases that require special exploration.

Because military interventions were widely seen as a denial of the democratic values and institutions which retiring colonial powers had hoped to establish in the new states, considerable scholarly attention was devoted to explaining why and how military coups occurred. Explanation was sought in the motives of coup leaders, the structure of the military, and in predisposing and facilitating socio-economic, political, and external conditions.[1]

Early scholarship sought the reason for military intervention in the relative 'underdevelopment' of civil political institutions. More specifically, some writers argued that in new states the military typically was more cohesive, better organised, more 'rational', and more strongly committed to modernisation than the rest of society, including politicians, and that military intervention was a predictable response to the inefficient and often corrupt administration, and political fractiousness, which characterised the civil government in many new states.[2] For those who saw a strong state as a necessary precondition for economic develop-

---

[1]   There have been numerous attempts to review the copious literature on military coups (see, for example Lowenthal 1974; Hoadley 1975; Nordlinger 1977; Perlmutter 1980; Ball 1981; Valenzuela 1985; Kennedy and Louscher 1991). We will not repeat that exercise here, though some features of the debate will be highlighted.

[2]   Among a number of studies which broadly pursued this theme, major contributions included Shils (1962); Pye (1962, 1966); Finer (1962); Johnson (1962); Halpern (1963); Riggs (1964); Janowitz (1964); von der Mehden (1964); Huntington (1968); Zolberg (1968); Daalder (1969); Dowse (1969); Lefever (1970); Bienen (1971, 1983); Lissak (1976); Perlmutter (1977, 1981); more recently see Crouch (1985) and Chazan et al. (1988).

For some dissenting views see Lee (1969); Welch (1974a); Mazrui (1976). Mazrui in particular saw the military, in Africa, as likely to 'retraditionalise'; similarly see Crouch (1979) on the 'neo patrimonialism' of the military in Indonesia.

ment, military intervention was not necessarily a bad thing (for example, see Lefever 1970). Such a viewpoint, however, raised some big questions: in particular, if the military intervened because the institutions of civil government were 'underdeveloped' or not working well, what chance was there of civil institutions ever developing? Although military coup leaders frequently presented themselves as intervening temporarily, once out of the barracks they were seldom in a hurry to return; moreover the actions of military rulers – banning political activity, suspending constitutions, imposing media censorship, and so on – were frequently inimical to the development of civil politics.

An alternative line of explanation saw military establishments as motivated less by a culture of rationality, sound management, and modernity than by its corporate interests. Military intervention was especially likely, they argued, when the military was marginalised or fiscally deprived, or its interests, autonomy, or 'professionalism' threatened. (See, for example, Janowitz 1964; First 1970; Bienen 1971; Hakes 1973; Thompson 1973; Nordlinger 1977; Horowitz 1980; Rouquié 1987.)

In both these approaches the military was seen essentially as a cohesive entity with a sense of collective identity. A third school of thought, in contrast, portrayed the military as simply an extension of the larger civil society, subject to the same class, regional and ethnic cleavages, prone to internal friction, and likely to side with particular political factions at particular times. Taking this argument further, Decalo (1976) suggested that the reasons for military coups were to be found in the personal ambitions of coup leaders. The idea that the military was at least potentially fragmented had particular salience in those states in which the military had a specific ethnic bias, often the result of deliberate colonial policies of recruiting from 'martial races' or from ethnic minorities rather than dominant ethnic groups which might thus be given the means to challenge colonial rule (Daalder 1969; Guyot 1974; Kabwegyere 1974; Mazrui 1976; Hansen 1977; Nordlinger 1977; Enloe 1980; Horowitz 1985; also see Gow 1991). The role of social class, on the other hand, was contested: while some saw the military as likely to pursue the interests of the middle class, others saw it as characteristically cutting across class interests. (Major contributors to this debate include Huntington 1968; Lloyd 1973; Halpern 1963; Nordlinger 1977; Alavi 1979; Luckham 1979; Perlmutter 1981; Nun 1967, 1986.) Inter-generational tensions, and rivalries between age cohorts and political factions within the military were seen to be increasingly significant as the number of coups – especially 'second round' coups – increased; Seitz (1991:70) estimated that 'intra-military elite factionalism' accounted for about a third of the plots, attempted coups and coups recorded in the Orkand Corporation study (see above).

Several studies distinguished various *types* of coup and coup attempt, ranging from those (typically first coups) which sought to set up new regimes, through internal military putschs, to 'coups' directed against regime change (for example, see Huntington 1968; Hoadley 1975; Chazan et al. 1988; Luckham 1991).

Of course, these various 'explanations' were not necessarily mutually exclusive: a state in which there was an imbalance in development between the institutions of state control and those of popular participation, for example, was probably more vulnerable to intervention to assert the military's corporate interests. 'Isolating "The Cause" of a *coup d'etat*', Welch (1974a:135) suggested, 'is a fruitless exercise. Personal, organisational and societal factors are intermingled'. Moreover, as Horowitz (1980:8) suggested, different explanations were sometimes appropriate to different *levels* of explanation (if in fact, they *explained* anything at all). Not surprisingly, then, a growing body of case studies provided support, in varying degrees, for all of these hypotheses, suggesting that while there were some recurring characteristics of military intervention, the explanation of individual cases required an understanding of their particular historical and social circumstances.

With military or civil-military regimes becoming increasingly the norm in Africa, Asia, Latin America and the Middle East, from around the mid 1970s students of the military began to shift the focus of their enquiry from explaining coups to a second enterprise, that of assessing the relative performance of military regimes. Early writings on military intervention in politics tended, as we have seen, to regard military intervention as essentially anti-democratic, but to see military regimes as probably more capable than democratic civilian regimes of achieving modernisation and development. A series of studies in the 1970s and early 1980s (for example, Nordlinger 1970, 1977; Schmitter 1971; Hoadley 1975; McKinlay and Cohan 1975, 1976; Jackman 1976; Zuk and Thompson 1982) addressed this question in fairly broad terms but found that, in terms of performance (variously defined), military regimes did not form a distinctive regime type. Heeger (1977:247) went further, suggesting that for Africa and Asia in the decade 1965-1975, 'most military regimes have hindered the development of their countries'. More recently Seitz (in Kennedy and Louscher 1991) has concluded from a study of 38 sub-Saharan African states that there is 'no significant discernible pattern separating the *economic* performance of military and civilian regimes' (ibid.:7, italics added). Crouch (1985, 1988), addressing the record of the military and development in Southeast Asia for the period 1970-1985, also dismissed the particular role of the military as a decisive factor; he went on to emphasise the significance for economic development of maintaining political stability but concluded that in this respect, too, the military's record was mixed.

Measures of *political* performance, on the other hand, seem to show a more definite pattern: Nordlinger (1977), for example, looking at four measures of political performance (legitimisation, noncoercive rule, minimisation of violence, and responsiveness to popular wishes), concluded that the performance of military governments 'is significantly and almost consistently poorer than that of civilian governments' (ibid.:197). More recently, Finer (1991), using Freedom House data, notes that all but two out of 36 military governments (i.e. 94 per cent) were ranked as authoritarian and lacking basic civil freedoms, compared to 60 per cent of 73 civilian regimes. Nevertheless, the only safe – if unexciting – generalisation seems to be that, as stated by Luckham (1991:22), 'Military regimes are usually but not invariably authoritarian, and authoritarianism frequently but not always involves rule by soldiers'.

As more and more states came to experience periods of military rule it also became obvious that stereotypical models of military rule were inadequate. In some countries the military, or factions within the military, had simply made a blatant grab for power; in others the military intervened to replace an ineffective or corrupt civilian government with the stated intention of handing power back to civilian rule; in still others the military and civilian authorities established a system of joint participation in government. Consequently, a third major endeavour of the literature on the military in politics has been to differentiate types of military and civil-military regime. Janowitz (1964) made an early distinction between five types of civil-military relations, which he labelled authoritarian-personal control, authoritarian-mass party, democratic competitive and semi-competitive systems, civil-military coalition, and military oligarchy. Welch (1974a) suggested a distinction between personalist, corporatist and interventionary professionalisationist military regimes. Nordlinger (1977) distinguished military regimes by their role, as moderators, guardians or rulers. (Similarly see Perlmutter's [1981] classification of arbitrator and ruler praetorian regimes.) Perlmutter (1980), arguing that, 'The modern military regime is distinctly and analytically a new phenomenon, restricted to the developing and modernising world' (p.96), suggested a fivefold typology, dividing military regimes into corporative, market-bureaucratic, socialist-oligarchic, army-party and tyrannical. Finer (1991), confining himself to countries in which the current regime is the outcome of a previous illegal usurpation and in which the head of state is a member of the military, and adopting a more structurally-oriented classification, divides military governments into three sub-types: the military junta (or stratocracy), the presidential type, and those (perhaps more properly regarded as authoritarian civilian states) which, while founded by a military coup, have a civilian cabinet and a (limited) competitive party system and legislature.[3] What is emphasised by these (and other) authors, however, is not simply the variety of military regime types (or in Finer's terms, subtypes) but the lack of a clear dividing line between military and civilian regimes. As Heeger (1977:243) put it:

> It has become increasingly apparent that the rigid dichotomy between 'civilian' and 'military' regimes cannot be maintained . . . the transition from military rule can be seen in one sense as a transition from one mixed system to another mixed system.

Similarly, Finer (1982:282) argued that 'the class of "military regimes" embraces a number of distinct subtypes which merge, gradually, into civilian regimes', and Bebler (1990) proposed a continuum of civil-military relations, whose opposing extremes he called 'civilocracy' and 'militocracy' and whose middle ground was occupied by equal partnership arrangements, dual hierarchies, and 'fused' systems. Bebler went on to observe:

> Whether officially recognised or not, the military everywhere constitutes an important part of the state apparatus and of the political system, and the soldiers, even when sound asleep in their barracks, participate in the political process and tacitly share political power with civilian rulers (ibid.:262-63).[4]

A further aspect of the discussion of military regime types lay in the recognition that the role of the military may change over time. Huntington (1968:221) observed:

> As society changes, so does the role of the military. In the world of oligarchy the soldier is a radical; in the middle-class world he is a participant and arbiter; as the mass society looms on the horizon he becomes the conservative guardian of the existing order.

---

[3]   In an earlier paper, Finer (1982) presented a 'morphology of [32] military regimes', ranging from 'military-supportive civilian regimes', through 'indirect-military regimes', to 'military regimes proper', based on an analysis of 'who governs'. Also see Luckham (1971) and Bebler (1990).

[4]   Also see Finer (1962, 1985); Lee (1969); Lloyd (1973); Bienen and Morell (1974); Heeger (1977); and Perlmutter (1981); however cf. Luckham (1991: 2): 'The more one looks at [the military], the more it decomposes like the vanishing smile of the Cheshire cat, into the turbulent social and political forces that swirl around it. Yet the more one seeks to explain its role in relation to those forces, the more its military specificity is brought (like the smile) back into focus'. Even Bebler, having introduced the idea of a civilian-military continuum, argues against those who deny the perceptual validity of the civilian-military dichotomy, that 'in every society, at any given moment, there is a demarcation line considered as "normal" by the leading political forces' (Bebler 1990:265). (Also see Nordlinger 1977:xii.)

On the other hand, Welch and others suggested that once in power military regimes changed systemically – in Welch's (1974a) analysis from personalism to corporatism to interventionary professionalism; in Perlmutter's (1981) analysis, from arbitrator to ruler and back to arbitrator. Studies of the military in Latin America in 1970s suggested that a more fundamental, secular change was taking place in the military's perception of its role: increasingly, Stepan and others argued, soldiers were taking on civilian roles of administration, management and economic enterprise.[5] Stepan (1973, 1978) referred to this as the 'new professionalism'. Such a military role expansion was evident in Southeast Asia in the 1960s, and Lissak (1976:13), writing about Thailand and Burma, spoke of 'the penetration of the officer corps, either collectively or as individuals, into various institutional fields, such as economic enterprises, education and training of civilian manpower, fulfilling civilian administrative functions, and engaging in different forms of power politics'. In Indonesia, the 'civilianising' of the armed forces had been anticipated even before 1960s.[6]

In part, the role expansion of the military in the Third World has reflected a shift in predominant concern, from external defence to internal security (embracing civic action programs and the growth of paramilitary forces).[7] But in part also it has been a strategy by which military regimes have sought to consolidate and legitimate their role in government, especially where that role has been challenged by civilians or external actors, or threatened by factionalism from within.

This suggested a further issue for investigation: the question of 'exit' – how can the army, once in power, be returned to the barracks? As early as 1962 Finer observed that, 'In most cases, the military that have intervened in politics are in a dilemma: . . . they cannot withdraw from rulership nor can they fully legitimise it' (1962:243). In fact, of course, some coup-makers did withdraw; indeed Finer (1985) later acknowledged that, 'Most military regimes . . . have very short lives', and went on to review the practice and theory of military withdrawal in terms of two principal alternatives – institutionalisation (essentially what other writers have termed 'civilianisation') and abdication. Following Sundhaussen (1984,

---

[5]   An early review of this literature is contained in Lowenthal (1974).

[6]   More recent discussions of the 'new professionalism' of the military in Southeast Asia are contained in Soedjati and Yong (1988) and Selochan (1990).

[7]   Some recent tendencies are discussed in Sarkesian (1981); Stepan (1988); Goodman, Mendelson and Rial (1990:Part III); Zagorski (1992); Burk (1993), and Ashkenazy (1994).

1985), Finer suggested that the conditions for military withdrawal parallelled, in reverse, those for military intervention, and identified two sets of dispositions and societal conditions for withdrawal; successful abdication, he concluded, required that the personal, corporate and ideological interests of the military be protected, and that the party or party system to which the military handed over be 'organised, not unwise, and in effective control of the country' (Finer 1985: 30). Contemporaneously with Finer's analysis of 'the retreat to the barracks', Clapham and Philip (1985) rephrased the dilemma for military regimes as being to develop a mechanism for succession without jeopardising their own supreme position; they saw six likely alternative outcomes – handback, civilian renewal, authoritarian clientelism, factional clientelism, and military party state, and 'just another impasse' (as when the military, under pressure, hands power back to a weak civilian state). (Also see Finer 1962; Huntington 1968; Welch 1971, 1974b; Bienen and Morell 1974; Heeger 1977; Nordlinger 1977; Needler 1980; Horowitz 1980; *Third World Quarterly* 7(1) 1985; Danopoulos 1988.)

However, as Heeger (1977:244) warned:

> . . . in speaking of the military's withdrawal from politics one risks exaggeration. The transfer of formal political power to civilians may be accompanied by a full-scale return to the barracks on the part of the military. More likely, however, is the emergence of the military in a somewhat less prominent, but no less political, role.

Typically, military personnel, having seized power, sought either to consolidate their position, penetrating civil society (sometimes setting up military-backed parties) and discouraging opposition, or to shift from a 'caretaker' role by restoring civilian governments while maintaining a guardian or veto role and strengthening linkages with civilian politicians and business people. Cases of a single military intervention, followed by consolidation or withdrawal, have in fact been unusual; more common have been cycles of greater and lesser military involvement of politics.[8] 'Proclaimed intentions', Finer (1985:17) observes,

> . . . usually bear little relationship to the outcome. Rulers who intend to hand power back to civilians and do so are rare . . . Rulers who say they so intend but in fact hang on to power are more common . . . Rulers who make no promises to hand back, or openly propose permanent military rule are very common . . . But rulers of this intention who actually succeed in carrying it out are most uncommon.

---

[8]   Thus, although Finer observes that most military regimes have very short lives, he also notes that: 'Few civilian successor regimes have lasted more than ten years' (1985:29).

At this point the literature on the military in politics converges with the burgeoning body of writing on regime change (see, for example, Linz and Stepan 1978; O'Donnell, Schmitter and Whitehead 1986; Diamond, Linz and Lipset 1988, 1990; Goodman, Mendelson and Rial 1990). Specifically, the recent perceived trend towards democratisation in parts of Latin America, Africa and Asia has revived interest in questions of military withdrawal, though as Luckham (1991: 12) reminds us, 'the installation of a military government [and, per contra, the withdrawal of the military from government] by no means always adds up to a change of regime'.

The questions raised here, and others, have, of course, been substantially addressed both at the theoretical level and in a growing volume of case studies, including comparative Asian and Pacific studies (among the latter, see Guyot and Willner 1970; Hoadley 1975; Zakaria and Crouch 1985; Olsen and Jurika 1986; Soedjati and Yong 1988; Heinz, Pfennig and King 1990; Selochan 1991b). In the light of the current discussion of 'transitions to democracy', however, and especially in view of the recent experience of some Asia-Pacific countries in resisting democratisation (Burma, China, arguably Indonesia, Singapore and Tonga) or moving away from it (Fiji, and arguably Malaysia), it seems worth revisiting some of the central concerns of the literature. More specifically, we have approached the topic within the framework of a larger interest in the processes of regime change and regime maintenance in Asia and the Pacific (see May 1994), since it is clear that the military has played a major role both in bringing about changes of regime and in forestalling change.[9]

The principal questions which this volume addresses, therefore, are, first, what role has the military played in regime change and maintenance in the countries of Asia and the Pacific, and, second, have differences in the degree of military involvement in politics been systematically associated with differences in the performance of the political system, particularly its performance in relation to democratic criteria?

Before turning to the case studies presented in this volume, however, it is necessary to reflect briefly on some key concepts.

---

[9]   Cf. Luckham (1991:10): 'Rather than analysing coups as such, we might do better to consider them as part of a much wider process of transformation: firstly as a subcategory of a broader class of regime changes or political transitions; and secondly as one among several different channels through which military power can influence politics'.

Democracy and the Military

Huntington (1957), in a study based primarily on the history of the military in Western societies), elaborated what was widely accepted as the liberal democratic model of civil-military interaction. '[T]he principal responsibility of the military officer', Huntington said, 'is to the state':[10]

> Politics is beyond the scope of military competence, and the participation of military officers in politics undermines their professionalism . . . The military officer must remain neutral politically . . . The area of military science is subordinate to, and yet independent of, the area of politics . . . The military profession exists to serve the state . . . The superior political wisdom of the statesman must be accepted as a fact (Huntington 1957:16, 71, 73, 76).

The idea of the subservience of the military to civilian authority, as Grundy (1968) has pointed out, follows a tradition going back to Plato.[11] Huntington, however, challenged the simple identification of civilian control with democratic government, and military control with absolute or totalitarian government: the military may undermine civilian control in a democracy, he argued, acquiring power by legitimate processes,[12] and within a totalitarian system the power of the military may be reduced by such means as creating competing military or paramilitary units or by infiltrating it with 'political commissars'. 'Subjective civilian control', he concluded, 'thus is not the monopoly of any particular constitutional system' (ibid.:82). Huntington went on to distinguish five patterns of civil-military relations, based on differing relative degrees of military/anti-military ideology, military power, and military professionalism (see ibid.: chapter 4), but as evidenced in his later study (Huntington 1968), for Huntington military 'intervention' represented an essential breakdown of the liberal democratic political order.

While Huntington's concept of military professionalism has remained influential, the spate of post-independence military coups in the new states of Africa and Asia from the late 1950s prompted a more critical examination of the relation between civilian government and the military. Some commentators, indeed,

---

10   In context, Huntington appears to equate 'state' with 'government'; the significance of distinguishing 'state' from 'government' is discussed below.

11   Also note von Clausewitz (1832/1968:405): '. . . subordination of the military point of view to the political is . . . the only thing which is possible'.

12   For a recent statement of this theme, drawing primarily on US experience, see Johansen (1992).

suggested that the presumed neutrality and separation of the military from politics was at best a Western concept, if not a complete fiction (see, for example Perlmutter 1980:119; Valenzuela 1985:142; Ashkenazy 1994:178). Not only did military intervention sometimes occur in response to the effective breakdown of democratic civil regimes – with the ostensible aim of *restoring* democracy, and often with substantial popular support – but in some new states, notably the communist 'people's republics' and the 'guided democracy' of Indonesia's President Soekarno, an alternative model of 'democracy' was espoused, in which the military was seen as an integral part of the political system rather than, as in Huntington's formulation, an agency outside the political realm.[13]

That a variety of political regimes, in which the pattern of relations between civilian politicians and the military covers a broad spectrum, should claim to be 'democratic' is testimony to the popularity of the term in international political discourse. Such popularity reflects the extent to which the term acts as an agent of political legitimation in a world where democracy is accepted, at least rhetorically, as a universal 'good'. But can military regimes ever be described as democratic? Or, indeed, are they necessarily anti-democratic? Gallie's (1956) formulation of democracy as an 'essentially contested concept' lends support to a relativist position, the extension of which is that democracy can mean all things to all people. As Hewison, Robison and Rodan (1993:5) point out, this effectively denies the possibility that any universal understandings can be reached and serves to 'indemnify the most scurrilous of dictatorships and to undermine the legitimacy of democratic and reformist oppositions'. On the other hand, too narrow a definition, especially with respect to institutional forms, is unrealistic.

One way of dealing with this definitional problem is to acknowledge that regimes measure up differently against various criteria of democracy, and that the idea of a continuum from more democratic to less democratic is the most useful and meaningful approach to the problem of analysing and comparing regimes. Diamond, Linz and Lipset (1990:6-7), for example, define democracy in terms of three essential and generally accepted conditions: meaningful competition for government office; a high level of political participation; and a level of civil and political liberties sufficient to ensure competition and participation. They recognise, at the same time, that 'countries that broadly satisfy these criteria, nevertheless do so to different degrees' and that the 'boundary between

---

13   See, for example, Albright's (1980) critique of Huntington's 'conceptual framework' on the basis of the experiences of sixteen communist states. On civil-military relations in communist states, also see Perlmutter (1982) and Herspring and Volgyes (1978).

democratic and undemocratic is sometimes blurred and imperfect' (ibid.:7; see also Dahl 1989:112; Hadenius 1992; Sørensen 1993; Lawson 1993).

For military rulers, however, the widespread association of democracy with civilian supremacy has created a particular crisis of legitimacy. A central pillar of modern democratic theory is the doctrine of constitutionalism which, in its simplest form, refers to limited government, a system in which any body of rulers is as much subject to the rule of law as the body of citizens. An important corollary to the democratic doctrine of constitutionalism is civilian supremacy (though this in itself is not a sufficient condition for democracy since, as Huntington pointed out, many non-democratic governments maintain civilian control over their military and police organisations). Democracy requires, therefore, not only that armed forces be subject to civilian control, but that 'those civilians who control the military and police must themselves be subject to the democratic process' (Dahl 1989:245). A fundamental principle of the democratic model of civilian supremacy in civil-military relations resides in the important distinction between the state and the legitimate government. It is to the latter that the military owes its primary allegiance, and any implicit distinction that the military might be tempted to draw between the goals of the government and those of the state must provoke a serious legitimacy problem (Harries-Jenkins and van Doorn 1976); this is so because the democracy model insists that the military's power is legitimate only in so far as it has been endorsed by society as a whole and that its practical objectives are those set for it by the government of the day. Van Gils (1971:274) states this succinctly:

> Under the conditions of pluralistic democracy, the relations between the armed forces and civilians are, at least theoretically, quite straightforward. Soldiers are public officials. They are not the embodiment of any particular set of values. They are not the chosen defenders of any specific social or political institution. They hold public office on the assumption that they will provide society with a specific set of services whenever society considers itself in the need of having such services performed.

This reflects the deeply embedded assumption of modern democratic theory, that it is the popularly elected government, and no other body or person, that is wholly responsible for deciding what policies are to be pursued in the name of the people. In so doing, the government is constrained by the limits to action set out under the law of the constitution, and is ultimately held accountable for its activities and decisions when it faces the judgement of the people at the polls.

But what if a constitutionally and popularly elected civilian government once in office abrogates the constitution and rejects the democratic values embodied in it (including genuinely competitive elections)? In such circumstances – which have been not uncommon in post-colonial states – the military may be the only entity within the country capable of reversing such a development and reinstating democratic government.

While contemporary democratic theory appears to be entirely at odds with the notion that the military has any role in unilaterally acting to 'safeguard the national interest', the most common justification for military intervention is just this. Such appeals to the national interest have frequently been coupled with references to some perceived crisis or threat involving the security of the state or serious economic or social problems. As Goodman (1990:xiii) observes for Latin America:

> The frequent military ascension to power has often been motivated by a perceived need to save their nations from weak, corrupt, and undisciplined civilian leadership.

Numerous commentators on the role of the military in politics have observed the tendency of armed forces to justify their intervention in terms of the national interest, and thereby to identify themselves with the desiderata of nationhood. Most have been sceptical. Lissak (1976:20), for example, notes that the military can acquire a self image as guarantor of the fundamental and permanent interests of the nation, thereby arrogating to itself the requisite legitimacy to assume the right to rule. Similarly, Nordlinger (1970:1137-8) highlights the manner in which the military's corporate interests can be defined, legitimised, and rationalised by a close identification with the interests of the nation, while at the same time portraying oppositional protests to their actions as 'expressions of partial and selfish interests'.

Nevertheless, authoritarian rule is not exclusive to military regimes and, as the case studies in this volume illustrate, armed forces have played a role in pro-democracy regime transitions (see also Chazan et al. 1988; Goodman 1990; Rial 1990a). The critical factor for most commentators on civil-military relations concerns the intention of military rulers to return to the barracks.

To legitimise their intervention, military regimes commonly contend that their rule is only a preparatory or transitory (but entirely necessary) stage along the road to a fully democratic political system, and promise an early return to civilian rule, thereby recognising, Dahl (1989:2) argues, that 'an indispensable ingredient for their legitimacy is a dash or two of the language of democracy'. In some cases, military rule has been justified 'as necessary for the regeneration of the polity to allow for stable and effective rule'; military regimes have even portrayed their role as that of 'democratic tutor' (Huntington 1968; Nordlinger 1977:204-5). Yet once out of the barracks military rulers have seldom been anxious to relinquish power and even where there have been transitions back to civilian rule the armed forces have typically retained an involvement in politics and have been more likely to intervene again if dissatisfied with the performance of civilian governments.

Observing processes of transition from authoritarian military rule to democracy in Latin America, Goodman (1990:xiv) comments that, 'successful transitions have utilised a process of incremental rather than immediate civilian control'; he goes on to suggest:

> For democracy to take root in Latin America, both military men and civilian leaders must take on new roles. . ... Recognition that the military is one of the strongest formal institutions in societies that are in dire need of political and social coherence poses challenges to Latin American civilian leaders that are very different from those confronted by their developed-nation counterparts (ibid.:xiv; see also Stepan 1988; Rial 1990a, b and Varas 1990).

Goodman, however, is not explicit on the nature of these 'new roles', and other contributors to the same volume suggest that recently democratised regimes in Latin America remain vulnerable to 'the rapid rebirth of military authoritarianism' (Rial 1990b:289).

In Asia and the Pacific armed forces have played a role in both democratising and anti-democratic transitions, and though, as elsewhere, their tendency as rulers has been towards authoritarianism, patterns of civil-military relations and degrees of authoritarianism/democracy in governance have varied widely. Any attempt at understanding this variety must begin with an appreciation of the particular historical and cultural circumstances under which military involvement in politics has developed in different countries.

The Case Studies

Within this volume we have selected nine countries for detailed study. All but one – Thailand – were former European colonies, and in all but the Thai case the liberal democratic model of military professionalism (the model elaborated by Huntington 1957) has at some stage been dominant. Not represented are those communist states of Asia in which the party and the military have dominated politics in such a way as to negate the essential conditions for democracy listed above. In all but two of the case studies (the Philippines and Papua New Guinea) there have been successful military coups, over a period stretching from 1932 (Thailand) to 1987 (Fiji) and 1991 (Thailand). In the two exceptional cases, there have been several unsuccessful coup attempts in the Philippines and occasional rumours of prospective coups in Papua New Guinea.

Of those which have experienced military intervention, all but Indonesia have made the transition back to at least nominal civilian rule and, with the arguable exception of Fiji, back again to military domination; Thailand has experienced several such cycles. While the Philippines has not experienced military rule since independence, it has experienced martial law and repressive authoritarian rule, under Ferdinand Marcos, and the military played a critical role both in maintaining Marcos in power and later in the transition which removed Marcos and restored democracy. The Philippines has not been alone in the experience of an authoritarian civilian regime; such regimes have also been experienced in (South) Korea, Pakistan and Bangladesh. Papua New Guinea alone has been able to maintain a robust democracy (notwithstanding several localised states of emergency and recent military action to suppress a rebellion on Bougainville), and it has been able to do so even though it has displayed most of the social and political features which coup theorists have suggested as preconditions and motivating circumstances for military intervention. In four cases (Thailand, Korea, Pakistan and the Philippines) the military, or sections of it, have been actively involved in pro-democratic transitions, and in another (Bangladesh) the military's non-intervention facilitated a pro-democratic regime change. In all cases the military itself has been subject to some degree of factionalism, and in most, ethnic divisions in society have had an influence on the role the military has played.

The case studies presented here thus provide a rich variety of military-civil interactions, ranging from the classic military coup to displace a civilian government, through military coups against military regimes and military intervention to change civilian regimes, to successful popular uprisings against military regimes.

In Indonesia the armed forces (ABRI) trace their origins to the revolution against Dutch colonialism. Following the surrender of the occupying Japanese forces in 1945, Indonesian nationalist leaders declared their independence and began a protracted battle against Dutch and Allied forces which ended with the formal recognition of the Republic of Indonesia in 1949. The Indonesian armed forces, created in 1945 to support the revolutionary struggle, were recruited largely from the military force, Pembela Tanah Air (Defenders of the Fatherland, PETA), recruited from amongst nationalist elements by the Japanese in 1943, but included also elements of the pre-war Dutch colonial army, Koninklijke Nederlansche Indische Leger (KNIL), and spontaneously-formed, politically-aligned militia units (*laskar*). Although lacking an effective centralised command, the military played a major role in the revolutionary war; it also inherited a distrust of civilian politicians, who, it believed, had been too ready to negotiate the nation's political status with the Dutch. Not surprisingly, given its origins, the military in the 1950s was a highly politicised and fractious organisation.

The early post-independence years saw growing tension between those (primarily ex-KNIL officers) who sought to build an apolitical, professional military along Western lines, and those (mostly ex-PETA and *laskar*) who favoured a continuing active role for the military in politics. This resulted, in the early 1950s, in a series of 'coups' within the armed forces, which shifted power towards the more politicised groups. At the same time, a series of local rebellions, and divisions within the government in Jakarta, produced political instability and led to the imposition of martial law in 1957, and the abnegation of the constitution and inauguration of a regime of 'Guided Democracy' two years later. Despite a greater centralisation of authority, however, political fractiousness and economic deterioration continued into the 1960s, and following the assassination in 1965 of several generals by middle-ranking officers associated with the Left, the military leadership moved against President Soekarno and his left-wing supporters; about half a million Communist Party supporters were killed, the president was removed from office, and a 'New Order' government, headed by General Suharto, was established. Suharto was installed as president in 1968.

Already in the 1950s army chief-of-staff, Colonel Nasution had put forward the idea of a 'Middle Way' for the armed forces, which combined their conventional role in the defence of the country with participation in government. After the overthrow of Sukarno this idea was formally embodied in the principle of *dwifungsi* (dual function); in the 'New Order' regime of President Suharto, ABRI is formally represented at all levels of government, military officers head many state enterprises and have business enterprises, and political support for the president is organised through Golkar, an effective 'state party' which was organised in the first place within the armed forces. With the assistance of foreign aid and investment, and a firm attitude towards political dissenters, the Suharto regime has achieved a fairly high level of political stability and economic performance, and as such has won some measure of legitimacy. But despite suggestions that the regime is becoming more open, it remains authoritarian, showing little tolerance of opposition, and there is a general consensus that when Suharto eventually goes his successor will have to be a person approved by ABRI.

The Burmese experience parallels that of Indonesia in a number of respects. As in Indonesia, nationalism flowered in Burma during World War II and Burma's post-independence leadership had been closely associated with the anti-colonial Burma Independence Army recruited and trained by the Japanese. Under somewhat different circumstances, but with common elements of ethnic fragmentation and class division, Burma also went through a period of considerable turbulence following independence in 1948 and in 1958 Prime Minister Nu stepped down, inviting the armed forces to set up a caretaker government. Elections were held again in 1960 but the political party which the military supported was defeated and two years later a military coup brought an end to parliamentary democracy and reinstated army commander General Ne Win as head of government. With some parallels to Indonesia's Golkar, the military's Burma Socialist Program Party (BSPP) became an effective state party (other parties were banned in 1964) and Ne Win and his military associates maintained tight control over what became – notwithstanding the semblance of a parliamentary system after 1974 – one of the most repressive and personalised regimes in Asia.

As in Indonesia, the Burmese army was initially composed of diverse elements. During the British colonial period the Burmese army was recruited predominantly from among the ethnic minorities, especially the Karen. During World War II, when Burmese nationalists joined the Japanese-trained Burma Independence Army and initially fought alongside the Japanese, many of the ethnic minorities fought with the Allies. There was also (comparable to the Indonesian *laskar*) a spontaneously-formed, largely-politically-affiliated Peoples' Volunteer Organisation (PVO) in the countryside. By the end of 1948, however, the PVO had split and declined. With the outbreak of communal violence between Burmans and Karens, the Karen head of the army was removed; Ne Win was given command, and the multi-ethnic composition of the army gave way to Burman domination. Indeed the suppression of ethnic minority revolts became the army's principal task.

Unlike the Suharto regime in Indonesia, however, that of Ne Win achieved neither political stability nor economic progress. Civil rebellion has threatened the Burmese state virtually since independence and its economy has deteriorated to the point that Burma has become one of the world's poorest countries. In 1988 a popular uprising occurred which seemed likely to topple the Ne Win regime; Ne Win in fact resigned the presidency (though initially remaining as BSPP leader) and some liberalisation seemed imminent. But in contrast to the Philippines, where two years earlier the 'People Power' revolution, supported by elements of the armed forces, had removed President Marcos, in Burma the army held firm; although Ne Win stepped down and the country briefly had a civilian head of state, when the government promised multiparty elections and other reforms the military staged another coup. Since then, Burma has been ruled directly by the military through a State Law and Order Restoration Council. Elections, which in 1990 gave an overwhelming majority to the pro-democracy National League for Democracy (NLD), have simply been ignored; the NLD's leader, Aung San Suu Kyi, was placed under house arrest and political repression has intensified.

The other country included in this volume with a long history of military involvement in government is Thailand. But unlike Indonesia and Burma, Thailand was never a colony and its first military coup took place in 1932 when the army intervened to replace Thailand's absolute monarchy with a constitutional system. Since then Thailand has gone through cycles of military and civilian rule, in which military intervention has been sometimes 'anti-democratic' (as in 1947, arguably 1958, 1976 and 1991) and sometimes 'pro-democratic' (as in 1932 and 1977), but consistent in seeing the military as having a 'guardian' role in the political system. That the military was able to mount a successful coup in 1991 after about fourteen years of parliamentary government and political liberalisation suggests, as Suchit Bunbongkarn observes below, that popular commitment to democratic norms and procedures is not strongly developed; however, the reversal of the military takeover (albeit with the intervention of the king) suggests the growing strength of civil society in Thailand, a development which is often identified with processes of democratisation.

The lack of a developed liberal democratic tradition has been even more obvious in the case of Korea, and Yung Myung Kim argues below that postwar attempts to impose Western-style democracy upon an unprepared nation simply did not work. Instead, the imported institutions of liberal democracy gave way to the authoritarianism of the Rhee Syngman regime. In 1960 Rhee was overthrown in a popular uprising, but in the ensuing political turbulence the army stepped in to reestablish control. What emerged, however, was not direct military rule but what Kim describes as a system of 'quasi-civilianised party politics' headed by Park Chung Hee. Between 1961 and his assassination in 1979 Park's regime became increasingly authoritarian and personalised. Referring to communist threats from the north and from within, Park denounced Western democracy as inappropriate to Korea's 'emergency' security situation. But the removal of Park Chung Hee did not bring fundamental changes in the political system. From the struggle between conservative military elements and popular pro-democracy forces, the New Military Group of Chun Doo Hwan and Roh Tae Woo emerged victorious. This group was committed to the continuation of a dominant role for the military in politics and saw democracy as a potential threat to political stability and rapid industrialisation. Confrontation between the repressive regime of Chun Doo Hwan and a growing democracy movement eventually produced a shift towards constitutional democracy in 1987-88, though conflicts within the opposition allowed Roh Tae Woo and a faction of the ruling party to achieve electoral victory, and divisions within the military enabled Roh to extend his authority there. The outcome, Kim suggests, has been a 'limited democratisation', producing a system 'somewhere between military-authoritarian and civilian-democratic'. But with the reversal of the relationship between the military and civil sectors – from one in the 1950s and 1960s where an 'overdeveloped' state, in which the military occupied a critical position, dominated civil society, to one in which the military is 'underdeveloped in comparison to the civil sectors' – Korea appears to have moved, tentatively, towards democracy.

In the two South Asian nations, also, the interaction between military and civil politics has been complex. Pakistan inherited the British traditions of military professionalism and non-involvement in politics, but the military became increasingly involved in decision making and eleven years after independence intervened, ostensibly to end the squabbling of civilian politicians and oversee the rehabilitation of parliamentary democracy. For the next decade Mohammed Ayub Khan, the first commander-in-chief of Pakistan's armed forces, ruled initially as chief martial law administrator and later as the country's first elected president, before resigning and handing over power to the then army commander, Yahya Khan. Two years later, following the defeat of the Pakistan army and the secession of East Pakistan (Bangladesh), Yahya Khan stepped down in favour of a civilian martial law administrator, Zulfikar Ali Bhutto. But in 1977 a further coup removed Bhutto and again placed the country under a martial law regime, headed by Zia ul Haq. Having 'legitimised' his position in a referendum in 1984, President Zia lifted martial law and introduced a system of 'controlled democracy', in which political power was, at least nominally, shared between the military and civilian politicians. Four years later, following the death of Zia, elections were held under the supervision of a military-dominated Emergency Council. The victory of Benazir Bhutto ended the military's direct role in politics, though it continued to play an active indirect part both during Bhutto's period in office and in her removal in 1990. After 1990 Pakistan was governed by a pro-military civilian government until 1993 when Benazir Bhutto was re-elected as prime minister. However, the military clearly still sees itself as having a 'guardian' role.

Indirectly, Bangladesh also substantially inherited the British Indian tradition of military professionalism, though as in Indonesia and Burma, the circumstances of the birth of the independent state left a division in the armed forces, between the professionalism of the former members of the Pakistan military and the politicisation of the former Mukti Bahini militia, reorganised after independence as a national security force attached to the ruling Awami League. But following a brief period of increasingly authoritarian civilian rule, and growing antipathy between the military and paramilitary forces, the army entered politics in 1975, ostensibly as guardians of parliamentary democracy. Having achieved power and initiated a partnership between the military and civilian politicians, General Ziaur Rahman moved to establish a multi-party system and to civilianise and democratise Bangladesh politics. However, splits with the ruling party following the assassination of Zia by a group of military officers, and opposition from within the military to the democratisation process initiated by Zia, led to another military intervention in 1981-82 and demands for a constitutional role similar to that enjoyed by the military in Indonesia. Martial law was lifted in 1986 but Chief Martial Law Administrator General Ershad continued to preside over an authoritarian regime until 1990 when a popular uprising forced his resignation and reestablished parliamentary democracy.

In all of these Asian states military intervention came at a fairly early stage, generally in a context of political instability or popular discontent, and not entirely unexpectedly. In the Pacific island state of Fiji, on the other hand, the military coups of 1987 came unexpectedly after seventeen years of stable parliamentary government. As Lawson argues below, the coups had less to do with praetorian challenges to civilian politics than with the army's reassertion of the dominant traditional-aristocratic pattern of Fjian politics following the electoral victory of an opposition coalition dominated by Fiji Indians and ethnic Fijians from outside the chiefly establishment. In the wake of the coups, Fiji's constitution was rewritten to further entrench the paramountcy of indigenous Fijian interests and consolidate the position of the chiefs. That achieved, the country returned to civilian rule and in elections in 1992 coup leader Sitiveni Rabuka was popularly elected as prime minister.

The remaining two countries, the Philippines and Papua New Guinea, have not experienced military rule since independence. Both inherited from their colonial regimes (US and Australia, respectively) a tradition of military professionalism which has been reinforced by close ties with their former mentors with respect to training and financial assistance.

In the case of the Philippines, the armed forces were involved at an early stage of the post-independence period in domestic security operations, and in subsequent years seemed at times on the verge of involvement in civil politics. The military did not become a significant actor, however, until 1972, when, faced with communist and Muslim insurgencies, and the prospect of being constitutionally unable to stand for a third presidential term, Ferdinand Marcos declared martial law. As Marcos sought to consolidate his authority he appointed loyal officers to senior positions and in doing so politicised the armed forces and created a division between the professional officers who had graduated from the Philippine Military Academy and the 'integré' officers whose careers rested largely on political patronage. When a popular uprising occurred in 1986, protesting the declaration of a fraudulent election, senior military personnel, including the then deputy commander of the armed forces, Fidel Ramos, broke with Marcos and joined the opposition; this split within the armed forces (in contrast with the pattern of events in Burma in 1988) was critical to the success of the so-called People Power Revolution which removed Marcos and returned the Philippines to parliamentary democracy. After her victory in 1986, however, the incoming president, Corazon Aquino, had to survive seven coup attempts from elements within the armed forces, notably among the younger professional officers who had supported the move against Marcos in 1986 and sought a role in post-Marcos government. Ramos, reinstated as commander of the armed forces, remained loyal to Aquino, however, and in 1992, as her chosen candidate, was elected to succeed her. Rebel former military leaders continue to pose a minor challenge to the Philippine government but the prospects of military intervention now seem remote.

By the time Papua New Guinea became independent in 1975 many of the newly-independent states of Africa and Asia had succumbed to military rule, and there were many who foresaw the likelihood of a similar development in Papua New Guinea. The classic preconditions for military intervention were there: a high degree of 'modernism' and coherence in the military relative to the institutions of civil society; threatened corporate interests as expenditure on the military lagged and the size of the force was reduced; personal ambition, and a highly fluid pattern of party politics. That a coup has not been attempted probably owes something to the successful working of Papua New Guinea's essentially Westminster-style political institutions and the fact that dissatisfied or ambitious officers (including the defence force's first three commanding officers) have chosen to resign from the military and contest elections (one becoming deputy prime minister); but it probably owes a lot, also, to the intensely fragmented topography and ethnic composition of Papua New Guinea. In recent years a growing perception that the military's likely role in defence against external aggression is less significant than the role it has come to play in maintaining internal security has led to a shift in attitudes towards the military, which has also become more politicised. Tensions have occasionally arisen in relations between the military and the civilian government, particularly in relation to the handling of the ongoing rebellion on Bougainville, but while the possibilities of a more substantial civil-military confrontation cannot be entirely ruled out, the prospects of military intervention seem remote.

Comparing experiences

It is tempting to conclude from this overview that each country's experience is explicable in terms of its particular historical and cultural circumstances, and to proceed directly to the individual country studies.

Certainly the range of civil-military interactions seems to be greater than that among the states of Africa and Latin America, a factor which might be at least partially explained by wide variety of colonial experiences.[14] Nevertheless, some common patterns, and some contrasting patterns, invite comparison.

Three countries – Burma, Indonesia and Pakistan – experienced fairly conventional military coups in which the army intervened after several years of fractious parliamentary politics, ostensibly to restore 'political order'. In Burma the army reinstated civilian politics after two years but soon after again intervened and has remained in power since, becoming one of the modern world's most durable military regimes. In both Burma and Indonesia the military had played a prominent part in the achievement of independence and soldiers had played an early role in government. In both countries, having intervened decisively, the military consolidated its position by expanding into civilian administration and business and by establishing a military-dominated political party. Both regimes have maintained strong central control, repressing opposition (especially on the ethnic peripheries), and both have had a poor record in terms of civil and political liberties.[15]

But there the similarities end. In Indonesia at least some of the trappings of a democratic system have been largely maintained, with three effectively state-approved parties contesting elections (which have been consistently dominated by the military-backed Golkar); fairly purposeful policy making has achieved an impressive rate and reasonable distribution of economic development, and since the late 1960s a fairly high degree of political stability has been maintained. This has contributed to a degree of performance legitimacy that has enabled President Suharto to remain in power for almost thirty years, despite criticisms of what Filipinos might have labelled cronyism and frequent predictions of his regime's imminent demise. In contrast, Burma abandoned any pretence of participatory politics after 1962 and has waged an ongoing war against non-

---

[14]   Cf. Sundhaussen (1985). Sundhaussen begins with the proposition that 'South-East Asian armies have failed to follow the trend in other regions to withdraw to the barracks', and seeks the explanation for this (following the lead of Huntington 1968:237) largely in cultural terms: '... there has never been a significant democratic tradition among the people of South-East Asia ... Thus the principle of civilian supremacy over the military ... was hardly ever a focal point in the politics of these countries' (ibid.:270, 277-78).

[15]   In the 1994 Freedom House 'Comparative Survey of Freedom', on scales of 1-7 (best to worst) for political rights and for civil liberties, Burma scored 7 and 7 and Indonesia 7 and 6. See *Freedom Review* 25(1) 1994.

Burman ethnic groups as well as, for some time, a communist insurrection. These factors, coupled with a record of economic performance which by 1987 had reduced Burma to one of the world's poorest countries, and a high degree of political repression, has severely undermined the legitimacy of the regime. This culminated in the unsuccessful popular uprising of 1988, from which emerged a more repressive military regime. In both cases the lack of pronounced divisions within the military (once Burma had effectively purged the army of its non-Burman elements) has been a factor in regime maintenance, though in Burma in 1988 it looked for a while as though a people power movement along the lines of that in the Philippines two years earlier might force a regime change with military acquiescence. Explaining the differences in regime performance is more difficult, though the serious ethnic cleavages which independent Burma inherited from the colonial period probably imposed greater obstructions to national unity than Indonesia's (not inconsiderable) ethnic diversity, and it is difficult to avoid the conclusion that Burma's opting for virtual economic isolation largely accounted for the disastrous economic record which denied any claim the military regime might have made to legitimacy based on performance.

In Pakistan, also, a politicised military intervened ostensibly to restore political order. But after a decade as martial law administrator, General Ayub Khan became elected president and what Pakistan has seen since is an increasing interpenetration of military and civilian politicians, compounded by ethnic divisions, and a succession of regimes on both sides of a mid point on Bebler's (1990) proposed 'militocracy'/'civilocracy' continuum. And there seems to be nothing to suggest that this pattern will change substantially.

In Bangladesh, on the other hand, the military initially intervened not to restore order among fractious politicians but to remove an increasingly authoritarian civilian regime. And having gained power the military proceeded to civilianise and democratise Bangladesh politics. Factions of the military again intervened, however, and though there were suggestions that Bangladesh was moving towards a fused system similar to Indonesia's *dwifungsi,* opposition to the authoritarianism of the Ershad regime instead led in 1990 to a popular uprising to restore democracy (though for how long remains to be seen).

In the two South Asian cases, as also in Thailand, the military (or factions of the military) has emerged as one of several key players in a fluid political system. Having expanded its role into civil administration, business and politics, and having formed linkages with non-military players (including linkages along established ethnic/regional and class lines), the military seems likely to continue to play a role in a broadly civilian-military mixed system, the nature of the role varying over time according to the political and economic performance of the government of the day. Much the same might be said of Korea, where an initially authoritarian civilian regime was overthrown by popular uprising and the military stepped in to impose order. Since 1961 Korea has experienced a series of mixed military-civilian, civilian-military governments, alike in their tendencies towards authoritarianism, though civil society seems to have become stronger since the 1980s.

In Thailand, and perhaps Korea, there seems to be some validity in the general proposition that military intervention is less likely as societies become more complex and the middle class expands; the proposition seems less relevant to Pakistan and Bangladesh – despite the often-cited common military professionalist heritage of British colonialism.

Fiji presents another example of decisive military intervention, but in this case not so much to restore 'political order' – since Fiji had enjoyed a considerable period of orderly parliamentary government – as to maintain ethnic Fijian (and chiefly Fijian) dominance. Once this had been achieved, by introducing a new constitution and holding new elections which returned coup leader Rabuka as prime minister, civilian rule was restored and further military intervention seems unlikely.

The Philippines under Marcos presents one of a number of cases of an authoritarian, repressive regime (yet one which largely preserved the formal semblance of democracy – elections, parties, a legislature and judiciary, a reasonably free press) in which the military played a relatively minor role. As in Bangladesh, the military's substantive entry into politics came in support of popular demands for the restoration of democracy. Having played a part in the removal of Marcos, elements of the military clearly saw themselves as having a continuing role in government, but notwithstanding a series of unsuccessful coup attempts the model of military professionalism was substantially maintained. Thus, what has to be explained in the Philippines – as in Papua New Guinea, where despite occasional rumours of an imminent coup military intervention has never been attempted – is why successful coups have not occurred. In both countries most of the classic preconditions and motives for coups have been present: imbalance between the military and civil political institutions and at least periods of arguable political instability, threatened corporate interests of the military, and personal ambition; factionalism within the military has also existed, though not on the same scale (and without the obvious ethnic or class divisions) that has been experienced elsewhere. Both countries inherited strong traditions of professionalism, but in that they were no different from Fiji or Pakistan. An attractive line of explanation perhaps lies in the vitality of civil politics in both countries – a vitality which in the Philippines even the repressive regime of President Marcos failed to stifle – and in the sheer logistical difficulties of maintaining centralised control. But in varying degrees both these arguments might be applied to other cases (for example, Pakistan and Indonesia) in which coups *have* occurred.

Indeed the case studies in this volume produce little to support systematically any of the common 'explanations' for military intervention, although elements of all such explanations can be invoked. In explaining the individual cases, history (especially concerning the role of the military in the colonial regime and its part in a struggle for independence) is obviously important, as is ethnicity in some cases (notably Burma and Fiji) and factionalism within the military (for example, Indonesia, Bangladesh).

On the question of performance, also, generalisation is difficult. In terms of economic performance, military or military-civilian fused regimes have performed well in Korea and, to an extent, Indonesia (though perhaps not as well as non-military regimes in the region such as Singapore and Malaysia), but have performed poorly in Burma and Bangladesh (though no more poorly than the civilian administration of the Philippines under Marcos); Thailand's record (as in many other respects) is mixed.

In terms of political performance, measured against the three criteria listed above – competition, participation, and civil and political liberties – there is stronger evidence of a military/non-military divide, but again the evidence is not clear cut. Comparing countries, Burma and to a lesser extent Indonesia have performed poorly against all three criteria, as have Thailand, Pakistan, Bangladesh and Korea under military rule. In Fiji, also, during the brief period of military rule there was a decline in political competition and a deterioration of civil and political liberties, though not to the extent experienced in the Asian states. On the other hand, the essentially civilian regime in the Philippines under Marcos also performed badly against the competition, and civil and political liberties criteria and, with some qualifications, against the participation criterion, for at least part of the period of the Marcos administration. Within the region, the civilian governments of Singapore, Malaysia and Tonga also have far from unblemished records.

As a rough comparative measure, the nine countries covered in this volume, together with nine other Asian and Pacific countries, are ranked below (Figure 1) on the basis of the 1994 Freedom House 'Comparative Survey of Freedom' (the two Freedom House gradings, for political rights and civil liberties, ranked on a scale (best to worst) of 1-7, have been averaged; those with a rating of 1-2.5 are categorised by Freedom House as 'free'; those scoring 3.0-5.5 as 'partly free' and those above 5.5 as 'not free'). The Freedom House ratings are not beyond question (it is not obvious, for example, why Papua New Guinea is classed as 'partly free', below Western Samoa and South Korea), but they are probably the most widely accepted measure available of comparative freedom, and thus of the degree of democracy (or relative 'democracidity'). They show the two long-time military-dominated regimes of Indonesia and Burma at the bottom of the list, along with Brunei and several communist states; most of the rest (including the two states – the Philippines and Papua New Guinea – in which coups have either failed or not been attempted) are grouped around the middle of the range, with Bangladesh and Papua New Guinea performing better and Thailand and Pakistan worse – but all outranking the civilian regimes in Singapore and Malaysia. South Korea alone is listed (contentiously, perhaps) among the 'free' countries.

FIGURE 1: Freedom House, 'Comparative Survey of Freedom, 1994'

1.0	(Australia)
1.5	South Korea
2.0	(Western Samoa)
2.5	
3.0	Bangladesh, Papua New Guinea
3.5	Philippines, Fiji
4.0	Thailand, Pakistan, (Tonga)
4.5	(Malaysia)
5.0	(Singapore)
5.5	
6.0	
6.5	Indonesia, (Brunei)
7.0	Burma (North Korea, PRC, Vietnam)

(Source: *Freedom Review* 25(1) 1994:14-15).

What is more pertinent, however, is how *changes* in regime within a single country affect political performance. Here the evidence is less opaque, but still not unambiguous. In general, military intervention has resulted in restrictions on both competition and participation and, sometimes with a lag but usually increasingly, in limitations on civil and political liberties. The arguable exceptions are Thailand in 1932, Korea in 1960-61 and Bangladesh in 1975, where the military ostensibly intervened to restore civil and political liberties and increase competition and participation, though even among these cases (notably Korea) it may be argued that the tendency to democratisation was shortlived.

It should also be observed, however, that the impact of military intervention on different parts of the population is uneven. Typically, the impact of military intervention is heaviest on those most actively engaged in politics, and these are often (but not always) a social as well as political elite. When military intervention does something to restore 'political order' and promote economic development, large segments of the population may perceive themselves (as the proponents of bureaucratic authoritarianism and its variants once argued) to be better off. It is this, perhaps, that helps explain the longevity of the Suharto regime and the acceptance, by much of the population, of martial law in the Philippines in 1972. Similarly, it has been argued by some that the Fiji coups of 1987 were welcomed by most ethnic Fijians as a reassertion of the paramountcy of Fijian (over Indo-Fijian) interests (although Lawson's analysis below suggests that this is an over-simplification). The broad question of who gains and who loses from military intervention has seldom been adequately addressed, either for the larger civil society or for those within the military itself.

Beyond these restricted comparisons, generalisations are hazardous. Nevertheless several low-level generalisations suggest themselves.

First, by virtue of their monopoly (or at least dominant control) over the means of coercion, and frequently because they are a relatively coherent organisation in a fragmented society, militaries can play a major role in bringing about changes of regime, not just in fluid political situations (such as in Burma in 1958 or Indonesia in the mid 1960s) but in fairly stable ones (Fiji in 1987 [though the 1987 coups were essentially regime maintaining], Korea in 1960-61). They may also play an important role in forestalling changes of regime (as in Burma in 1988).

Second, in 'explaining' military intervention, it is evident that the relative strength of civil and military institutions, larger divisions in society, corporate and factional interests of the military, personal ambitions, and external factors may all be relevant in different proportions, but none provides a reliable indicator of military intervention (as the Papua New Guinea and Philippines cases show).

Third, while a shift along the continuum from civilian to military regime is not strongly correlated either with economic performance or with the degree of democracy, there is, not surprisingly, substance to the general proposition that military regimes are oriented more towards maintaining 'order' – against which criterion, however, they perform variably, with Indonesia and Thailand providing polar examples of regime stability – and to maximising their corporate (or perhaps more correctly their collectively individualised) interests, than to promoting the liberal democratic values of competition, participation, civil and political liberties, and more egalitarian distribution of wealth.

Fourth, although these case studies provide varying instances of military withdrawal, the general conclusion seems to be that having once intervened military leaders are likely to seek to maintain a political role, either as guardians, with the implication that further interventions are likely, or by the interpenetration of the interests of military and civilian personnel in politics, civil administration and business. This conclusion, which is amply recognised in a growing body of literature on the morphology of civil-military regimes, suggests there is scope for further research in at least two major areas of civil-military relations. One of these concerns the role of the military in civilian administration and in the military/civilian borderland of paramilitary, internal security, and law and order type operations.[16] The other has to do with the involvement of militaries institutionally, and soldiers individually, in business. In both these areas, the almost universal tendency towards expansion of the role of the military suggests the possibility of gradual change in regime type without major discontinuities in government.

The military seems likely to continue to play an important role in the politics of the countries of Asia and the Pacific, notwithstanding predicted tendencies towards democratisation. To comprehend that role it will be increasingly necessary to shift the focus of research from the military per se to the activities of soldiers in the complex of military-civil relations. It is towards this endeavour that our volume is directed.

---

[16] 'Paramilitary forces' are a major concern of Janowitz (1977) and 'military civic action' is the subject of a volume by de Pauw and Luz (1991). The role of officially-recognised 'vigilantes' in the Philippines is discussed in May (1992).

2

THE MILITARY AND DEMOCRACY IN INDONESIA

Michael R.J. Vatikiotis

At the close of the 1980s, Indonesia's military was in a state of flux. Over a decade of declining political fortunes for an institution considered the fulcrum of President Suharto's New Order regime was generating something of an identity crisis. Yet as the political edifice which the military helped erect in the mid 1960s showed signs of age and decline, the military moved awkwardly to adapt its image and role in order to preserve its perceived position as the principal body in the political constellation. In doing so, new interpretations of the civil-military relationship evolved.

To understand the Armed Forces of Indonesia (*Angkatan Bersenjata Republik Indonesia* or ABRI) – and its attitude towards democracy – it is important to grasp the relationship between the military and the state in Indonesia. Basically, this relationship developed under stress. The earliest independent civilian government of the new republic, as Kahin (1952) and more recently Salim (1991) describe, hesitated to form a national army and prevaricated over its form. At the same time, the armed revolutionary youth groups (*pemuda*) which had launched the armed struggle almost as soon as the Japanese imperial occupation collapsed in August 1945 were suspicious of the civilian nationalists who not only hesitated to declare independence, but were keener to organise political parties than a national army. This reluctance on the part of the civilian government to deal with the army in the early days of the revolution created, Salim (1991:33) suggests,

> a particular pattern of civilian military relations, and all subsequent efforts to bring the army completely under its control failed.

This bifurcation of the two most important elements of the Indonesian polity at so formative a stage of its existence provides a useful guide to the country's subsequent political history.

Essentially, the history of Indonesian government since independence has been the progressive emasculation of the multi-party, parliamentary democracy envisaged by nationalist leaders, like Soetan Sjahrir, imbued in various degrees with the European liberal socialist orthodoxy. Sjahrir, as expressed in his influential 1945 pamphlet '*Perjuangan Kita*' ('Our Struggle') specifically wanted to see Indonesia shun a one-party system under a monolithic executive.

> He feared the development of a totalitarian government in Indonesia because of the legacy of feudalistic authoritarianism which had been kept alive and reinforced by the long period of colonial government (Kahin 1952 :166).

Herbert Feith (1962:313) argues that the adoption of a system of constitutional democracy in the first decade of independence reflected the influence of men like Sjahrir and Mohammad Hatta. But he is careful to distinguish between the idea of democracy as a 'legitimating principle' and actual majority rule. There was never any substance lent to the 'characteristic principles and mechanisms of constitutional democracy'.

Imperfectly implemented, Feith argues that this early and only era of constitutional democracy in Indonesian political history was nonetheless reasonably effective. The parliament may not have been an elected body, but cabinets were accountable to it. The press was free, the courts operated independently, and a semblance of non-political bureaucracy emerged.

However, disillusionment with this system quickly developed. The 1955 general election, considered by many Indonesians to be the only genuinely representative election the country has ever held, etched out the country's religious and communal elements with alarming clarity. The two main Muslim parties obtained almost 40 per cent of the vote; the Communists 16 per cent and the Nationalist Party (PNI) just 22 per cent. The results laid bare potentially divisive forces in the infant republic. The country was already afflicted by regional rebellions and the army grew restless, forcing Soekarno to step in with an alternative to constitutional democracy in the form of 'guided democracy'. Indonesia turned its back on constitutional democracy and began developing the strong executive rule inherited by Suharto's New Order.

The military's attitude to this early period of post-independence politics was very much governed by its role in the independence struggle. ABRI considers itself the progenitor of the state , having fought a war of independence against the Dutch from 1945-1949. As stated in Law No. 20 on Members of the Armed Forces (1988):

> The history of the Indonesian struggle has been a series of armed resistance put up by the people against colonialism.

As such ABRI projects itself as the guardian of the nation, a definition which, as Finer (1974:535) points out, imbues a tradition of loyalty to the state, rather than obedience to the rulers of the day. Indeed, as part of the soldier's oath taken by every member of ABRI, loyalty is sworn only to 'the Unitary State of the Republic of Indonesia that is based on *Pancasila* and the 1945 Constitution'. There is no mention of the government or the executive.

In crude terms, ABRI still regards itself as a people's army. Central to ABRI thinking, however, is a doctrine crystallised in the soldiers' oath, or *Sapta Marga,* which endows the army with guardianship of the state. To justify this, ABRI must be shaped as a people's army, using a strategy of close cooperation with the people. In summary, the strategy of total defence and the *Sapta Marga* theoretically positions ABRI with the people and above the state. To understand why this is so, some consideration of national history, as seen through ABRI's eyes, is essential.

ABRI considers that independence was achieved by the armed struggle against the Dutch, which not only had to contend with the colonial army, but also the treachery of Indonesian communists, and the weakness of civilian nationalist leaders who were prepared to fall back in the face of Dutch aggression. One of the events of the war most drummed into army cadets is the 19 December 1948 capitulation of the civilian government after the first capital, Jogyakarta, was occupied by the Dutch. It was only ABRI's resolve to continue the fight 'with or without the government', that persuaded the world that Indonesia would not return to Dutch hands, the cadets are taught. The implication is clear; ABRI, not the civilian government, saved the infant republic.

Soon after independence the army was called on to suppress a series of regional revolts which threatened the unitary state. Barely had these revolts been sup-pressed when another threat to the state in the shape of the Indonesian Communist Party (PKI) loomed. The events of 30 September 1965, which lit the short fuse to the end of President Soekarno's rule, saw the military once again step in to restore order and save the nation. This view of their own history has endowed the military with a deep suspicion of politicians and dissenting groups.

The birth of the New Order brought ABRI for the first time a leading role in Indonesian political life. As Sundhaussen points out, the army's entry into formal politics came after twenty years of civil-military tensions (Sundhaussen 1982: 257). Underlying this tension, as senior commanding officers of the period have subsequently described, was a perpetual hesitancy on the part of senior officers to be dragged into running the country. It may have been that opportunities were scarce, or that prior attempts at intervention were unsuccessful. But former army chief of staff T.B. Simatupang argues that there was a distinct aversion to military rule among the military intellectual elite:

During the 1950s there was originally a strong reluctance and a feeling of scepticism and uneasiness among the army leadership when the army had to perform an expanded role in view of the continuing political instability. They were haunted by the spectre of creating what was perceived then as a 'Latin American situation' in Indonesia (Simatupang 1989:135).

Suharto and his somewhat less educated, less travelled followers were clearly not imbued with such notions. As Crouch (1978:26) aptly points out, they represented a new class of officer from small towns in Java, less formally educated but with strong claims to prominence because of their role in the struggle against the Dutch. Though much questioned by his detractors, Suharto participated as a local military commander in some of the key actions against Dutch forces in and around Jogyakarta. If he was not, as claimed, a key figure in the campaign, he certainly played a role.

Yet it would be incorrect to assume the New Order core group clustered around Suharto was intent on the crude seizure of power. To this day, Suharto is adamant that his accession to power after the 11 March 1966 Order did not amount to a *coup d'état*. Rather, he argues in his 1988 ghost-written autobiography, he was pushed along by events beyond his control:

> I was pushed in an atmosphere of political conflict to step forward. Some politicians were impatient for a change of leadership to the point of proposing that I assume power just like that. I responded to this proposal at once; 'If that's the way things are, I'd better step down. Such a method is not good. Seizing power by military force will not bring about lasting stability. I am not going to bequeath a history indicating that there was once a seizure of power by military might' (Suharto 1989:185).

This highlights one of ABRI's persistent concerns under the New Order. For one of the key inputs to civil military relations has been the legitimising of ABRI's intervention in 1965 in ideological, nationalistic terms. At the outset there seemed to be an awareness that Soekarno's sudden ouster could set a dangerous precedent, and every effort was made to cloak it in constitutional trappings. Suharto may have assumed executive powers in March 1966, but it was not until 1968 that he was formally appointed president of the republic, and not until 1971 that a general election was held.

Delicate manoeuvres to remove Soekarno – whom many suspected could still command substantial popularity even within the armed forces (Legge 1972:405) – was followed by a reworking of ABRI's doctrine. At an Army Seminar in 1966, ABRI's dual political and military function (*dwifungsi*), which was first proposed in the late 1950s, was sharpened. Earlier definitions of ABRI's dual role had sought to establish ABRI's right to participate in national development using the dual function principle formulated in 1958. According to Simatupang (1989:136), it was 'an attempt to provide a rationale . . . at the same time laying down limitations to the expanded role'.

The events of 1965 elevated ABRI's right to assume a non-military role from a choice into an obligation. The seminar declared that ABRI was forced by circumstances to stand by the people, because 'all the people's hopes for well-being are focused on the armed forces in general, and the army in particular'. As Jenkins (1984:4) points out, the 1966 seminar acted as timely ideological justification for what in effect the army was already practising.

On reflection, though, it is important to note that civilian aspirations at the time also helped the army assume control of the government. Civilian intellectuals and professionals bore the brunt of Soekarno's relentless politicisation of society; his so-called 'politics as commander' strategy which forced people to choose sides as the Indonesian Communist Party grew in strength and numbers. The prominent writer and journalist, Goenawan Mohamad recalls :

> Recurrent calls for '*indoktrinasi*' (indoctrination) took place in almost every poli-
> tical circle, with Marxism and Sukarno's writings being the main components of the
> teaching. No one, it seemed, was free from them. 'Revolution' became a highly
> hypnotic word: it could immediately make one either combative or submissive
> (Mohamad 1989:72).

The atmosphere prevalent at the time helped ABRI acquire a political role. First, because before Soekarno's fall, the military, with encouragement from friendly Western powers, had begun setting up social organisations to counter the spread of Communist influence. One of these, Sekber Golkar, eventually formed the nucleus of the New Order's principal mass political organisation, Golkar.

Once in power, however, ABRI also found that popular reaction against the politicisation of the Soekarno era aided moves to dismantle civilian political structures, among them most of the political parties of Soekarno's 'Old Order'. Quite simply, the civilian elite was willing to see the army assume power in the hope that order and stability would be restored. Such was their desire for stability, many civilians were blind to the implications of army rule for the function of democratic institutions enshrined in the 1945 constitution.

It would also be misleading to assume ABRI had a plan or strategy for the execution of their role in politics. It now seems clear from contemporary diplo-matic reports that ABRI was divided over what to do about Soekarno's headlong tilt towards the Communist fold. Concern about the situation ran up against a reluctance to intervene and actually usurp power, probably because no one was certain whether any attempt to do so would attract solid backing within the military.

Once in power, the military had no clear idea of how to proceed either. Some elements of the armed forces, probably an intellectual minority led by chief of staff General A.H. Nasution, envisaged their political role as only temporary, in line with the original 'middle way' formulation of the dual function. He was overruled by Suharto and his group, who seemed to have an informal popular mandate to restore order and stability as quickly as possible and using whatever available means.

> For all practical purposes . . . during the initial period of the New Order, national leadership was identical with army leadership, not as the result of a usurpation of power through a *coup d'etat* or the like, but simply because the alternative would have been anarchy and chaos (Simatupang 1989:135).

As measure of the confused thinking about the army's role, it is interesting to note how some of those who participated in the early development of the New Order are capable of reconsidering ABRI's position.

> It was never the philosophy of ABRI to perpetuate the crisis situation that existed in October 1965. The intensity and involvement of ABRI in political life is completely dependent on the political situation of the moment. If we feel it is no longer needed, we have to release all jobs to civilians (interview with General (retd.) Sumitro, 6 February 1988).

If thinking along these lines existed among the ranks of senior ABRI officers when the New Order came to power, it should not be confused with the aims of the core group clustered around Suharto, which proceeded to erect the New Order's political edifice. In fact, judging from the early disaffection of officers like Nasution, Kemal Idris, H. Dharsono, and others who supported Suharto in his rise to power, there was disenchantment over how the New Order was proceeding right from the beginning. Subsequent interviews with these men reveal a common thread; they felt that civilian functions of the government should have been restored and fostered. Instead, Suharto and his men proceeded slowly but steadily to dismantle the civilian political infrastructure, first by banning the parties which existed in the Soekarno period, and then by gradually introducing stringent legislation controlling the freedom of political expression.

Yet if certain quarters in ABRI felt the New Order was taking the dual function too far, neither was ABRI given a free hand to run the state. Instead, the state became progressively dominated by Suharto and his inner circle. Probably unsure of ABRI loyalties, Suharto deployed tactics of divide and rule which often favoured civilian bureaucratic interests at the expense of ABRI. Thus ABRI began losing power almost as soon as they achieved it. To understand why, the Suharto-ABRI relationship must be looked at in more detail.

Suharto and ABRI

President Suharto dates his official entry into the Indonesian Army on the same day it was founded, 5 October 1945. His subsequent military career bears some examination, because it tells us something about his own attitude towards the army and the army in politics. Suharto drifted into the new republic's army after brief service in the Dutch colonial army (KNIL) and a spell in the Indonesian militia organised by the Japanese occupation forces. Like many young men in Java at the time, he claims to have been drawn to the cause of fighting for independence. His prior formal military experience under the Dutch and Japanese almost certainly explains why he was given a local command in Central Java.

Suharto's actual role in the war of independence is a subject of controversy. The official history grants him a leading role in the 1 March 1949 'general attack' on Jogyakarta, when Indonesian forces surprised the Dutch and briefly occupied Jogyakarta. In his autobiography, Suharto relates how he was at the centre of things, discussing strategy with the revered army commander, General Sudirman. Others have subsequently cast doubt on his importance during the campaign, arguing that he was but one of many local commanders, and even casting aspersions on his capabilities in the field. General Nasution claims, for example, that Suharto was reluctant to follow orders, preferring to wait and see what others did first.

Naturally, both sides of the story are heavily cloaked in later political interpretations. Any objective assessment, however, must assume that Suharto's presence in Central Java at the height of the war placed him in a position to participate in significant military action, and the fact that soon afterwards he commanded troops to put down a regional revolt in Makassar suggests that his abilities and experience were recognised by the high command.

The more interesting period of his military career began with his transfer to Central Java in 1952. After a spell as chief of staff of the regional divisional command, he was elevated to regional commander in 1957, with the rank of full colonel. These were difficult times for ABRI. The fledgling state was unable to find funds to finance a fully-equipped professional army, so ABRI was encouraged to seek independent financing by establishing its own businesses. To do this, ABRI officers formed business liaisons with local Chinese businessmen.

The nationalisation of Dutch companies declared by Soekarno in 1957 also saw many lucrative enterprises fall into ABRI's hands.

Suharto demonstrated consummate skill at satisfying the quartermastering demands of the division, striking up a relationship with one businessman, Liem Sioe Long, who later became the largest corporate player under the New Order. Here too he established the core group of officers who were later to serve as his closest aides after 1966, men like Ali Murtopo and Sudjono Hurmurdani. The period was therefore formative for Suharto, and determined some of the methods he applied to his rule after becoming president. The conditions faced by Suharto in Central Java represented the harsh realities of ABRI's struggle to survive. Confronted by budgetary difficulties and the threat of Communist-led insurrection, ABRI was forced to adapt and deploy unconventional methods. The territorial system developed to combat regionalism and Communism ensured that the military presence was pervasive right down to the village level. Yet it was less a strategy of warfare than of the imposition of strict control over the population.

To fund military operations, deals were cut with local businessmen. They helped set up local foundations to act as fronts for the imposition of taxes on most economic activities. The activities of Suharto's division were so lucrative they attracted the attention of the Jakarta high command, which had Suharto quietly removed from the position in 1959 and sent to staff college. Suharto continued to use social foundations, *yayasans*, after coming to power; in fact they became a major source of funding for the military elite, and provide the lion's share of funds for important political institutions like Golkar. The fact that Suharto was effectively fired because the army considered these practices corrupt in the late 1950s, seems to have had no effect on the perception of the system as it is applied on a much larger scale today.

The important point is that Suharto brought with him to the presidency both the methods and the men from this period in Central Java. Neither was looked upon as orthodox by the intellectual military elite in Jakarta at the time. General Nasution relates that Suharto told him in 1968 : 'General, my politics are at the point of a bayonet'. Nasution contends that from the beginning Suharto surrounded himself with men who were not from the army's mainstream:

> Soeharto became more or less presidium of the army's political think tank, *Panitia Sospol*, led by Basuki Rachmat and Sutjipto. Into this Soeharto brought in Murtopo as his *asintel* (assistant for intelligence). With him came the Tanah Abang Group (mainly Chinese Catholic students under Murtopo's wing) with their strategic plans for the future. Not the army. We had no plans. In this sense, the army more or less

faded away in its influence on Soeharto (interview with General A.H. Nasution, 11 November 1989).

Nasution himself was perhaps by this stage less representative of the mainstream. But his point underlines the extent to which the generation of officers with more educated and intellectual backgrounds had been marginalised – or eliminated – by 1966.

1970-1988: ABRI Under the New Order

This brief look at Suharto's military origins provides a useful springboard from which to examine the development of ABRI's role and position under the New Order. For if the New Order is considered in general terms as a military-backed regime, closer examination of the more recent period reveals that it has been Suharto rather than ABRI which has reaped the fruits of power. Compounding this sense of impotency was the progressive division of ABRI thinking into two schools: one closely associated with Suharto and enjoying the benefits of his power and patronage, the other increasingly estranged from the ruling group and advocating ABRI's gradual withdrawal from politics (Jenkins 1984:255).

For much of the 1970s and early 1980s, ABRI found itself torn between these two poles. The steady consolidation of the Suharto group saw military men attain considerable power and prestige, but in the process, arguably, the military tenor of the regime became diluted. If one examines the methods of men like Murtopo and Sudharmono – two of Suharto's closest aides over this period – much of what they achieved was at cross-purposes with the military. Murtopo's *opsus* (special operations group) favoured unorthodox methods of intelligence and subterfuge to execute policy, often leaving the military high command in the dark. Sudharmono's legalistic mind helped erect an array of legal props to Suharto's legitimacy and gradually strengthened the civilian bureaucracy at the expense of the military. He engineered a presidential order (number 10) which deprived ABRI of considerable financial clout by diverting lucrative government tenders to businessmen close to the palace.

Those on the periphery of the ruling group grew steadily uncomfortable with what they saw as Suharto's entrenchment in power. Some have since suggested that Suharto was not expected to last by the military elite.

> I never thought he would last so long. In 1971 I expressed the view that the president should run only for two years, because otherwise his vested interests would take over. Suharto may also have seen the sense in this, but those around him told him to go on (interview with General Kemal Idris, 16 January 1990).

The effect this had on ABRI's relationship with the leadership and the civilian elite cannot be underestimated. Arguably, growing disaffection towards Suharto in certain ABRI quarters by the mid 1970s lent strength to the view that ABRI should be less engaged in politics, for this implied a distancing from the leadership. In doctrinal terms, it produced by the late 1970s a move to purify ABRI's position in the state above all groups.

Suharto's grasp of the implications of such a position in terms of loyalty to the leadership prompted him to lash out at ABRI in 1980 for failing to see that defence of the constitution could not be achieved without supporting the New Order. Therefore, he said, ABRI must choose sides; it could not consider voting for any group other than Golkar, of which ABRI is a component part. The implications shocked many senior officers: ABRI a part of the Golkar family? ABRI serving the New Order? Such notions flew in the face of ABRI doctrine. But realistically speaking, they accurately located ABRI's position under Suharto.

Against this background of diverging views and loyalties within ABRI, questions about ABRI's role in politics and support for a more democratic style of government in Indonesia began to surface. From the above, it would appear that the stimulus for ABRI's questioning of its political role was derived from the realisation in certain quarters that Suharto's entrenchment in power was no longer serving ABRI's interests, and indeed was hindering ABRI's own ability to serve the people. Initial attempts to put a distance between ABRI and the Suharto regime surfaced in the mid 1970s. Suharto was able to check these potential threats to his position by his judicious manipulation of senior appointments in ABRI. Those generals considered a threat were sidelined. But this served only to define more sharply the distinction between those in ABRI who believed the military should play a less overtly political role, and those – considered close to Suharto – who had no intention of altering the status quo.

In his seminal monograph on the Indonesian military, David Jenkins concludes that however divided ABRI was becoming because of the power struggle at the top, ABRI was, as he put it, 'dug in on the commanding heights of the political, economic and social landscape' (Jenkins 1984:263). The anatomy he presents of the debate about ABRI's role seems dominated more by semantics than substance. Arguably, the concerns were more political than real. Can the same be said of the more recent period? Is ABRI moving any closer to significant change in attitude towards its role in politics?

1988-1991: ABRI Faces an Uncertain Future

The end of the 1980s saw Indonesia recover its composure after the disastrous fall in oil prices which sent the economy hurtling into decline. A combination of artful macro-economic reform and full support from the country's aid donors not only has helped the economy to recover, but also shows signs of at last living up to its considerable potential. But with the economic boom of the late 1980s came calls for political liberalisation. Some intellectuals saw little point in granting the private sector more freedom without accompanying political reforms.

Pressures for political reform surfaced against a background of mounting concern in elite circles about Suharto's tenure in office. Soon after his re-election for a fifth term of office in March 1988, debate focused on the succession. Suharto entered his seventieth year in 1991 showing no signs that he intended to retire before the next election in 1993, and behaving as if he wanted to stay the course for a sixth term. This intensified concerns about how to manage the succession smoothly. Talk of succession has been a perennial feature of the New Order's political cycles, but this kind of talk surfacing so soon after Suharto's 1988 re-election suggested new urgency. Altogether, calls for more openness and debate over the succession generated a highly charged political atmosphere, one in which ABRI found itself to some extent intellectually outclassed and encumbered by anachronistic ideas.

While senior ABRI officers continued to harp on vigilance against the Communist threat and 'national discipline' as the keys to stability, civilian intellectuals were arguing that democratisation was needed to renew and preserve the New Order. It was not long before certain military leaders saw the political advantages of adjusting to this new thinking and coopting those who were behind it. Far from being ideologically inspired – or necessarily committed to democracy – as will be argued below, ABRI needed a political constituency.

The year 1988 taught ABRI just how low their political stock had sunk under the New Order. A move to pass a new soldiership law through parliament was blocked in late 1987 after the executive branch mobilised the parliamentary factions to raise objections to the draft. The draft bill included alterations to the soldier's oath which emphasised allegiance to the constitution and by implication de-emphasised loyalty to the government of the day. It also sought to neutralise the president's notional powers as supreme commander by sharpening the authority of the ABRI commander. The draft bill, for instance, proposed increasing the mandatory retirement age from 55 to 60 (Vatikiotis 1987:35). Subsequent revisions to the draft were forced on ABRI after lengthy debate in parliament, which ironed out these conspicuous attempts – using constitutional means – to enhance military power, and the bill was passed.

Worse was to come. When ABRI signalled its objection to Suharto over his choice of vice president in the 1988 presidential election, they once again found their influence much weakened. Suharto had earlier indicated he wanted Sud-harmono, the chairman of Golkar and state secretary, to have the job. Sudhar-mono, the shrewd ex-Army lawyer who was the architect of much of the New Order's legal and bureaucratic edifice, was considered unsuitable by ABRI. As Golkar chairman he had worked assiduously to reduce ABRI's influence over the party. Using the state secretariat, he had effectively drained a good deal of ABRI's pool of extra-budgetary funding. In the eyes of the military, Sudharmono represented a dangerous threat to their political supremacy.

ABRI was overruled. By demonstrating so openly his disregard for ABRI's ad-vice, and insisting on Sudharmono becoming vice president, Suharto demonstrat-ed that he no longer needed ABRI as a prop to sustain his power. The political fallout made a deep impression on the military and triggered introspection on ABRI's role in politics and its relationship with the national leadership on one side, and the people on the other.

ABRI's catharsis was expressed in two ways. The political setbacks of 1988 almost immediately led to further disaffection within the ABRI leadership. Most notably, the former ABRI commander, General L.B. Murdani, smarting from his curt dismissal before the presidential election, signalled that his patience with Suharto was wearing thin. He joined the ranks of the dispirited, but retained a cabinet position as Defence minister. Showing how much more important per-sonalities can be than institutions in Indonesian politics, as ABRI commander Murdani overshadowed the Defence minister. Once he was in the job, the position once more assumed importance.

Murdani, aided by his extensive intelligence network, set about laying am-bushes for Sudharmono almost as soon as he was elected vice president. Rumours surfaced, for example, of his involvement in the Communist uprising at Madiun in 1948. Sudharmono took these seriously enough to publicly deny his Communist sympathies in late 1988. For a political culture steeped in the art of discretion, the anti-Sudharmono campaign broke all the rules. One prominent retired general even refused to hang his portrait beside that of President Suharto.

Arguably, though, the ABRI leadership's sniping at the vice president was wasted ammunition. For Suharto, the advantage was two-fold: the campaign against Sudharmono drew some of his opponents out into the open, and it also drove a wedge into Golkar. Ironically, this was useful because it served to weaken Sudharmono's strong grip over the party – thus denying him a power base. He lost the chairmanship of Golkar in November 1988, in spite of a furious campaign mounted by his supporters. It also ensured that some of the smart – and increas-ingly popular – civilian politicians fostered by Sudharmono would not fall into the arms of ABRI. Interviews with senior Golkar officials, like Secretary General

Rachmat Witoelar, and his predecessor Sarwono Kusumaatmadja, conveyed a sense of ambiguity towards ABRI, despite the traditionally close relationship between the two institutions. Sarwono's view in May 1988 was:

> In a tactical sense, the army is losing out. Suharto is increasingly civilian in his outlook, if not by concept then by association (interview with Sarwono Kusumaatmadja, 16 May 1988).

The boldness of such views jeopardised popular attitudes towards the military simply because of the influence Sarwono and other prominent civilians in Golkar were beginning to have on the debate about the country's political future. At the same time ABRI also embarked on a re-appraisal of its role and standing in society.

There seems little doubt that the younger generation of ABRI officers harboured misgivings about the dual function. This has been apparent since at least the early 1980s, when Jenkins (1984:261) detected that younger officers took more pride in their professional role as soldiers and paid less attention to their socio-political role. The logical consequences of this trend were partly offset in the past by the fact that many such officers once injected into the socio-political role soon lost their misgivings about the system.

However, by the end of the 1980s the government was faced with a chronically demoralised civil service, low on esteem because all the plum jobs went to ABRI personnel. Civilian elements in the cabinet clamoured for the injection of more *esprit de corps* and some sort of career-track policy. They argued that the government's economic reform programme would be jeopardised without the back-up of a more efficient, dedicated civil service. In response, the government took steps to limit the number of ABRI personnel in civilian posts. Ironically enough, one man who helped implement the policy was a former army chief, General Rudini, in his new capacity as Home Affairs minister. In August 1990 Rudini announced that military appointments to civilian posts, known as *karyawan* – 'cadres' – would be decreased gradually 'in areas where they are not needed'. Already in force was a policy which reduced the number of military district officers to 40 per cent of the total, and insisted that posts below that of deputy governor in provincial seats must now be held by civil servants. His argument drew on ABRI's historical justification for political intervention :

> ... *kekaryawan* is a small part of the dual function. It existed because of the situation and conditions. In 1965, after the coup, many civilian officials were afraid to execute their jobs. They were afraid of Communists. Only ABRI wanted to do the job. After the situation stabilised, everyone agreed that *kekaryawan* could decrease step

by step in areas where they are not needed (speech by General (retd.) Rudini to the Jakarta 'Executive Circle', 7 August 1990).

While the actual participation by the military in civilian administration was being reduced, there was no sign that the military was relinquishing its function as a 'dynamiser' of society. Senior military officers, if anything, intensified their efforts to influence society by speaking up on a range of political issues. However, in a marked departure from the familiar ABRI catechism on security, stability, and the need for national discipline, senior ABRI leaders began echoing the debate in civilian intellectual circles about openness.

The change often seemed more of a nuance than a *volte face*. For example, in a speech he made on 20 May 1987, with the title 'National Discipline and Development of our Democracy', Murdani started out with the familiar theme of national discipline. 'The role of discipline in national and constitutional life is to guarantee the creation of peace and order in daily life', he intoned. But later in the speech he noted :

Discipline must not cause initiatives and creativity to disappear. Obedience and loyalty must not produce passive ... people ... there is indeed the fear that the obligation to do everything with full obedience and loyalty might produce humans who are like robots/automotons that move only when commanded (speech by General L.B. Murdani, 20 May 1987).

By 1989, with the debate on openness in full swing in civilian intellectual circles, Army chief of staff, General Edi Sudrajat had this to say:

Having enjoyed better education, our people want differences discussed more openly. As such they want more active participation in the decision-making process on national problems and in social control (speech by General Edi Sudrajat, at Magelang Military Academy, 5 December 1990).

In December 1990 Sudrajat presided over an army seminar which attempted to project the make-up of what was euphemistically termed the 'human resources' (*sumber daya manusia*) of Indonesia in the years ahead. Some of the seminar's recommendations and conclusions indicated the army's understanding of society's more liberal urges:

1. The concept of development should not be static.
2. The people will become more critical and desire more participation as society becomes more open.
3. They will want more of a say in electing the leadership.
4. Current social and political institutions are not fully developed.

5. They are characterised by too much paternalism.
6. Education is unevenly distributed.
7. Officials must know when to step down.
8. Their period of office must be clearly defined.

ABRI's embrace of the need for more openness, and acknowledgement of the need for reforms in this direction took some people by surprise. In the first place, the perception prevalent among the civilian elite was that ABRI's continued belief in a 'security approach' to the safeguard of national stability ruled out their espousal of so-called 'Western liberal ideas of democracy and free speech'. More savvy commentators understood ABRI's strategy as less to change the system as to bring about a change of leadership:

> Apparently the game, even at this late hour still seems to be to try again with words to trigger somebody's senses into realising that it is time indeed to change (*Indonesian Observer*, 5 December 1990).

Indeed, some of ABRI's actions appeared to contradict the new political rhetoric of its leaders. Whilst tacitly supporting student demonstrations on campuses in Central Java, West Java and Jakarta, in the course of 1989 the incidents of local discontent were dealt with in the familiar harsh fashion dictated by the 'security approach'. In March 1989 a minor disturbance in the South Sumatran province of Lampung resulted in an army assault on alleged Muslim extremists in a village, leaving at least forty, and possibly as many as two hundred, dead.

ABRI's decision to adopt a kinder, gentler approach to the people of East Timor after international diplomatic pressure forced the government to open up the disputed province in early 1989, did not bring a halt to army intimidation of those suspected of disloyalty to the state. Faced by increasingly militant Timorese youth in urban areas, the army showed little leniency. On 12 November 1991, troops fired on mourners in a cemetery on the outskirts of the capital, Dili, leaving by a later official account at least fifty dead. When a low-level insurgency re-erupted in the North Sumatran province of Aceh in early 1990, the army's response was as fierce and uncompromising, leaving hundreds dead.

While ABRI debated openness and democracy with intellectuals in Jakarta, senior officers were maintaining that when it came to threats to national security, ABRI was above the law (attributed to a senior ABRI staff officer by a representative of a humanitarian organisation in Jakarta October 1991). In this respect, ABRI's true orientation with regard to the democratic tendencies emerging in Indonesian society was not easy to define. Some observers felt that the assertive action taken by the military against irredentist movements in Timor and Aceh was partly a product of knowing no other means to deal with the situation. Political enlightenment may have seeped into the upper ranks, but at the local command level the legacy of basic training which emphasised the use of brute force to deal with social disturbances still prevailed. Some recognition of this by 1990 was evident after the military sanctioned for the first time the use of civilian university teachers to enhance the curriculum at the military academy at Magelang.

ABRI's Dilemma

Arguably, by the beginning of the 1990s ABRI was confronting a dilemma. The New Order with which the military rode to power in 1966 was under pressure to renew itself. In common with other longserving regimes in the region, it was fast becoming a victim of its own success. There was a limit to how much longer the people could be convinced of the need for stifling order and stability at the expense of individual freedom to sustain national development. For once national development had been achieved to the successful degree so evident in the ASEAN states, the people possessed more materialistic means for assuring their own security, however intrinsically unstable the fabric of society was deemed to be. In this context, ABRI was torn between the reality of its role and the ideals of its doctrine.

To resolve this dilemma, the ABRI leadership sought a way of preserving its political pre-eminence in advance of the coming succession struggle. Thus ABRI's articulation of the need for more openness seemed to be driven less by a desire to relinquish power, than by the necessity of maintaining their relevance in politics to enhance their popularity. As suggested above, this latter period of the New Order was characterised by a blending of society's desire for political change with the elite's more narrow concerns about political succession. In this respect, it remains to be seen whether ABRI's commitment to political change survives the change of leadership.

Whether the future prospects for democracy are linked to the military's reduced role in any future Indonesian power structure is a tempting area of speculation. Based on the above analysis it seems reasonable to assume that ABRI will be reluctant to yield its position as a key political institution and its role as guardian of the state. As stated by one senior officer in 1980:

> ... it is clear that the armed forces would never abandon what it perceives to be its responsibility towards the people, which is to be active in the total life of Indonesian society (Nugroho 1980:95).

In fact, the signs are that though its room for manoeuvre has been weakened by Suharto's canny use of divide and rule tactics, ABRI continues to dominate the competition for power at the top. Few Indonesians believe that the next president will not be drawn from among its ranks. Although the notion of a civilian vice president gained currency towards the end of President Suharto's fifth term, the most likely contenders for power in a post-Suharto power-struggle are either in the armed forces, or are retired senior officers.

Indeed, Suharto's selection of former armed forces commander General Try Sutrisno as vice president in March 1993 was interpreted in ABRI circles as a signal that a military successor was guaranteed. But nothing in politics is guaranteed, and Suharto's concession to ABRI esteem was skilfully counterbalanced by his promotion of civilian interests soon after his re-election as president in March.

As Suharto embarked on his sixth presidential term, he seemed once again to be juggling his political support, and keeping the military at bay. The political leeway he granted to men like Professor B.J. Habibie, the artful minister of Research and Technology whose ambitious – not to mention costly – schemes for Indonesia's technological development irked the innately conservative military establishment, had parallels with Sudharmono's role in the previous five-year period.

In political terms, the licence Suharto appeared to grant Habibie guaranteed that ABRI would be preoccupied with attempts to block him, leaving Suharto free to focus on his broader national and international agenda. The succession question was, in this way, neatly shelved for the time being.

The crucial question is whether the current democratisation debate, and the slight relaxation of freedom of expression accompanying it, is a function of this competition for power, or a manifestation of actual progress towards more democracy in Indonesia. One of Indonesia's most respected civilian political figures, head of *Nahdlatul Ulama*, the vast rural-based Islamic organisation, is optimistic:

> Once you open the door you can't shut it completely – that's the lesson, what happened to Nikita Krushchev after he opened the door by criticising the Communist Party. It accumulates you see, during the Brezhnev era and after that Gorbachev and then the emergence of Boris Yeltsin. All those things show that, however little, sediments of democratic spirit will come through the filter and accumulate. So I don't think the next government will be able to reverse the situation (interview with Abdurrahman Wahid, *Inside Indonesia* October 1990, pp. 4-6).

Such optimism may be justified in the light of the changing global situation, and specifically in the light of persistent international pressure on the Indonesian government after the 12 November 1991 incident in East Timor. But so long as the armed forces act as the principal agent in the filter Wahid refers to, it is hard to imagine a radical departure from the current patterns of social and political control practised by the New Order.

3

THE MILITARY AND DEMOCRACY IN THAILAND

Suchit Bunbongkarn

A stable democracy requires public commitment to democratic norms and procedures, a strong and institutionalised party system, and active pressure groups. Such conditions have yet to be fully developed in Thailand. Since the ending of absolute monarchical rule in 1932, the fragility of representative institutions and public political apathy have allowed the military to take control of state power. Over the past sixty years the struggle for power between men in uniform and civilian politicians has been reflected in a series of coups and continued military control of the state. The armed forces have been concerned not only with national defence but with other dimensions of national security such as political stability. Through effective control over state apparatuses, particularly the police force and civil service, the military has dominated political decision-making; the course of political change has not been set by civilian politicians or political parties. The party system is far from institutionalised and its lack of mass support is clearly evident. As a result, the separation between democracy and military rule remains fragile in Thailand.

In the last ten years, however, Thailand has undergone dramatic changes which perhaps have provided the preconditions for democracy: pluralism, open politics, and rapid industrialisation. These developments have not put an end to authoritarian rule. A coup occurred in February 1991. The military subsequently appointed a civilian government, but pro-democracy forces have become very active in campaigning against the pro-military constitution and General Suchinda Kraprayoon's assumption of the premiership. Thus, although the military continues to play an important role in politics, it faces increasing competition for state power from civilian politicians. It is being forced to tolerate the increasing strength of representative institutions and extra-bureaucratic forces and to adjust its role accordingly. A 'guardian' role continues to be advocated by the military, but that role is unlikely to enjoy as much public support as in the past. In discussing the role of the military in the democratisation process in Thailand, the interesting questions therefore are: what role does the military have to play in the process of democratisation, and under what circumstances will its political role change?

Coups and the Military's Struggles for State Power

In Thailand, coups, not elections, have become the norm for change of political leadership and government (Bunbongkarn 1987a:42-52). Since 1932, political change has evolved in a cyclical pattern – starting with a coup, followed by an election and a short period of open politics, before a crisis leading to another coup. In most cases, the coups provide a channel for the Royal Thai Army (RTA) to exert influence on the political situation, and have little to do with political transformation. They reflect struggles for power among the top military officers and civil servants among the political class. Some coups have been launched to oust civilian governments; others have been the result of competition for state power between factions within the military establishment. Rarely have political norms and practices been altered.

The first coup in modern Thai political history, which took place in 1932, can be considered one of the very few military interventions which led to a regime change, since it overthrew the absolute monarchy and replaced it with a form of constitutional rule. Although a democratic government was not installed, some democratic norms and practices were introduced. Subsequent military interventions were staged simply to provide opportunities for military leaders to acquire senior political positions. The 1947 coup was a case in point. It provided an avenue to power for a new group of army officers who were not previously involved in politics (Samudavanija and Bunbongkarn 1985:83). These officers were much more traditionalist than the 1932 coup leaders. Most of them did not have the same degree of exposure to Western education and culture and they lacked political vision and a blueprint for political development. Apart from personal ambition, the motive behind the coup was to return to military rule and restore the prestige of the armed forces. At the end of World War II, the armed forces were in disarray as the government was under Allied pressure to demobilise the army which had cooperated with Japanese troops in military operations during the war. The army was humiliated and the civilian-led, anti-Japanese underground Free-Thai Movement was the hero.

After the 1947 coup, the armed forces split into factions, each competing for power. But although the military elite was divided by personal interest, the military's political dominance remained unaffected. The group supporting democracy was small and confined to elected parliamentarians and some intellectuals. In the 1950s, the Thai public was politically apathetic and viewed politics as a matter for the ruling class. Political parties were unorganised and lacked mass support; they did not present a threat to the military.

Military rule in Thailand was further strengthened when Marshal Sarit staged a coup in 1958 (Chaleamtiarana 1979). The distinctive characteristic of this coup was the combination of conservatism and capitalism. Sarit, who had been a key member of the 1947 coup group, rose rapidly to power after this coup. He later came into conflict with senior leaders, particularly Field Marshals Pibul and Phin and Police General Phao. Sarit launched a coup to oust those three from power in 1957. A second coup the following year, however, dealt a heavy blow to all liberal and progressive elements as well as to the representative institutions. Sarit soon realised that political instability in part derived from the fact that the armed forces lacked cohesiveness. An ideology was needed to reunify the armed forces and to guide the direction of political change. Sarit's response was a conservatism which raised the prestige of the monarchy, consolidated bureaucratic rule, abolished constitutionalism, and limited political activities.

Most analysts agree that Sarit's military rule was detrimental to democratic development, as democratic institutions and practices were not given a chance to survive. Sarit believed that what the country needed most was not political but economic development. Nevertheless his emphasis on economic development eventually strengthened the business community and other extra-bureaucratic forces, which in turn contributed to the strength of civil society. An influx of foreign investment, more systematic national economic development plans, and the expansion of economic infrastructure strengthened the business sector. The student organisation which led the historic uprising in October 1973 gained strength from the expansion of higher education initiated during Sarit's period.

Coups and Democratisation

The coup in 1977 was different. While other coups were staged to enhance military rule, this intervention was intended to allow greater democratisation, with the promulgation of a democratic constitution, elections to a House of Representatives, and the granting of political freedoms. The coup occurred a year after the military had seized power from the civilian government in a volatile political situation created by a series of clashes between left- and right-wing groups. The civilian government emerged from an uprising in 1973 which overthrew military rule, but the government could not cope with the political violence and internal bickering in the government parties, which characterised open politics. The seizure of power by the military in 1976 terminated the three-year period of the civilian regime and installed an ultra-rightist civilian government under the supervision of a military junta. The new government lasted only one year before being ousted by the same group of military leaders who had installed it.

One of the major reasons for the military staging the 1977 coup was the political suppression practised by the government. Most liberal and progressive groups were labelled communists or communist sympathisers and severely suppressed. A number had to flee to the jungles, where they joined the Communist Party of Thailand. Military leaders came under pressure from various groups in the civil society, and from a powerful faction in the army which could not tolerate this ultra-rightist policy, to replace the government with a more liberal one.

Following the 1977 coup parliamentary rule lasted almost twelve years, the longest period of civilian rule since 1932 (though the government survived two attempted coups). Political parties gained strength and legitimacy. Commitment to democracy among the educated Thai was on the rise and the military seemed close to accepting democratic norms and practices (Boonprasert 1990).

In February 1991, however, the military staged another coup, putting an end to parliamentary rule. Like the coups in 1947 and 1976, the military justified the intervention in terms of the weakness of the civilian government. It also cited the excessive corruption of civilian politicians, which had clearly undermined the legitimacy of the government. But the real reason behind the coup was the mutual distrust between the military and the government. A number of leading military officers felt insecure when Prime Minister Chatichai appointed ex-army chief General Arthit Kamlangek as deputy Defense minister in early 1991 to tighten control over the armed forces (Bunbongkarn 1992:132-33).

Prime Minister Chatichai came to power in 1989 after General Prem declined an invitation to continue in the premiership. As the leader of the biggest party in the National Assembly after the 1989 general election, Chatichai was the only legitimate successor to General Prem. He had maintained good relations with the military until the second year of his term, but his intention to exert more control over the military caused concern in the armed forces.

After the coup, the military was faced with a problem of how to deal with the growing democratic forces. Protests led by pro-democracy parties, student organisations, and other civic groups against the draft constitution signified the growing commitment to democracy within those groups and forced the coup leaders to grant concessions (such as agreeing not to let active military officers hold political posts).

The Military's Mission and Its Political Involvement

To hold on to power, the military had to adjust its mission and organisation to changes in political and social circumstances. Before 1932 the armed forces' mission was to safeguard the king and defend the country from outside aggression. After the People's Party overthrew the absolute monarchy the military's mission was changed to that of protecting the new constitution and the new regime. The military's guardianship mission expanded for the first time into political affairs. It became a key instrument of support for politicians in uniform.

Between 1932 and the end of World War II the armed forces expanded and developed not only to meet the government's defence needs but also to strengthen the support for Field Marshal Pibulsongkram, who emerged rapidly after the 1932 coup as a strong political leader. After the war a communist threat provided the armed forces with a new justification for its expansion and involvement in national affairs. The victory of the Chinese Communist Party in 1949, the outbreak of the Korean War in 1950, and the Vietminh's struggle for Vietnam's independence in the early 1950s forced Thailand to ally itself with the US. Postwar Thai militarism grew to meet the challenge of communism and Thailand was integrated into the US collective security system. The Thai armed forces were modernised and expanded further with the assistance of the US. Between 1950 and 1971 US military assistance averaged $US46 million per year, which represented 50 per cent of the Thai Defence Ministry's total budget (Snitwongse 1990:91). As a result US influence was pervasive in the Thai military, especially in education, training programs, strategic thinking and military hardware.

One aspect of US influence in the 1950s was the perception of the communist threat. The Thai military shared the US view that the communist threat would come in the form of overt aggression from outside. The domino theory and John Foster Dulles's containment policy received much attention within the government and the military establishment. As a result, the development of the armed forces was geared to the threat of conventional warfare.

The development of the armed forces further strengthened the political position of the military elite. During the 1950s and 1960s civilian political forces were unorganised, fragile and unable to challenge the military. They lacked mass support and linkages to groups in the society. The Democrat Party was the only organised political force but it was popular only in Bangkok. The military establishment was expanded in part to provide a basis of support for military leaders. Since coups had become a method of changing government, the military organisation was an important political resource for those officers who sought to use the coup as an avenue of control over state power.

Among the three armed forces, the army enjoyed the strongest growth. The navy, which had been powerful before World War II, suffered from its abortive coup in 1951. The air force had always been a close ally of the army and supported the army in becoming the leading service. It is not surprising, therefore, that army leaders have acquired more political posts than the other services.

US military assistance did not affect the political attitudes and thinking of Thai military officers. US assistance up to the 1970s included training programs for Thai officers at major military educational institutions like West Point and Fort Leavenworth, and American advisers were sent to Thailand to organise training programs for military personnel. But these programs did not result in transformation of the political outlook of Thai military officers. Liberal-democratic attitudes, military professionalism, and the concept of civilian supremacy did not emerge within the military establishment. American assistance coincided with an increase in the military elite's involvement in political affairs and, perhaps because the US made no effort to dissuade them from political involvement, the political outlook of the military elite remained the same.

Without challenge from the democratic forces it is impossible to see the military furthering the development of democracy in Thailand. The modernisation and strengthening of the armed forces has led only to an increase in the political power of the military elite, strengthening their advantage in the struggle for state power. For three decades after World War II, the armed forces were split and became the personal power base of military leaders. Sarit, Thanom and Prapas, who first came into politics through the 1947 coup and reached the peak of their power in the 1960s, were known to have used the armed forces as their support base. Political parties like the National Socialist Party of Sarit and the United Thai People of Thanom and Prapas did not have political significance and were used as a façade to give their regimes the appearance of legitimacy. Personalisation of politics bred factionalism within the armed forces.

The Communist Insurgency and Military-Initiated Liberalisation

The military's failure to suppress the communist insurgency is one of several important factors which contributed to the military-initiated liberalisation which brought a relatively long period of parliamentary rule in the 1980s. Thai military leaders were concerned with the communist insurgency from the early 1960s. But they believed that it was external in origin and consequently that the success of the insurgency depended in large part on the communist movement's success in Vietnam and Laos. To counter the insurgency in Thailand, the RTA saw improvement of the people's livelihood in the affected remote rural areas as essential. Political solutions to the problem were not considered (Snitwongse 1990: 93-94).

Marshal Sarit's action reflected the military elite's perception of that period. Communist suspects were severely punished. The military launched rural development projects in peripheral areas where the state was not in evidence. The military believed that the communist insurgents were merely bandits, without an organisation, and could be easily dealt with by the police force. In 1965 when overt armed insurgency broke out in the northeast, armed suppression was carried out on the assumption that military means were the only way to wipe out the communist movement. This response only fuelled the insurgency which expanded rapidly in other parts of the country in the late 1960s. Military campaigns against the communists intensified in the 1970s, but further encouraged the spread of the armed struggle. Civic actions were carried out against poverty and hardship in peripheral areas, but these did not stop the expansion of the insurgency.

After 1977, when General Kriangsak staged a coup which overthrew the rightist regime of Thanin Kraivixien, a new strategy of counter-insurgency was initiated to replace military campaigns. Intensification of the insurgency in response to the sweeping suppression of liberal and leftist movements during the twelve months of Thanin's rule became a major concern to the military. In addition, an exodus of more than a thousand students, intellectuals and laborers to join the Communist Party of Thailand, following the ruthless suppression of the student protest on 6 October 1976, expanded its support base and convinced the military that a new counter-insurgency policy was needed.

The military-initiated liberalisation began in 1978 when Kriangsak's government lifted the suppression order on the CPT and its sympathisers and enacted an amnesty law for those who joined the CPT after the 1976 coup. As a result, defectors, many former student leaders and intellectuals, left the Communist Party and resumed their normal lives. The political offensive strategy became official when the government of General Prem Tinasulanond issued Prime Ministerial Order No. 66/2523. This detailed a counter-insurgency policy which stressed the priority of political means over military actions to suppress the CPT. It laid down operational guidelines, such as the elimination of social and economic injustices, promotion of political participation, promotion of democratic institutions and movements, and assurance of political freedom. In short, the order made it clear that building full democracy was the only means to defeat communism.

Attempts were made to implement the order. Several mass organisations were established in rural areas to mobilise the people in support of the government's insurgency suppression program. The military claimed that these organisations were evidence of democratic development at the grassroots level since the people were encouraged to participate in the administration and the development of their villages. The Thai National Defense Volunteers, Volunteer Development and Self-Defense villages, and the Military Reservist for National Security organisation were set up as centres for mobilisation and training of villagers for democratic participation (Bunbongkarn 1987b:53-58).

It is difficult, however, to see these projects as catalysts to democratisation in Thailand when the administrative structure at the village and *tambol* (sub-district) levels remained unchanged. Although the village headman and *tambol* officer (*kamnan*) were elected by the people, they came under the authority of the provincial administration, and the village and *tambol* administrations were parts of the provincial administration and received their budgets from the central government. The people were not given the authority to decide the future of their community and the local administrative structure and the principle of development from above remained unaffected.

The Military, Society, and Democratisation

More important, however, was the liberalisation and democratisation at the national level. After the 1977 coup, Prime Minister Kriangsak promised to promulgate a permanent constitution within a year and hold a general election a few months later. Pressure for liberalisation came from a group of middle-ranking officers, known as 'The Thai Young Turks', which was formed within the army after the October 1973 uprising. Their demand for democratic reform was less ideological than pragmatic: they favoured strong leadership and coups, but liberalisation and democratisation were acceptable if they could resolve national conflict and promote political stability.

The twelve years of liberalisation and parliamentary rule after 1979 would not have been possible without the initiative of the Kriangsak government. Despite liberalisation Thailand still faced instability, partly because the military continued to maintain strong political influence throughout that period. The military regime initiated liberalisation because it wanted to ease the political tension which had resulted from the rightist policies of the Thanin government. But assurance had to be given to the military that its corporate interests would not be endangered. Open politics in this period allowed representative institutions to develop and gradually made inroads on the military-dominated regime. Coups staged in 1981 and 1985 showed that the military was disturbed by the decline of the bureaucratic polity and the development of political parties. The army's attempt in 1983 to have the constitution amended to allow serving military officers and civil servants to hold cabinet portfolios was further evidence of this. (The 1978 constitution permitted active government and military officers to assume political posts for four years only after the 1979 general election.)

Prime Minister Prem, who took the helm of the country from 1981 to 1989, had to maintain a delicate balance. It was a period during which liberalisation and democratisation were put to the test. Although the military's power was waning, it was still powerful and was a major force in the state. But as civil society was becoming more influential, the army had to review its role in the political arena. While factions like the Young Turks accepted coups as a strategy, others believed that they had to play the game by the rules. They agreed that since the Thai political system was in a transitional phase, the military could not withdraw itself from the political scene; it had to take part in politics to make democratisation possible. The army's role as political broker and supporter of the Prem government was emphasised. Nevertheless the military was not willing to let political parties take full control of the state. Army leaders were involved in forming the government in order to make sure that the prime minister and other key cabinet members were on their side. Political parties were not allowed to interfere in matters of the military's domain such as the defence budget, counter-insurgency operations, personnel reshuffles, and control of the electronic media. Stability during this liberalisation period, though delicate, was maintained because the boundary between the military and civilian politicians was observed by both sides.

The breakdown of the democratisation process in 1991 and the pro-democracy protests against Prime Minister General Suchinda Kraprayoon in mid May 1992 showed that although the military was able to seize state power, as it did in the February 1991 coup, civil society was strong enough to curb the military's influence in government. The 1991 military intervention reflected the armed forces' disaffection with the increasing influence of political parties and the civil society's attempt to exert more control over the military. It did not meet resistance because the Chatichai government had lost the support of the people. Nevertheless, when General Suchinda resigned from the army and assumed the premiership after the April 1992 election the civil society was able to force the former army chief to step down. Opposition parties and other pro-democracy groups launched a protest with the support of the urban middle class, including businessmen, intellectuals, and people from various professions. It was the biggest protest witnessed in Thailand since the student uprising in 1973. The demands of the pro-democracy groups were strengthened by the ruthless suppression of the demonstration by the military, which led to stronger public condemnation.

One of the problems of democratisation in Thailand has been that, because of a long period of bureaucratic and military domination, a democratic regime often has difficulty establishing legitimacy in relation to the traditional political culture. Economic and social changes in recent years have produced a new urban, educated middle class which subscribes to the principles of democracy; but the possibility of an *effective* democratic government could hardly be expected. The Chatichai government (1989-1991) gained legitimacy because it was popularly elected, but it later lost legitimacy because it could not tackle effectively the corruption in the government. Anand's government, which succeeded it after the 1991 coup, assumed power without legitimacy because it was appointed by the military junta. But it went on to gain public recognition as one of the most reliable, transparent and efficient governments. The fact that all democratic regimes in Thailand have been weak and inefficient has affected their legitimacy. And if they cannot improve their performance and accountability, their popular support will be easily undermined.

With this in mind, the military has generally preferred a non-partisan prime minister, and has given him full support in order to ensure the government's stability. This implies a preference, on the part of the army, for effectiveness over legitimacy. After the 1992 general election the military wanted to continue its control of the state and to insulate the state mechanisms from popular forces. What the military leaders did not anticipate was the strength of the civil society. Attempting to force the political parties and the people to accept Suchinda as the government leader was a big mistake. It reflected the inability of the military elite to understand the development of societal groups which were determined to fight for democratisation and a weakening of the political power of the military.

The May 1992 Uprising and the Prospect of Democratic Development

The downfall of General Suchinda has again raised one of the important questions which arises whenever there is a breakdown of authoritarian rule: is Thailand going to have a stable and long-lasting democracy? The answer is probably no. It is difficult to anticipate sustained democratisation. One reason is that changes have yet to take place in the military establishment to make it more conducive to democratic development. The concept of civilian control is still unacceptable within the armed forces. More important, the military continues to insist on its political guardian role, which implies a right to intervene whenever it feels that national security is threatened. During the 1980s there were signs that the army was about to accept a civilian-dominated regime, but as one expert on Thai security affairs said, the change in the military's political thinking was 'in a very formative stage, incoherent and inconsistent' (Snitwongse 1990:103). Thus, when the Class 5 Group (the fifth graduating class from the Military Academy under the West Point curriculum) assumed leadership in the RTA, liberal attitudes in the army began to erode. Class 5 officers led by Suchinda and Issarapong Noonpakdi, the former army chief, are not known for their liberal political ideas. The group was first formed to counter the Young Turks group, but later transformed itself into a powerful pressure group to work for the benefit and promotion of its members. The group has firm control of the army and has not been much affected by the pro-democracy protest and the downfall of Suchinda.

Having been resurrected, Thai civil society now poses a real threat to the military. The business community is expanding and becoming more complex. Several professional and societal groups, including doctors, lawyers and teachers' associations, are demanding an end to the military's political involvement. It can be argued that these popular uprisings have been largely a phenomenon of Bangkok and other major urban areas, and that they are unlikely to have a strong impact in the country. However, it has always been the urban people who have led public opinion and successfully pressed for political reforms. The May 1992 uprising was a product of the politicisation of urban groups. Now that authoritarian rule is fading, the question of whether democratisation will be consolidated remains to be answered. The military establishment is still unified and reform from within cannot be expected in the immediate future. In the long run, if the politicisation of societal groups continues, military reform will become inevitable, and as a result political democracy will be given more chance to consolidate itself.

The triumph in the September 1992 election of the pro-democracy forces – comprising Chuan's Democratic Party, the New Aspiration Party (NAP), the Palang Dham Party and Solidarity – and the subsequent establishment of the democratic government led by Chuan, marked another important development in civil-military relations. The armed forces have pledged to support the government and to remain in their barracks. The military leaders once again have reiterated that the military will not interfere in political affairs; modernisation programs and professional development will be their main priorities. Chuan also recognises that civil-military relations are a delicate matter and civilian control can hardly be achieved if the prime minister and defence minister are unacceptable to the armed forces.

To placate the military, Chuan appointed a retired and respected general to head the Defense ministry. In addition, he has been very cautious in dealing with technical matters such as national security policy, strategic issues, defence budgets, and military personnel appointments, in the hope that the relationship is not jeopardised. Despite these efforts, however, the relationship continues to be delicate and a lot needs to be done to strengthen it.

Among other things, the civilian government must improve its efficiency, accountability and stability. The Thai political experience suggests that the fragility of democratic governments encourages military intervention. To change the military mind-set into a more democratic one, the civilian democratic government must prove itself strong and responsible.

Democratic reforms should be carried out gradually. The military and other conservative elements are not in favour of radical changes. The vote by the military-dominated Senate in March 1994 against the government parties' bill to reduce the number of the senators showed that the military, though supporting the government, would not let the democratisation process go too far or too fast. The pro-democracy groups which advocate more drastic reform should keep in mind that the military and the conservatives are still influential and control a variety of political resources. Even the urban middle class, which supported the pro-democracy groups during the May 1992 event, does not agree with radical political reform. The politics of compromise is likely to be essential during the initial stage of democratisation.

Democratisation involves institutionalisation of the competitive process by which the people elect their leaders. This can be done by allowing continuity of the representative government and elections. The military should learn how to tolerate the democratic processes and play the game by the rules. The more elections Thailand has, the more developed the competitive process will be. Once the process is institutionalised, coups will find no place in the Thai political system.

4

THE MILITARY AND THE FRAGILE DEMOCRACY
OF THE PHILIPPINES

Viberto Selochan

On 4 July 1946 the US granted independence to the Philippines, in keeping with its promise of self-determination for the islands after a period of Commonwealth administration. The Philippines thus became the first independent democratic country in Asia. During its colonial administration the US had encouraged the development of political parties, though the two major parties which developed differed little in ideology – the main differences concerning their attitudes to US administration of the islands.

At independence the Philippines political system was modelled on that of the United States, where the constitution required the armed forces to uphold civilian supremacy. As in the US, elections were held every four years in the Philippines, and presidents were limited to two terms in office. This constitutional requirement was initially upheld and the military played a minor role in politics, except to guard polling stations against fraud during elections. Threats by the communist-inspired Hukbalahap movement soon after independence to seize political power and disrupt national elections required the military to play a more active role in monitoring elections. As a result of its success in curbing the insurgents' threat to the country, the military was co-opted into playing a larger role in the administration of former defence secretary, Ramon Magsaysay.

When he was elected president of the republic in 1965, Ferdinand Marcos believed that in a developing country where the military was not occupied with external threats, it should assist in developing the country. He used the military in civic action programs and to enhance his chances of being re-elected. Marcos was the first Philippines president to be elected to a second term in office. Constitutionally deprived of seeking a third term, Marcos declared martial law in 1972 and facilitated the military's playing a larger role in government. When he was forced to leave office in 1986, elements in the military found difficulty in adjusting to the requirements of the democratic system restored by Corazon

Aquino. To assist in this process, military personnel were subjected to instruction in democratic principles and the role of the military in a democracy. Yet Aquino had to endure seven attempts by the military to seize political power. The survival of her government was due to some extent to the belief among elements of the Armed Forces of the Philippines (AFP) that the military must remain subservient to civilians in a democracy. The military's adherence to democracy was again tested during the national elections in May 1992. There were fears that it would attempt to seize power if the elections were seen to be fraudulent, but with free and fair elections the military adhered to the restored democracy.

Strong leadership and a weak central state have been the hallmarks of Philippine politics. Whether democracy will continue to flourish in the post-Cold-War era, when authoritarian rule is generally in retreat, remains to be seen.

Origins of Democracy in the Philippines

When the United States colonised the Philippines in 1898 it planned to gradually grant self-determination to the country as the principles of democracy were imbibed by the population. As education was not widespread, the elite and the educated benefitted most from the system instituted by the US, which was largely executed by officers of the US army. Filipinos worked in the American administration and quickly came to value the concept of self-government. By 1917, when the US decided to institute its policy of 'Filipinisation' , the elite was ready to assume positions vacated by departing US military officers. Between 1917 and 1935, when the Commonwealth came into existence, political parties were formed and most of the population was educated into accepting the principles of democracy, which meant having a ruling party and an opposition. In this respect, the Philippines was significantly different from many Asian countries which gained independence a few years later. As Apter (1962:154) points out: these countries did not generally accept an opposition as a normal feature of a democracy. The small elite who controlled the political process realised that each party would have its turn in government. The Nacionalista and Liberal parties, which differed little ideologically, dominated politics, and politicians switched parties to gain office. But the democratic system that developed did not represent the majority of the population.

The Philippine Commonwealth was inaugurated in 1935 under a democratic constitution patterned after the United States bicameral system. 'The ideology of American 'democracy' which emphasised the limitation of state power was very different from the philosophy of the French in Indo-China, the Dutch in the Indies and the British in Malaya. It played into the hands of the elite to whom the Americans, always ambivalent colonial rulers, proceeded to hand over political power as soon as possible' (Overholt 1986:1136).

> For most Filipinos, American-style democracy meant little more than elections every few years. Beyond this, the colonial authorities made sure that only the candidates who represented colonial interests first and last won. This practice did not die with colonialism. The ensuing political order, which persisted long after independence, was one where a handful of families effectively and ruthlessly ruled a society riven by inequality. It was democratic in form, borrowing as many American practices as it could, but autocratic in practice (World Bank report cited in Chomsky 1991:237).

The first duty of the Commonwealth government was national security. President Manuel Quezon procured the services of General Douglas MacArthur, who was about to retire as US Army Chief of Staff, to establish the Philippine military. MacArthur and his US military advisory team used the Swiss army as a model for the Philippine army. A military academy, patterned after the US military academy at West Point, was designed in which officers were to be instructed in the techniques and skills of the military and taught that the proper role of the military in a democracy was one of subservience to civilian government. In practice, however, these ideals were not easily imparted to the new recruits, many of whom attained their place at the academy through political patronage rather than merit (Selochan 1990:57). Courses at the academy were oriented towards equipping cadets to maintain internal law and order through combat techniques. The curriculum did not address subjects in the humanities. Maintaining law and order, more a policing than military function, required more emphasis on domestic politics than military skills. Officers recruited from the Reserve Officers Training Course (ROTC) conducted at the universities were more amenable to humanitarian considerations, but they did not generally hold command positions in the military as they were seen as part-time soldiers. Yet with a liberal education they were possibly more attuned to the democratic process than the officers trained at the Philippines Military Academy (PMA) under an authoritarian military system.

Officers' adherence to democratic practices also suffered under the Commission on Appointments (CA), instituted to vet appointments under a functioning democracy. Politicians who were members of the CA sought and gained allegiance from officers in exchange for approving their promotion. Many officers consequently remained indebted to politicians and were unable to conform strictly to the military chain of command. While the Philippine military was still being developed World War II abruptly interrupted the military training and education program. To defend the islands, the fledgling Philippine military was incorporated into the United States Armed Forces for the Far East (USAFFE) under the command of General MacArthur.

At the termination of the war, the Philippines had suffered severe damage. It also had over one million people claiming to be guerilla fighters and thus seeking a place in the military. Reconstruction of the Philippine economy and the reconstitution of the military became priorities of the newly-installed government under President Osmeña. Independence was also granted during this period. But the country was inadequately equipped to assume full sovereignty.

The 1935 constitution, which was adopted at independence on 4 July 1946, provided the framework within which a democratic state could develop.

> The Constitution was supplemented by laws enacted by legislatures at the national, provincial, and city/municipal levels of government. A centralised court system which was headed by the Supreme Court performed the judicial function of the state and a career national bureaucracy administered the policies of the government. In other words, the political and institutional infrastructure of a democratic government was in place in the Philippines at the time of independence. What was not altered was the distribution of wealth, economic power and social status (Lapitan 1989:236).

The American-style democracy exported to the Philippines was bound to encounter problems: 'Except in rare instances, democracy does not work when foreign models are imposed, and many features of American democracy are ill-suited to poor, unstable and divided countries' (Diamond 1992:27).

The President, the Military and Democracy

Soon after independence, Philippine democracy was threatened by the communist-inspired Hukbalahap movement. The insurgents who had fought against the occupying Japanese forces resumed their fight against the newly-installed administration; they had little confidence in the Philippine democratic process which they saw as favoring the ruling elite. Appointed Defense secretary, Ramon Magsaysay was, however, determined to restore faith in democracy, and especially the electoral system. Historically, elections in the Philippines were characterised by vote-buying, vote-rigging and the use of private armies to intimidate voters. Magsaysay used the AFP extensively to ensure that the 1951 elections were conducted fairly, and indeed they were alleged to have been the fairest in Philippine electoral history. Although he did not completely restore the Huks' faith in democracy, Magsaysay reformed the military with assistance from the US and defeated the Huks.

Having worked closely with the military, Magsaysay realised that the skills of the officers could be harnessed to develop the country. When he became president in 1953 Magsaysay decided to use the military in government. He appointed active duty officers to perform a range of functions in his administration. By 1954 Congressman Bengson claimed that over 122 active duty officers were performing duties formally the prerogative of civilians (Selochan 1990:118). Justifying this action, the president said that he was weary of the civilian bureaucracy as a whole. Furthermore,

> I have needed men of my absolute confidence to undertake delicate missions of investigation and cleaning up . . . In other cases, specialised skills and technical know-how were required for quick and official results . . . In still other instances, the new administration came upon officers so deeply entrenched in dishonesty and corruption that only the most ruthless, uncompromising kind of military discipline could redeem them from the mire and restore them to gainful usefulness to our people (Magsaysay, quoted in Abueva 1971:315).

Magsaysay, who probably would have been re-elected in the presidential elections of 1957, died in a plane crash that year. Knowing Magsaysay's attitude to the vice-president, Carlos Garcia, many officers who had been closely associated with Magsaysay were reluctant to allow Garcia to assume the presidency. Abortive plans to seize power before the inauguration were hastily and poorly designed (Selochan 1990:122-23), and Garcia assumed the presidency, aware of the military's attitude to him and to the democratic process. For these and other political reasons, Garcia was determined to rid the administration of officers appointed to government by his predecessor. By this stage AFP officers were pervasive in the government. They were in the cabinet positions normally occupied by civilians. After acrimonious debate, Garcia was able to persuade some officers to return to the AFP; others retired their commissions and ran unsuccessfully for office in the 1961 congressional elections.

Many of the officers who had been in Magsaysay's administration believed that they were more capable of governing than civilians. Some officers also believed that these civilians had achieved their positions as a result of political patronage rather than merit. That civilian politicians were corrupt was evident from their activities during elections and from the manner in which they used their positions to acquire favours from businessmen and the AFP. Democracy in the Philippines, according to many of these officers, benefitted the elite who controlled the political process. The majority of Filipinos, they argued, did not understand the concept of democracy; for them it meant being paid to vote for a candidate at elections. Many officers believed that Philippine-style democracy could not contribute to the economic development of the country but was being abused for the benefit of the elite. Authoritarian rule provided the means of addressing the situation. But the military was neither united in this view nor capable of seizing political power.

Abrogating Democracy

A civilian politician, Ferdinand Marcos, was elected president in 1965. Marcos, who claimed a distinguished career as a guerilla fighter during World War II (later disproved), courted the AFP while he was a congressman, but was generally believed to be suspicious of the AFP, which was rumoured to be planning to seize power in 1965. These rumours were taken seriously by many including the Garcia administration, as there was a series of successful coups in Asia during this period. Concerned about the military's political ambition and believing that a closer relationship with senior officers would serve his long-term interests, Marcos retained the Defense portfolio for the first thirteen months of his administration. During this period he reshuffled the officer corps, promoting officers favourable to his political agenda and retiring others less amenable. The military was subsequently enlisted to assist in his re-election campaign. Marcos became the first Philippine president to be re-elected in what became one of the most violent and fraudulent elections in the country's history. Increasingly during his second term he became dependent on the AFP to remain in office. To serve the interests of the president, the military harassed the opposition and violently quelled demonstrations against the government.

Constitutionally prevented from remaining in office for a third term, Marcos declared martial law in 1972, with the consent of the military, under the pretext of saving the country from Communist and Muslim insurgencies. Martial law allowed the AFP to play a larger role in government. Because democracy was so easily abrogated it has been argued that it had not in fact taken root in the Philippines. But then, 'A democratic constitution does not make a democracy; only democratic, constitutional behaviour that follows a long period of experience and education can truly constitute democracy' (Gastil 1985:161). Although the 1935 constitution had enshrined democratic principles and structures of government, political practice differed considerably from the theory (Reyes 1988:268).

Marcos argued that the democratic system would not allow him to develop the 'New Society' he envisaged for the Philippines. For him, the practice of democracy was 'energy-consuming' and 'time-wasting'; authoritarian rule allowed him to make the changes he wanted without having to endure democratic procedures (Hernandez 1985:243). Under his self-styled constitutional-authoritarianism the institutions of democracy were dismantled: Congress was disbanded, political parties were declared illegal, and civil and political rights were suspended. Freedom, a fundamental tenet of democracy, was taken away from Filipinos. As commander-in-chief, Marcos directed the AFP to carry out martial law functions. The military was, according to the principles of democracy, to remain subservient to the civilian head of state. But the head of state had abrogated the constitution under which he was elected and which officers were sworn to uphold. Third World armed forces have typically justified seizing political power in terms of preserving the constitution and the nation. In the Philippines, however, the military was incapable of governing. Having played a large part in the Magsaysay administration, where it developed its abhorrence of civilian politicians, the AFP was willing to resume a role in government decision-making.

Martial law gave the military the opportunity to get rid of civilian politicians who they believed were self-serving and had little respect for the majority of the people. Junior officers found themselves performing duties for which they were not adequately trained. Reservist officers were considered more capable of performing civilian functions as they had acquired a more liberal education.

To better prepare PMA officers to perform martial law duties, Marcos shortened the cadetship and modified the academy's curriculum in the early 1970s. Courses on democratic principles had still not been introduced to the Academy, but cadets were taught the concept of civilian supremacy over the military. Other significant changes to the curriculum included placing more emphasis on courses in the humanities as opposed to engineering. This, according to some officers, was designed to better equip cadets to work with civilians and in many cases to replace them. In fact, as martial law became entrenched in the Philippines, AFP officers replaced civilians in many government departments, and also in private corporations which Marcos sequestered from his opponents.

Martial law lasted from 1972 to 1981. These nine years had a profound effect on the society and the AFP. The AFP was no longer the protector of the nation. Instead, like a private army, it served Marcos and his cronies. Officers became deeply involved in politics as they rigged elections and suppressed the opposition. Self-interest led officers to pursue activities which lost them the respect of the people. And in turn the military lost its *raison d'être*. More concerned with government than military duties, the AFP was incapable of defeating the growing Communist and Muslim insurgencies; by 1985 the Communist Party of the Philippines (CPP) was claiming control over most of the *barangays* (villages) in the country. The AFP was even incapable of performing the functions of a conventional armed force in conjunction with American forces.

By and large the AFP remained loyal to an authoritarian civilian leader who satisfied its corporate interests and had no intention of restoring democracy. But some officers came to the conclusion that the prolonged period of martial law was working against the president. Widespread dissatisfaction among intellectuals and the middle-class finally surfaced after the 1983 assassination of popular opposition leader Benigno Aquino. Concurrently, factionalism developed in the military as the gap between those benefitting from the system and those fighting the insurgency in the war-torn areas of the countryside increased. The result was that soldiers lost interest in fighting the insurgents, who they believed were justified in their claims, though the military resented their ideology.

A consensus therefore developed among the senior military leadership that 'if the country was to survive as a political system', especially with the CPP/New Peoples Army rapidly gaining ground against the regime, Marcos had to be replaced (Lapitan 1989:237). These views were shared by secretary of defense, Juan Ponce Enrile, and AFP vice chief of staff, General Fidel Ramos. Plans to replace Marcos by a military coup were hastily abandoned when he suddenly announced on television that elections were to be held in February 1986. Surprisingly, the opposition was able to unite against Marcos, backing the widow of Benigno Aquino.

The battle to stop Marcos from cheating Aquino of victory and the defection of elements of the AFP, including General Ramos, culminated in what became popularly known as the 'EDSA revolution' of February 1986. Yet this was not the outcome envisaged by the senior military leaders who had conspired to replace Marcos. Defense Secretary Enrile had nurtured a group of reform-minded officers who shared some of his frustrations with the Marcos regime. These officers formed the Reform the Armed Forces Movement (RAM). With Enrile, they planned to seize political power and install an interim military-civilian council. Aquino was considered a likely member of the council. But when the coup was discovered by Marcos, Enrile joined General Ramos at the armed forces headquarters in Manila and they declared their support for Corazon Aquino. People power resulted from this rebellion which saw the military conceding its desires for political office to Aquino.

The accession of Aquino to the presidency, however, did not stop elements in the military from conspiring to seize political power. Enrile's actions while in the Aquino government, and his subsequent links to a number of the coup attempts, clearly demonstrated his – and the RAM faction's – desire to have a continuing role in government. RAM believed that its claims to a place in government decision-making were justified because it was responsible for assisting Aquino to achieve office (Selochan 1989:8). Enrile also believed that his role in the rebellion against Marcos justified his having a greater role in decision-making. Vice-President Salvador Laurel shared a similar belief, having conceded his presidential ambitions in the interest of Aquino in 1985. Having united in their opposition to Marcos, divisions now appeared in the groups that were contending for power – a pattern common in countries that have experienced transition from authoritarian to democratic systems (Huntington 1991).

Reconstituting Democracy

Much was expected of the Aquino administration. It was anticipated that the government would revive the institutions of democracy abrogated by Marcos in 1972; however, Filipinos also expected the government to take steps to eradicate economic and social inequities. The government promised to reinstate democracy 'but there were no specific social and economic programs that were identified to accomplish the goal of democratisation' (Lapitan 1989:238).

Aquino assumed office with a provisional government under a provisional constitution. This meant that both legislative and executive power was vested in the president until a new constitution was enacted. With the promulgation of a new constitution on 11 February 1987, a new era dawned for democracy in the Philippines. The constitution, which has many similarities with the 1935 American-inspired constitution, has a number of important provisions for the armed forces. Most important of all is the stipulation that active duty officers cannot participate in government.

As promised, elections for all government offices were held throughout the islands under the new constitution by mid 1987. But similarities to the pre-Marcos era were clearly evident as many candidates elected to office were 'former elected officials, relatives of powerful political families and/or members of the powerful economic elite' (Hawes 1989:72). Nevertheless, the elections were competitive and all citizens had the franchise.

Educating the military (which had voted overwhelmingly to reject the constitution) to democratic principles, became one of the issues to be addressed by the 'new' AFP chief of staff, General Ramos. A Training Command was established on 10 December 1986 to coordinate a range of programs to reform the armed forces (Selochan 1990:193). The principal objective of these programs was to restore the tarnished image of the AFP, improve morale and, under a value-formation course, teach the military to respect human rights. Little interest was taken in teaching the military about the need to adhere to democracy.

This did not change even when Marcos supporters and disaffected military elements joined with RAM on July 1986 to stage the first attempted coup against Aquino. It was not until three attempts had been made to seize power, largely by RAM and its supporters, between July 1986 and August 1987, and after PMA cadets had shown a willingness to join in the putsch, that any attempt was made to conduct courses for the AFP on the military's role in a democracy (Selochan 1991a:109). Soon after the first coup attempt notices began appearing at all military establishments and courses were taught at the PMA on democracy. Debates about the military's role in a democracy were conducted in the media as retired officers became columnists, arguing for and against the necessity for the AFP to uphold democracy under Aquino. Politicians were invited to talk to soldiers, and seminars on democracy were conducted for AFP personnel. Suddenly, democracy was an issue in the AFP.

Rhetoric, however, differed from reality as elements in the armed forces, backed by politicians and business groups which had profited under the authoritarian regime and were now unable to acquire the same privileges, were implicated in four further attempts to seize political power. The alliance of politicians and business reflected a common economic interest (Wurfel 1989:681). The factions they supported in the military, however, were incapable of convincing the majority of the AFP that they would benefit from a return to authoritarian rule.

When her term in office ended on 30 June 1992, Aquino proudly claimed that she had achieved her objective of restoring democracy to the Philippines. Elections were scheduled for 11 May 1992. With seven candidates running for the presidency, there were expectations that the military might again attempt to seize power. In fact, however, the elections were peaceful and former AFP chief of staff, General Ramos, was elected to the presidency. Aquino had been confident that democracy was now firmly in place. In her valedictory state of the nation address in June 1992 she said: 'This is the glory of democracy ... that its most solemn moment should be the peaceful transfer of power'.

Conclusion

Elected president in May 1992 by a quarter of the voters, General Ramos is again faced with protecting a fragile democracy. Given his limited mandate, threats from the RAM and the Communist movement, and a host of economic and social problems, Ramos is likely to ensure that democratic principles are upheld in his administration. Otherwise, challenges will quickly eventuate from those who appear still to prefer authoritarian rule. More unified than in recent years, the AFP leadership appears ready to accept democracy as the only system that will contribute to the economic and social development of the Philippines. For them, it is time that the Philippines shared in the economic dynamism of the Asia-Pacific region and that the military be seen not as a supporter of authoritarianism but as a supporter of democracy in a country that was once put forward as Asia's showcase of democracy.

5

BURMA'S STRUGGLE FOR DEMOCRACY:
THE ARMY AGAINST THE PEOPLE

Josef Silverstein

The decade of the 1990s opened with the people cautiously hoping for change in the future of Burma. After twenty-eight years of military rule, in one guise or another, many were optimistic that the 1990 scheduled elections would begin a process by which they would recover power and restore democracy.

Almost from the day they regained their independence from British rule in 1948, their nation has been torn by civil war, which persists to this day, foreign invasion and slow economic recovery from the devastation wrought by World War II. The people were sorely tested in 1988 when they demonstrated for freedom and change but were met with the guns and bullets of the army as it suppressed their peaceful revolution. And even though they complied with martial law, and participated in the election of May 1990 to vote for members of a national assembly as a first step toward the restoration of democracy, their patience went unrewarded as the military found one excuse after another to delay change. All real hopes for peaceful change were dashed in September 1991, when Major-General Tin U said, 'We cannot say how long we will be in charge of the state administration. It might be five or ten years' (*South China Morning Mail* 11 September 1991).

On 23 April 1992 the State Law and Order Restoration Council (SLORC) began a series of actions which were intended to signal that political change was beginning. Under a new leader, SLORC started to release political prisoners and took the first steps toward writing a new constitution. These and other changes provide a preview of the future political system which the military rulers in Burma are trying to establish, a system where the military will play the leading role and the people will be the approving chorus. The model the soldiers-in-power have in mind derives from the present Indonesian system (*The New Light of Myanmar* 24, 25 June 1993). This is the political burden the people carry as they continue to struggle to free themselves from tyranny and dictatorship.

Democracy and its Roots

Before Burma regained independence on 4 January 1948, an uneven leadership struggle developed between the older leaders of the prewar period and the young men who had formed and led the wartime Burma army and the coalition nationalist party, the Anti Fascist People's Freedom League (AFPFL). While the former were prepared to work within the framework of change offered by the British, the latter were not. The people backed the AFPFL from the outset, and its legal right to lead was confirmed in the 1947 election and in the constituent assembly.

Before the authors of the 1947 constitution took up their task they had, at least, three traditions to draw upon. They could have returned to some form of monarchy, such as existed before British rule (Koenig 1990:65-97). But that idea had been rejected during the war period when the Japanese granted Burma independence (Cady 1958:4-5) and again by Aung San, the nationalist leader, when he addressed the AFPFL on the eve of the constitutent assembly (Silverstein 1972: 92-100). They could have created a bureaucratic-authoritarian system, after the model the British instituted at the end of the nineteenth century or that of the constitutional dictatorship fashioned by Dr Ba Maw, under Japanese tutelage, during World War II (Christian 1945:60-76; Maung 1959: 54-62). This, too, was rejected. They had a third model, parliamentary democracy, which the British introduced as early as 1921 to put the nation on a course to self-rule (Christian 1945:77-105).

Most amongst the young elite were Buddhists and were influenced, to various degrees, by Buddhism's values and traditions. Many, however, like their leader Aung San, were Western-educated, holders of university degrees and believers in liberal democracy with its emphasis upon separation of church and state. They came to maturity in a period when democracy was evolving in Burma and they were able to study and debate the political ideas of their day – democracy, fascism, communism – and the meaning and content of Burmese nationalism. Overwhelmingly, they were drawn to socialism, secularism and democracy (Khin Yi 1988; Silverstein 1980:134-161). These ideas were foremost in the thinking of Aung San when he addressed the preconstituent assembly meeting of the AFPFL and committed the party to their support (Silverstein 1972).

But there were divisions within the AFPFL. In a barely disguised struggle between communists and socialists rival leaders and member parties fought for control of the AFPFL and influence in shaping the future constitution. In 1946 the communists were expelled from the AFPFL and the ideas of the socialists, together with those of Aung San, were influential in the writing of the basic law.

The constitution of 1947 created a parliamentary system with two legislative chambers. It included a renunciation of war as an instrument of policy, a set of socialist-influenced unenforceable goals – called directive principles, a definition of relations of the state to peasants and workers, and fundamental human rights for all.

The AFPFL leaders had a special problem in that nearly 40 per cent of the population were members of various minority groups who lived either amongst the Burman (the Karens and Mons) or in the hill areas which surrounded the heartland (the Shans, Kachins, Chins and others). Because the minorities either had been given special treatment under British rule (the Karens formed a separate electorate and were given a specific number of seats in the legislature) or had been excluded from the evolving political process during the same period (the various hill peoples), the question of uniting everyone in the territory of Burma proved vexing. Discussions leading to promises made by the Burman leaders to the minorities resulted in the creation of a unique federal union, which was more unitary than federal, and led to most Karens and Karennis rejecting it. It also promised the right of secession to the populations of two areas but denied it to all others. Failure to solve the problems of national unity at the outset was a major cause of minority revolts after independence (Silverstein 1980).

Internal wars tested the nation. Between 1948 and 1952 the government nearly collapsed as it fought to recover control first of the heartland and then of the hill areas. Yet even as it faced the threat of being overthrown and the union destroyed, the legislature met and acted, a national election was held, the High Court and Supreme Court upheld civil and political rights against the effort of the government to ignore them in its determination to restore control and domestic peace, education expanded at all levels, and the press flourished as one of the freest in all of Asia.

Religion and politics were never far apart. The 1947 constitution established religious freedom, but in the same chapter it declared that Buddhism enjoyed a 'special position'. As early as 1949, a Ministry of Religious Affairs was created and ecclesiastical courts were established. The state also conducted religious examinations and sponsored an international Buddhist celebration to commemorate the Buddha's 2500th birthday (Mendelson 1975:112).

Although the state was declared to be the ultimate owner of all the land, in fact agricultural lands were in private hands and the farmers were free to buy and sell and to make all farming and marketing decisions. While some economic enterprises, such as transportation and power generation, became government monopolies, there was a private economic sector which flourished alongside government businesses and cooperatives.

Despite a non-aligned foreign policy and the illegal invasion and occupation of some of its territory by remnants of the Chinese Nationalist Army – causing the government to divert resources from economic recovery and development to the expansion of the army and the purchase of weapons – the economy slowly recovered to near prewar levels in all areas; many of the groups in revolt either ended their war and returned home or, if they continued to fight, were driven into the hills and the delta area. In 1956 the nation held a second national election which generally was free and fair and produced an opposition party in parliament which generated lively debates and moved the nation from a one-dominant-party to a multi-party system (Silverstein 1956). The institutions of democracy began to grow in an atmosphere of peace and stability.

But unity and stability in the AFPFL leadership did not last. In 1958 the leaders split and, in their struggle to win control of the party and government, the rivals provoked a constitutional crisis. Prime Minister Nu tried to resolve it through a vote in the parliament; but even though he won, his margin was small and his backing came mainly from the minorities rather than the Burman members. Having no dependable majority in parliament, on 26 October Nu stepped down as prime minister and recommended General Ne Win, the military commander, to form a caretaker government and restore political conditions under which new elections could be held to resolve the political crisis.

This was not the first time that Ne Win was brought into government. In 1949, at the height of the rebellions, Nu asked him to serve as deputy prime minister and take charge of several ministries following the mass resignation of the socialists from his cabinet. Ne Win held those posts for nearly seventeen months.

The multiple internal wars in the decade of the 1950s gave Ne Win's army the opportunity to exercise political authority under martial law. In 1952 martial law was proclaimed in parts of the Shan state; it lasted for two years. The army abused the people and acted corruptly, giving rise to its reputation of ruthless and autocratic behaviour. Whatever popularity it had in the hill areas at the outset of its rule vanished as it exercised power.

Ne Win's caretaker government of 1958-60 ruled without party support. It drew upon senior military officers and respected civil servants to serve in the cabinet and administer government offices. Ne Win scrupulously adhered to the letter of the constitution, even demanding its amendment to allow him to serve beyond six months as a nonelected member. But his strict enforcement of the law, insensitivity to the people, and impatience with the democratic process, turned the public against his rule even though his administration brought law and order to a good portion of the country and improved the economy.

Like the government before his, Ne Win's had no compunctions against using religion for political ends. In 1959 it published a booklet entitled *Dhammantaraya* (*Dhamma in Danger*), which declared that the Burmese communists posed a threat to Buddhism, and mobilised 80 800 monks to hold meetings and denounce the local communist movement (Ba Than 1962:71). It also continued the practice of mixing religion and politics by placing religious affairs under the deputy prime minister and enforcing all laws pertaining to religion.

When elections were held in 1960, the party favoured by the military suffered an overwhelming defeat while its opponent, led by U Nu, returned to power (Director of Information 1960; Silverstein 1977). A major issue was U Nu's promise, if elected, to make Buddhism the state religion.

Between that election and the military coup on 2 March 1962, Nu worked hard to strengthen democracy and address the causes of national disunity (Silverstein 1964). But before he could accomplish his goals the military struck, seized power, and replaced democracy and the constitution with a military dictatorship.

Although the democratic experiment lasted only fourteen years, it established an important watershed for Burmese political thought and action. Three national elections had been held and a multiparty system proved workable; leaders coped with major economic and political problems and adopted pragmatic solutions. Human and civil rights generally were honoured, and when questions arose the courts acted independently in defence of the constitution.

Divisions in the ruling party were a major cause of criticism of the democratic process; however, it must be remembered that the AFPFL started life as a broad coalition of conflicting leaders and ideas. In the face of multiple rebellions which threatened to destroy the union as well as the democratic system, the leaders generally remained united. In 1958, when the nation began to enjoy real peace and thousands of people in revolt began to put away their weapons and drift toward a peaceful way of life, Nu tried to convert the AFPFL into a coherent and unified party; but divisions amongst its leaders already were evident and barely concealed in the party congress of that year. Three months later, AFPFL unity was shattered. A similar phenomenon occurred in U Nu's party during his last administration and reinforced the idea that personal rivalries outweighed commitment to democratic rule. If the people did not rise up to defend democracy against the military in 1962 it was because most of those who thought about it recognised the reality of a totally successful lightning coup and because many of them believed that a new caretaker government was going to be established.

The Military and its Roots

The modern military in Burma began as part of the independence struggle in the 1930s. In 1940 the Thakins, the political movement of the students and young intelligentsia, secretly sent one of their leaders, Aung San, to China to seek aid for their revolt. Picked up by the Japanese in Amoy, he was taken to Tokyo. There he met leaders of the Japanese Army command who were aware of the independence aspirations of the Thakins; Aung San entered into an agreement with them: 'Japan would help Burma to gain her independence by supplying her with necessary arms' (Ba Than 1962:15; Yoon 1973). At the same time, an underground revolutionary movement began to form inside Burma in preparation for the anticipated uprising against the British.

Aung San returned in 1941 and recruited twenty-nine Burmans to go secretly with him to Hainan Island where they would be given military training by the Japanese. These 'Thirty Heroes' formed the nucleus of the present Burma army. When the Pacific War broke out, they returned to Thailand, recruited the first members of the Burma Independence Army and followed the Japanese into Burma. Some of their units fought the British and the experience gave them pride and confidence. During the war the army's name was changed, first to the Burma Defence Army, then the Burma National Army and at war's end, to the Patriotic Burmese Forces. On 27 March 1945 it revolted against the Japanese and joined with the Allies in their final phase of the war against the Japanese in Burma.

There was a second strand to the modern Burma military: the ethnic minorities who were recruited and served in the pre-war Burma Defence Forces. During peacetime the colonial rulers recruited very few Burmans. Only in times of emergency – World War I and at the beginning of World War II – were the armed forces open to Burman recruits.

Following the defeat of British forces in Burma in 1942, minority recruits who did not escape to India returned to their villages in the hill areas and, there, were regrouped by British officers who stayed behind or were dropped by parachute to prepare for the return of the British army (Morrison 1947; Mountbatten 1960).

Shortly after the British were driven out of Burma in 1942, there were serious clashes between the Burma Independence Army and Karens living in the delta region. To overcome racial tensions, Aung San and other Burman leaders convinced some Karen leaders of their determination to build racial harmony by recruiting Karens into the new indigenous army and commissioning a few Karen officers. Following independence, a British-trained Karen officer, Smith Dun, was named the first head of the Burma army.

After the war, the Supreme Allied Commander, Admiral Mountbatten, met with Aung San and other Burman leaders in Kandy, Ceylon, where they agreed that the new Burma army would be created out of the two different military groups. It would contain approximately equal numbers from both and would be organised along racial lines on the model of the Indian Army. At the outset, it would employ British officers while Burmese officers were being trained to British standards. The armed force would be limited to approximately 10000 officers and men.

The two elements brought different values and attitudes to the new army. The

Burmans drew upon the ideas of the Thakins – opposition to colonial rule, independence and socialism. From their wartime experiences, they adopted the Japanese military ideas of loyalty, instant obedience to commands from above or punishment for their failures. They also learned to respond unquestioningly to authority and not to act independently in battle, no matter what the conditions. Their experiences in battle against the British and the Japanese gave them a sense of self-confidence, a belief in themselves as the leaders who played an important role in bringing the AFPFL into being, and pride in their patriotism for having fought for the political freedom of Burma.

The minorities brought a different tradition: loyalty to the British monarch, military professionalism, separation between politics and military affairs, and fear of Burman domination.

There was also a third element of the military – private armies. Such forces existed in the 1930s and were nothing new for Burma. Aung San formed the Peoples Volunteer Organisation (PVO) from the Burman soldiers who were not taken into the new army, as a home guard to help maintain law and order in the countryside. But its real mission was political: to give the AFPFL a vehicle by which to intimidate the colonial rulers in the growing struggle for independence. Because PVO members shared the ideas and values of and had close personal ties to the leaders and men in the new army and the rival political parties in and out of the AFPFL – the socialists and communists – doubts were raised in many minds as to whether there was a real separation between the professional army, the political army and the parties. So long as Aung San lived, the PVO remained united and loyal to him and the AFPFL. Aung San's assassination in 1947 left the PVO leaderless and subject to the persuasions of rival political groups seeking to lead the nation.

The communist uprising in 1948 split the PVO, with members divided between the government and its opposition. The PVO eventually faded as a military and political force, but not before its involvement in the civil war nearly tipped the scale on the side of those in revolt.

During this same period the minorities, too, were torn between loyalty to the new state and loyalty to their ethnic groups. The Karens, in particular, experienced a sense of abandonment by the British to their historic oppressors, the Burmans. This helped raise their ethnic consciousness at the expense of full identity with the new national army. In 1947 the Karens formed a paramilitary group, the Karen National Defence Organisation (KNDO) to defend their villages. At the same time, the other large minorities, the Shans, Kachins and Chins, gave their full loyalty to independent Burma. In the early phases of the rebellions their loyalty to the Union of Burma and their unwillingness to join the Karens and others in revolt was a major factor in saving the union.

The Kandy Agreement, which emphasised federation rather than full integration, had a second defect. It took no account of the political divisions and competing ideologies amongst the member groups in the AFPFL and their reflection in the new army. Thus, when the Communist Party went into revolt on 28 March 1948, less than three months after independence, the army began to come apart. The 1st and 3rd Burma Rifles – two Burman battalions – deserted with their weapons and joined forces with the revolutionaries. Two months later the PVO split, one part joining the communists in revolt and the other remaining loyal to the government.

Following independence and the failure of the constituent assembly to solve the problem of the Karens' place in the new union, communal violence erupted between Burmans and Karens. As the violence increased, in January 1949 the KNDO went into revolt. Three battalions of Karen Rifles deserted and joined the KNDO.

These events brought a change in military command; Smith Dun was placed on indefinite leave and Ne Win was placed in charge of the army. The government authorised the recruitment of PVOs loyal to the state, and other former World War II soldiers to form territorial units (*Sitwundans*) to buttress the depleted army (Tinker 1961:38). Under Ne Win's leadership, a process of Burman domination in the army began. Despite the loyal support given by Kachin, Chin and Shan battalions, their units gradually were reformed with Burman officers in command and Burman soldiers in their ranks. Aung San's federated army gave way to Ne Win's Burman-dominated and integrated army. The new army became more professional with the establishment of a military academy in 1954, and later a National Defence College. As its size grew, so too did its strength in arms.

In the midst of the political turmoil caused by the 1958 split in the AFPFL, the military feared that the primary loyalty of the Union Military Police (UMP) and paramilitary forces was to political parties rather than the state and that UMP units might take sides and even displace the army as the nation's defender. It also was alarmed at the divisions in the ranks of the nation's leaders. In this deteriorating environment the army saw itself as the only national institution ready to sacrifice itself to preserve the union and protect the constitution.

On the eve of the formation of the caretaker government the military leaders held a conference at which they defined the national ideology, as they understood it, and their role in upholding it (Director of Information 1960: Appendix I), declaring that so long as their strength remained, 'the Constitution shall remain inviolate'. They held that the nation's goal was to build a political-economic system on the principles of justice, liberty and equality. To gain that end, they set three priorities: first, to restore peace and the rule of law; second, to construct a democratic society, and third, to create a socialist economy. They pledged to pursue the aims of national politics as distinct from party politics. When Ne Win presented himself to parliament as candidate for the office of prime minister on 3 October 1958, he said:

> I wish deeply that all Members of Parliament would hold as much belief in the Constitution and democracy as I do. I wish deeply that all Members of Parliament would sacrifice their lives to defend the constitution as I would do in my capacity of Prime Minister, as a citizen and as a soldier (Director of Information 1960:547).

The caretaker government gave Ne Win a chance to put the army's ideology and theories into practice; and as discussed earlier, while he followed the letter of the constitution, he violated its spirit.

Military Rule: First Phase, 1962–1974

The military justified the coup of 2 March 1962 on three grounds: to preserve the union, to restore order and harmony in the society, and to solve the economic problems facing the nation (Silverstein:1977:80). The men who made the coup were not the same as those who stood close to Ne Win in the caretaker period. Several had been sent abroad as ambassadors a year earlier. And those who remained were divided in their view of what the military should do with power. Brigadier Aung Gyi wanted to continue along the lines of the caretaker government, while his rival, Brigadier Tin Pe, wanted to turn the nation immediately down the road to socialism. A year later Aung Gyi was dismissed and Ne Win adopted Tin Pe's position.

If the coup leaders were divided on their immediate course, they were agreed on abandoning their earlier commitment to the constitution and democracy in favour of dictatorship with no limits on their right to make rules and exercise power.

A month after the coup the leaders promulgated a new ideological statement, *The Burmese Way to Socialism*. In their new analysis they argued that Burma's problems were the result of the economic system, which not only deformed society and the personal values and attitudes of the people, but contributed to disunity and social unrest (Silverstein 1964:716). Parliamentary democracy also contributed by failing to produce political stability and lent itself to misuse and personal profit by those in power. Thus, the priorities were altered: economic change and the creation of a socialist democracy – on the lines of the Eastern European states – must come before all else. Gone were all pretences of upholding constitutionalism and the liberal democracy of the past.

From the outset, the military displaced the institutions created at independence, replaced the civilian leadership with members of their own organisation, and substituted their thought for that of their political predecessors. The constitution was suspended and became inoperative in areas where the Revolutionary Council, the military governing body, issued decrees and promulgated orders. The courts were changed. The old parties were outlawed and replaced by the military's own new party, the Burma Socialist Program Party (BSPP), the only political party allowed after 1964. The free press eventually was outlawed and replaced by an official publication, the *Working Peoples Daily*. Most of all, the federal system, while remaining in name, in fact became a centralised administrative system. Security Administration Councils, composed of representatives from the army, civil service and police, replaced state political and administrative organs. The new system was organised hierarchically with control located in Rangoon.

The changes were more than institutional. The people were cut off from contact with foreigners as the military's propagandists and educators sought to change people's beliefs, values and attitudes to those expressed in the new ideological documents. A police state emerged; people were required to inform on one another while a national network of domestic spies reported the activities and statements of ordinary citizens.

To bring an end to the various revolutions still in progress, the military rulers used both 'carrot' and 'stick', holding peace negotiations in 1963 and, following their failure, resuming their military campaigns.

The Burmese way to socialism failed both to improve the economy and to gain real support amongst the people. By the end of the decade Ne Win and his co-leaders gradually shifted to a new direction.

In 1971 the BSPP was converted from a cadre to a mass party and Ne Win gave it responsibility for writing a new constitution. Despite changes in structure, the party remained a political vehicle for the military with General Ne Win as its head and senior military officers monopolising all subleadership posts.

In April 1972, while the party pursued its tasks, Ne Win and nineteen senior military officers retired from the Defence Services. At the same time the government changed its name from the Revolutionary Council to the Government of Burma. U Ne Win remained prime minister and most of the same senior military leaders, now retired, continued as government heads; four civilian cabinet officers were added to their ranks. During this period Ne Win abolished the secretariat inherited from the British colonial system, and transferred its responsibilities to the ministers. In terms of who led the nation, these changes were more nominal than real as the military retained its near exclusive control of power. A new constitution was approved by the people in a referendum in December 1973, and in elections held the following month candidates for seats in the national assemby and the three sublevels of government were elected. On 2 March 1974 the second phase of military rule began.

Military Rule: Second Phase, 1974–1988

Despite the fanfare, the military did not return power to the people. The constitution institutionalised the power of the BSPP. It was directed to lead the nation; no other parties were allowed. It selected all candidates for seats in the national assembly, the *Pyithu Hluttaw*, and the deliberative bodies at the three lower levels; and it was empowered to give advice and suggestions to government. If there was any doubt that the new system was a continuation of its predecessor, Article 200 declared that when the People's Assembly interpreted the constitution, it had to do so in accordance with the General Clauses Law promulgated by the preceding government.

Like the army, government was centralised and hierarchical. The various levels of administration were tied together by the principle of democratic centralism. The people were given rights and duties. They had the right to stand for election and to recall their representative; they had the right to freedom of thought, conscience and religion; the right to freedom of speech, expression and publication 'to the extent *that the enjoyment of such freedom is not contrary to the interests of the working people and of socialism'* (author's emphasis). In carrying out one's rights, the constitution declared that persons 'shall be under a duty ... to abstain from undermining any of the following: (1) sovereignty and security of the State; (2) the essence of the socialist system; (3) unity and solidarity of the national races; (4) public peace and tranquility; (5) public morality'.

With no right to organise a political party to express legal opposition to the ruling party and the government it controlled, with the requirement to report the speech of others as well as one's own conversations with outsiders, with police informers everywhere, the rights were nominal, at best, and meaningless in this constitutional dictatorship.

The system remained intact, with relatively little change until 1988. At the Fourth Party Congress (August 1981) Ne Win announced his intention to give up the office of president of the nation, but to continue to serve as head of the party. As this was where real power was located, it did not represent any real change. His potential successor, U San Yu, was a former subordinate officer from the time he served under Ne Win in the 4th Burma Rifles. Other nominal changes were made but, as always, power remained in the hands of serving or retired military officers under Ne Win's leadership (Silverstein 1982).

The first sign of real change came in August 1987, when Ne Win startled the nation by admitting 'failure and faults' in the management of the economy and called for open discussion about the past and change. Within weeks the heavy hand of socialist economic control was partially lifted as the government removed restrictions on the sale, purchase, transport, and storage of foodstuffs. This was followed by demonitisation of three units of currency, which was intended to disrupt the black market but in fact had a devastating effect upon the general population because most did their business in cash and kept their reserves at home instead of in a bank.

Developments came to a climax in July 1988 while the nation was in turmoil and an emergency party congress was in session. Ne Win announced his resignation as party head and urged the leaders to consider the creation of a multiparty system, among other changes. He also warned the nation not to demonstrate, for if they did, the army would not shoot over their heads.

Although the party permitted Ne Win to resign, it did not adopt his recommendations. Instead, it appointed as its new leader General Sein Lwin, another protégé of Ne Win. He had the reputation of having led his military unit in suppressing dissent on the university campus in 1962, and again in 1974 where hundreds of students were killed or wounded. To put down the growing national unrest, which had been building up during the year and was about to culminate in a national strike on 8 August, Sein Lwin ordered the military to suppress the strike of unarmed civilians; it resulted in the death of thousands.

The resignation of Sein Lwin brought the first true civilian to leadership. Dr Maung Maung, a legal scholar and strong supporter of Ne Win, became head of state and sought to end popular unrest by promising elections for a multi-party system and other reforms. But his offer came too late as dissent grew and threatened to topple his government; more important, defections from the air force and the navy to the side of the people were a prelude to defections from the army. During this period, the government released criminals from jail and crime rose; at the same time, it spread rumors that the water was poisoned and the city was unsafe. Instead of drawing the people back to BSPP rule, this only hardened their resolve to continue peaceful demonstrations for immediate change to a democratic multiparty system.

At this critical stage, when the people felt that they were on the verge of victory, General Saw Maung, the head of the army, organised a coup and on 18 September seized power and ordered the armed forces to suppress all dissent. Again, the number killed and wounded is unknown, but is reported to have reached 3000 or more.

Thus, within a year, from Ne Win's 1987 announcement to the Saw Maung coup, the military's carefully constructed constitutional dictatorship crumbled and the army found it necessary to abandon the façade of constitutional government in favour of naked power to restore its leadership. As in 1962, it abandoned all pretences of legality and democracy to create a new dictatorship based on martial law and backed by soldiers and guns.

Opposition to Military Rule: 1962–1988

Despite having complete political power and the backing of the armed forces, military rule in its various guises was never free of opposition. The civil war between the minorities and the government persisted even though the armed forces increased in both size and strength. In the heartland, Buddhist monks and university students resisted openly at various times. As the military was fashioning its dictatorship in 1962, the monks refused to register and carry identification cards; and in the Mandalay area some monasteries resisted with force. Eventually, in 1980 Ne Win was successful in bringing the monks and the various sects under government control and marked the event by holding a national celebration, granting amnesty to dissidents and imprisoned felons.

The opposition of the university students lasted longer and was more influential in bringing the constitutional dictatorship to an end. It began in June 1962, with resistance to harsh new university regulations and the killing of an unknown number of students as the army dislodged them from their barricades on the campus and blew up the Student Union Building – the historic centre of student resistance during the British period. Skirmishes between the military and students erupted over the next several years, with the most serious occurring in 1974. When the remains of U Thant, the third secretary-general of the United Nations, were returned to Burma, students and monks seized the coffin because the government did not intend to properly honour his remains. They took them to the university where, after a few days, the army used force, and killed more than a hundred students and monks in recovering the coffin (Selth 1989).

In 1987 the students, most of whom lived on the cash in their pockets, demonstrated against the demonitisation. A few months later, a minor fight between students and townfolk grew into large-scale student-army clashes and a major demonstration in Rangoon, which was suppressed by force, with forty-one students known to have died of suffocation in a police van; others were killed or jailed in the conflict.

The demonstrations of March did not end, despite the closing of the universities. When the universities were reopened in June, the students demanded an accounting of the missing and the arrest of those who inflicted injury upon them; this provoked new demonstrations. At the time, there were rice shortages and skyrocketing prices of basic goods in the cities; there also was large-scale unemployment. These and other issues finally brought the people onto the streets to join the student-led demonstrations. Martial law had been declared in several urban areas outside Rangoon. With the students at the head of the demonstrations and demanding real change in the political system – a return to democracy and constitutional government – the situation slipped out of the control of the military and threatened to bring down the nearly three-decade-old dictatorship (Lintner 1989).

On the Unity of the Army, 1948–1988

It often has been noted that throughout the period of military rule the army remained united and intact. Ne Win could appoint and dismiss leaders with no fear of army resistance. He could call upon it to carry out the most brutal suppression of the people without fear that it would reject his command.

The officers in the Burma army have come from three sources: from the ranks; from students and graduates of the universities of Rangoon and Mandalay, who were given ROTC training and after entering the armed forces completed the Officers Training School (OTS) course. Under Ne Win, the first category were the most trusted, especially if they had served under him in his first postwar command, the 4th Burma Rifles. They formed a close camaraderie, and such men as Aung Gyi, Tin Pe, San Yu and Sein Lwin rose to leadership this way. The academy graduates were intended to be the army elite; they were carefully selected and given an education comparable to that offered at the universities. The ROTC produced engineers and doctors mainly; however, some, upon entering the armed forces, became line officers and they represent the best educated amongst the senior command. Enlisted men have been drawn almost exclusively from amongst the rural population. They have had less education generally than urban youth and the military has offered an opportunity to live better and earn more than if they remained peasants. They have proven to be very loyal soldiers who respond faithfully to command. The army has also recruited soldiers from amongst some of the minorities who were thought to be less political and most loyal to the national government. The Chins are believed to be the most numerous at the present time.

The persistent unity within the army can be traced to three sources: training, ideology, and its self-declared special position in society. As noted earlier, the initial Burman component of the army was trained by the Japanese and absorbed its traditions of absolute authority, brutalisation of the troops and officers who delayed or questioned orders, and centralisation of command. This was the glue that held the units together and punishment for individual initiative ensured that no deviation occurred.

The special position in society was a by-product of the army's central ideology. It saw itself as the most patriotic and loyal body in the nation. It had fought for independence and was in the front line of defence against both external and internal enemies. Because of its willingness to sacrifice everything for the people and the state, it saw itself as entitled to good housing, pay and benefits. During the democratic period, a two-class society emerged, with the army bases better built and cared for than the housing of the ordinary people. Through the Defence Services Institute the army expanded into the economic realm, where eventually, during the caretaker government, it organised and ran several large economic enterprises. From this period, the army argued that it not only defended the nation from its enemies but was the friend and helpmate of the farmer and worker, sharing in the harvesting and in building roads and dams. Throughout the period of the constitutional dictatorship this theme of friendship and partnership dominated in the press and at public events.

For all the apparent internal unity in the army, there was dissent in its officer ranks. In 1976, a coup against Ne Win was launched by more than a dozen junior officers. They were intent upon returning civilian leaders to power and the military to professional tasks. In court, the accused argued that they were dissatisfied with the political and economic system imposed on Burma by their leaders and with the corrupting influence of politics in the army. The failure of the coup and the conviction of the accused placed Academy graduates under suspicion, and many were diverted to administrative and party duties. Until 1988, military leadership remained in the hands of officers who rose from the ranks, from the OTS and from close association with Ne Win (Silverstein 1977); since then, Academy graduates have risen to leadership in SLORC, and General Maung Aye, a member of the first class at the Academy, is the second-highest ranking officer in the army.

Military Rule: Third Phase, 1988–1993

On the day before the 1988 coup, the minister of Defence ordered all members of the armed forces to resign from the BSPP and resume performing their 'original duties', working for the perpetuation of the state, for national unity and for the consolidation and strengthening of sovereignty. This was the first step towards ending party control, dismantling the constitutional dictatorship and reasserting the army's determination to rule directly. Immediately following their seizure of power, the coup leaders explained their action as halting the deteriorating conditions in the country and announced three immediate goals: (1) restoring law, order, peace and tranquility; (2) easing the people's food, clothing and shelter needs; and (3) holding democratic multi-party elections, once the first two goals were established. It also declared that all parties and organisations willing to accept and practise genuine democracy could make preparations and form parties. It abolished the state institutions and, in their place, created a State Law and Order Restoration Council (SLORC) comprising nineteen senior military officers under the leadership of General Saw Maung, the former minister of Defence and army chief of staff.

Also following the coup, the army dropped the original ethnic names of its military units. This was the last step in erasing its original federal structure.

Under martial law and arbitrary decrees, parties were able to form, but they were limited in their access to the media, and in their ability to hold rallies and communicate with their constituents. During the period of registration, 234 parties formed and all but one went onto the electoral rolls. Only a few were genuinely national, with leaders who attracted a wide following and offered some sort of program if they came to power.

The electoral law was highly restrictive and limited the ability of the parties to campaign and get their messages to potential supporters. Yet, despite the impediments to free and open campaigning established in the electoral law, the people took full advantage of the free election and voted overwhelmingly for the party which was recognised by all as being anti-military and pro-democracy. The National League for Democracy, led by Daw Aung San Suu Kyi and former General Tin U gained 392 of the 485 seats in the new People's Assembly, even though its leaders were either under house or direct arrest and the party was harassed in its efforts to reach its supporters.

Despite the coup leaders' promises to return power to the people and permit the People's Assembly to convene, the military had no real intention of doing that if the party and leaders it favoured did not win.

On 27 July 1990 they tore away their democratic mask and revealed their true authoritarian character. In their Announcement 1/90 they declared that SLORC was not bound by any constitution; it ruled by martial law and gained legitimacy from international recognition both by the United Nations and individual states. It declared that while it continued to rule, the elected members were responsible only for drafting 'a constitution for the future democratic state'. Nearly a month later, General Saw Maung said in a press conference that all previous constitutions ceased to be effective after the coup leaders seized power in 1988 (International Human Rights Law Group 1990:26-27).

While the elected members of the People's Assembly wait to assemble, SLORC continues its abuse of human rights by arbitrary arrest and imprisonment of the electees as well as citizens at large. Under Martial Law Order 1/89, military courts were established with power to severely punish, including issuing the death penalty for violators of SLORC decrees and pre-existing laws. In November 1989 Amnesty International reported that thousands of people had been arrested and convicted; other sources reported that more than 100 had received the death penalty (Amnesty International 1990a:1).

In the hill areas, the military pursues a dual policy to bring the civil wars to an end. Since 1989, it has offered individual ceasefire agreements that allow ethnic insurgents to retain their weapons and control local administration and economy in exchange for halting their wars against the state. All political issues remain unresolved until a new constitution and elected government are in place. For those who refuse the offer, war continues. By 1996, fourteen opposition groups had signed. Only the Karens have refused; the Karenni resumed warfare after the Burma army broke the agreement.

A key tactic of the military to force acceptance of an agreement is the persecution, torture, rape and murder of non-combatant old men, women and children of the minorities. By using innocent villagers as forced labour both in warfare and behind the lines, the army violates the human rights of civilians. These abuses are widely documented and reported by government agencies and non-governmental organisations.

Since 1989 the UN Commission on Human Rights in Geneva has pursued the issue of human rights violations in Burma. After listening to the reports of its special rapporteur and the testimony of representatives from various countries and non-governmental organisations, beginning in 1991 and continuing through its 1996 sessions the Commission adopted strong resolutions. Initially the Commission acted under a rule of secrecy, but the failure of Burma's military rulers to give full cooperation to its special rapporteurs and to make appreciable progress in correcting identified abuses led the Commission, in 1993, to make public its proceedings and reports.

SLORC's rule in Burma has drawn the continuous attention of the UN General Assembly since 1992. Following discussions in its Third Committee, it unanimously adopted strong resolutions calling on Burma's military regime to release Daw Aung San Suu Kyi, the Nobel laureate, and other political prisoners, to halt human rights violations, and to restore democracy.

Faced with growing hostility from the world community, and in need of foreign aid, investment and technical assistance, on 23 April 1992 SLORC began a series of steps it hoped would indicate that political change was in progress and that the military's iron grip was relaxing. Change began at the top, with General Than Shwe, the minister of Defence and commander-in-chief of the armed forces, replacing General Saw Maung as leader of SLORC. At the same time, SLORC announced that political prisoners who no longer were a threat to the regime would begin to be released. It also announced that Daw Aung San Suu Kyi could receive visits from her immediate family, and that if she promised to end her involvement in national politics she was free to leave the country.

Earlier in the same year, Muslims of Indian origin living in Arakan, many of whom are citizens of Burma, harassed and under pressure from the Burma army, began fleeing the country and seeking refuge in Bangladesh. The outflow led to a border incident between the two states and the mobilisation of tens of thousands of troops on both sides of the border. But tensions began to relax following the change in SLORC leadership and on 28 April the two countries agreed to an orderly return of the refugees if they could prove their citizenship or right to be in Burma.

Also, about the same time, General Than Shwe announced a halt to the military campaigns against the Karen, although he did not declare a ceasefire or take steps to halt fighting against other minorities.

But the change that attracted most attention was SLORC's announcement that it would shortly begin a protracted process of writing a new constitution as the first step towards transfer of political power. On 23 June 1992 it convened a pre-convention assembly of forty-three selected individuals, including candidates elected in 1990 to the parliament which they were never allowed to form, and fifteen representatives of the military. Their assignment was to decide who should be invited to the next stage of constitution-making, the drafting of principles and agreeing on chapter headings (Silverstein 1992).

To prepare for this second stage, SLORC promulgated Order 13/92 which set forth the six principles which the military rulers wanted the delegates to adopt as the basis of the new constitution: the unity of the territory, the people and the state; a multi-party democratic system; the incorporation of the principles of justice, liberty and equality, and 'the participation of the Tatmadaw [army] in the leading role of national politics of the State in future'.

With these and other instructions, the national convention of SLORC-selected delegates assembled in January 1993. From the start it did not go as planned. The military managers were forced to adjourn after two days when some of the delegates wanted to talk against the sixth principle and about other topics. The meeting reassembled but adjourned four times during the first six months of the year. By 1994, the national convention had adopted more than 100 principles. On the future rule of the military in government, it agreed that one-quarter of the representatives in parliament would come from the military. They would be named by and responsible to the Commander-in-Chief; he would also name the ministers of defence, interior and border affairs, as well as have absolute power in times of emergency (*New Light of Myanmar*, 9 April 1994). The president must have long military experience. The armed forces budget would not be reviewed by the parliament.

More than four years have passed since SLORC announced its intention to oversee the writing of a new constitution. The people have yet to have a say. Their elected representatives were screened by SLORC, and when any of them refused to go along with the military representatives and spoke out they were disqualified; some left of their own accord, fearing that their outspokenness might land them in jail. On the basis of progress made thus far, General Tin U's prediction about the length of time that might pass before the SLORC gives way to some other ruling body may not be too far from the mark. And when the soldiers-in-power get the signatures of their hand-picked delegates on the document they are readying for them, and have the document ratified by the public, they will have the legal basis for a new constitutional dictatorship under which they can rule indefinitely.

Conclusion

The five-decade-long history of independent Burma is one of struggle both to establish a modern democratic political system and to unite the people under its rule. Thus far, it has failed on both counts. But the struggle has not been in vain. Military rule has convinced even the most sceptical that a true democracy is the only way domestic peace, freedom and personal safety can be restored. If democracy failed in its first trial, most people in Burma are more than ready to give it a second trial.

Military dictatorship and human rights violations have destroyed the myth of the unity between the soldiers and the people; today, the army is the most hated and feared organisation in the country. And while the military has fashioned a jail out of the once free country, the people, as demonstrated in the 1990 election, will do what they can to recover the freedom they thought they achieved when Burma became independent in 1948.

The minorities, too, have concluded that their future lies in a union with the Burmans and not outside. They are willing to lay down their weapons and join the Burmans in forming a viable federal state, based on equality, autonomy and self-determination. They want modernisation and development to come to their areas and people, but on terms they can accept and live with.

Six years ago a handful of elected representatives fled to Manerplaw, the Karen headquarters on the Burma-Thai border, and with the backing of the Democratic Alliance of Burma – a political front of minority and Burman groups – established the National Coalition Government of the Union of Burma (NCGUB) as a rival to SLORC. The leader, Dr Sien Win, is the cousin of Daw Aung San Suu Kyi. Although it has not received formal international recognition, its members travel widely and speak often to parliaments, political leaders and the press; they have a headquarters in the US and lobby at the UN, keeping the issue of Burma before them. Both the Burmans and the minorities want to see the military return to the barracks, leaving politics to civilian elected representatives. Until democracy is re-established, there will be disunity, warfare and economic decline in Burma.

6

PAKISTAN: CIVIL-MILITARY RELATIONS
IN A PRAETORIAN STATE

Hasan Askari Rizvi

Pakistan can be described as a praetorian state where the military has acquired the capability, will, and sufficient experience to dominate the core political institutions and processes. As the political forces are disparate and weak, the military's disposition has a strong impact on the course of political change, including the transfer of power from one set of the elite to another. Such an expanded role is at variance with the traditions and temperament of the military at the time of independence in 1947.

The Pakistan military inherited the British tradition of civilian supremacy over the military, aloofness from active politics, commitment to professionalism, and assistance to the civilian authorities with respect to law and order and national calamities. Its role expanded gradually. At first, it emerged as an important actor in the decision-making process, especially in defence and security affairs. In 1958 General (later Field Marshal) Mohammad Ayub Khan, Chief of Army Staff [COAS] from 1951 to 1958, overthrew the tottering civilian government. He ruled under martial law until June 1962, when a new presidential constitution was introduced which civilianised military rule through co-option of a section of the civilian elite. In March 1969, General Yahya Khan, COAS from 1966 to 1971, took power after Ayub Khan's resignation in the wake of mass agitation against his rule. Yahya Khan abolished Ayub's constitution and ruled the country under martial law until December 1971, when he was forced to hand over power to a civilian leader, Zulfikar Ali Bhutto, following the surrender of the Pakistani troops in East Pakistan (now Bangladesh) to India.

Zulfikar Ali Bhutto was temporarily successful in asserting the primacy of civilian government. He enjoyed popular support in the early stages of his rule while the military's reputation had declined dramatically owing to the East Pakistan debacle. However, Bhutto's assertion of civilian supremacy did not prove durable for three major reasons. First, his efforts to personalise power rather than work towards establishing viable participatory institutions and processes eroded his popular support. Second, in their determination to dislodge Bhutto, some of the opposition leaders made it clear in the later stages of anti Bhutto agitation in 1977 that they would not challenge the military in the event of his overthrow. Third, by 1977 the military had recovered from the shock of 1971. When the senior commanders found that the Bhutto regime was discredited and could not survive without their support, they retrieved the political initiative.

This was accomplished when General Zia ul Haq, COAS from 1976 to 1988, staged the third coup in July 1977, and governed under martial law until 1985. During this period he tailored a political system and carefully stage-managed partyless elections to ensure the continuity of his rule after the termination of martial law. When Zia ul Haq died in an aircrash in August 1988, the military allowed the constitutional process to become operative, facilitating the holding of elections and transfer of power to an elected leader, Benazir Bhutto. However, the military monitored the elected government's actions and periodically commented on its performance. Differences developed between the military commanders and the civilian government over the government's performance, which was considered unsatisfactory. The military joined with the president to dismiss the government in August 1990.

In addition to the privileges of exercising power, other considerations which impel the senior echelons of the military to maintain interest in politics include overall political stability, the size of the defence budget, security and foreign policy, professional interests, especially the autonomy of the military in its internal affairs, and corporate interests, including the privileges and benefits for military personnel, especially senior commanders.

The Heritage

The military was organised on modern lines by the British. Towards the end of the nineteenth century the three armies of the presidencies of Bombay, Calcutta, and Madras were amalgamated and put under the Commander-in-Charge of India. The Indian Navy and the Indian Air Force were organised as independent forces in 1928 and 1933 respectively; much of their expansion took place during World War II. The British emphasised the principle of civilian supremacy over the military and the military's aloofness from politics. They did not let the nationalist movement in India impair military professionalism and discipline, and the military was kept away from the nationalist struggle. The formation of the Indian National Army by Subbas Chandra Bose and the naval strike of 1946 could not be described as concerted efforts to dislodge the British as these were confined to a section of the armed forces and took place under exceptional circumstances. The armed forces as a whole remained loyal to the government.

A logical follow up to the decision to partition India and establish the independent states of India and Pakistan was the division of the British Indian military. Military personnel were given the option of joining the armed forces of either country, with one exception: no Muslim from the area that became Pakistan could opt for India and a non-Muslim hailing from the area that constituted independent India could not opt for Pakistan. The division of arms, weapons and equipment proved a more complicated affair. However, the whole task was completed in a couple of months.

Despite the vicissitudes of partition, the military in Pakistan reorganised itself quickly. It adopted five major strategies to overcome its initial problems. First, a large number of British officers was retained on contract. Second, competent officers were given accelerated promotions. Some non-commissioned officers were promoted to the commissioned ranks. Third, a large number of released personnel was called back. Suitable personnel of the armies of the princely states that acceded to Pakistan were also absorbed into the Pakistan Army. Fourth, the regiments with common traditions, common class composition and common recruiting areas were amalgamated. Fifth, the gaps were filled by fresh recruitment (Rizvi 1986:30 34). These measures were coupled with continued emphasis on centralisation, hierarchy, discipline, and *esprit de corps*. Professionalism, training in Pakistan and abroad, and the principle of civilian primacy continued to be the hallmark of its organisation.

The military in Pakistan views itself as the guardian of independence and territorial integrity against external and internal threats. Its training program aims at producing servicemen dedicated to national values and state symbols and who are prepared to make sacrifices for their professional ideals. There is a strong emphasis on the ideological foundation of leadership. Leadership traits as enunciated in Islam are emphasised in the military. These include, *inter alia*, faith and trust in Allah alone, a firm belief in the basic principles of Islam, piety, humility, honesty, bravery, selflessness, forgiveness, competence and steadfastness. Islamic ideology, values and history constitute an integral part of the training program (Army General Headquarters 1990).

The Gradual Rise of the Military

What helped the military most to maintain its professional disposition was Pakistan's syndrome of insecurity, which is due mainly to the strained relations with India dating back to the early years of independence. The Pakistani elite viewed India's policies as a threat to Pakistan's security and survival as a nation-state. A strongly held view was that India wanted to subdue, if not dismantle, the Pakistan state. Perceptions of India based on antagonism and fear influenced Pakistan's domestic politics and foreign policy.

Pakistan became more security conscious in the post Bangladesh period because India had clearly demonstrated its military superiority in defeating Pakistan in the 1971 Indo-Pakistan war. Pakistan was reduced in size and it suffered from a crisis of confidence. The power balance in South Asia, which already favoured India, further tilted to its advantage as New Delhi embarked on a massive military expansion in the 1970s. Moreover, despite the restoration of peace through the signing of the Simla Accord in 1972, mutual distrust and conflicting national aspirations often disrupted dialogue between India and Pakistan.

Pakistan's national security policy was also shaped by Afghanistan's irredentist claims on Pakistani territory and intermittent troubles in the tribal areas. India's support for Afghanistan's policy towards Pakistan was a source of further concern. As Pakistan joined the US-sponsored defence alliances in the early 1950s, the Soviet Union retaliated by openly supporting Afghan territorial claims on Pakistan. The Soviet military intervention in Afghanistan in December 1979 and the intensification of the civil strife in Afghanistan exacerbated Pakistan's security problems and led it to seek support from the West and from Muslim countries.

These security compulsions had several important implications for civil-military relations. For one, defence requirements enjoyed top priority in Pakistan. Whether the government was under a civilian or a military leader, Islamabad always allocated the largest percentage of its national budget to defence. When it functioned, the national legislature underlined the need to maintain a strong defence posture and supported the high budgetary allocations for defence. General Zia ul Haq argued that defence was not merely important in its own right 'but the economic prosperity of a country depended on the military's capability to defend its geographical frontiers' (*Dawn* 6 February 1987). He further maintained that the armed forces guaranteed a secure environment for national development in industry, agriculture, education and allied fields (*Pakistan Times Overseas Weekly* 28 February 1988).

Second, security pressures were often cited by the military governments to deflect demands for political participation and suppress dissent. The standard official argument was that there were serious threats to Pakistan's territorial integrity and the opposition groups should not make political demands. The military regimes also raised the spectre of linkages between external adversaries and dissident groups within the country who were alleged to be serving the cause of the 'foreign masters'.

Third, the maximum possible allocation of resources to defence facilitated modernisation of the armed forces. The military also benefited from Pakistan's decision to join Western-sponsored pacts in the 1950s as well as by the reinvigoration of Pakistan-US relations after the Soviet military intervention in Afghanistan. The new weapons, military hardware, and extensive training that the three services obtained under these arrangements improved their professional disposition and gave them greater confidence.

And finally, these developments served to accentuate the imbalance between the disciplined, cohesive and self-confident military and the weak and fragmented political institutions. The military grew in stature and continued to enjoy respect in society. The reputation of politicians declined and the political institutions degenerated over time. They were unable to control the military. 'It was too powerful for civilians to tamper with and virtually ran itself without outside interference' (Cohen 1987). It was therefore not surprising that when the military decided to displace civilian governments in 1958, 1969 and 1977, it faced no opposition and many groups welcomed the assumption of power by the military.

The Political Institutions and their Degeneration

Pakistan introduced a parliamentary system of government at the time of independence, under the interim constitution of 1947. This system was maintained in the 1956 constitution which the Constituent Assembly of Pakistan approved after about nine years of deliberations. However, it was not long after that the decline and degeneration of the civilian institutions set in, making it difficult to sustain the principle of civilian supremacy over the military.

Pakistan faced a serious crisis of political leadership within a couple of years of attaining independence. Mohammad Ali Jinnah, a charismatic leader who led the independence movement, died in September 1948, just thirteen months after independence. His lieutenant, Liaquat Ali Khan, partially filled the gap but he was assassinated in October 1951. There was thus insufficient time for these leaders to establish and legitimise participatory institutions and processes. This was in contrast to what occurred in India where Jawaharlal Nehru led the country from 1947 until his death in 1964. Although Nehru's personal appeal was more powerful than the political institutions he established, the fact that he insisted on developing institutions and processes provided a firm foundation for the political system and guaranteed civilian supremacy.

The Muslim League of Pakistan failed to transform itself from a nationalist movement into a national party which could lead the way to democracy and political stability. Given its weak and divided leadership, the lack of a clear socio-economic program, and the absence of procedures to resolve its internal problems, the Muslim League was not instrumental in nation building. The roots of these problems can be traced back to the pre-independence period. Founded in 1906 mainly by a Western-educated Muslim elite, the Muslim League could not establish a popular base among the Muslims of South Asia until 1939-40, and functioned as a popular mass party for only seven to eight years. As a result, it could neither bring forward a group of leaders who had sufficient experience of working together at the popular level as members of a party, nor evolve procedures to resolve internal conflicts and aggregate diverse interests. It relied heavily on the towering personality of Jinnah, and soon after his death the Muslim League began to become disunited and lose direction. Other political parties, established mostly by those defecting from the Muslim League, suffered from similar discord, indiscipline and weak organisation. They were neither able to bring forward a national alternative to the Muslim League nor evolve a broad-based consensus on the operational norms of the polity, and thus failed to produce a coherent government.

The interim and permanent constitutions of Pakistan adhered to democratic and participatory norms but when it came to putting these into practice the political elite floundered and often engaged in a free-for-all power struggle. The sole objective of the ruling party was to hold on to power at any cost, while the opposition groups sought to dislodge them by any means. Such conditions were bound to compromise the ability of civilian governments to assert their leadership over the military, and the military consequently had ample freedom to deal with its internal affairs and consolidate its position. Political leaders also attempted to cultivate the military so as to strengthen their own positions vis-à-vis their adversaries.

The civilian governments frequently relied on the army for the restoration of authority in law and order crises and in coping with natural calamities. These operations helped to enhance the image of the military and exposed the weakness of the political leaders. Senior commanders were able to get firsthand knowledge of the politicians' inability to manage their affairs. These situations provided the military with useful experience in handling civilian affairs. The experience also provided the military with the impression that it could perform the job when the civil governments failed and that the civilians were surviving because of the military's support. Three periods of martial law – 1958, 1969, and 1977 – were preceeded by law and order disruptions and serious legitimacy crises for the existing governments. The military thus never had any problem in justifying its assumption of power while blaming the displaced governments for political chaos, misadministration and corruption.

The military's strength is also a result of its strong ethnic and regional cohesion. The Punjab provides the majority of officers, followed by the North West Frontier Province (NWFP) and the tribal areas. The army consists largely of Punjabis and Pakhtuns (Pathans). These two groups have not only developed strong mutual ties but have also established links with the civilian bureaucratic elite, most of whom have a similar ethnic background. In fact, only two COAS in Pakistan's history have come from outside the Punjab and NWFP areas. These were General Mohammad Musa (from Baluchistan but not a Baluch) and General Mirza Aslam Beg (an Urdu-speaking refugee from Uttar Pradesh, India, who settled in Karachi-Sindh). The traditional Punjabi-Pakhtun composition of the army has been a major source of grievance for Sindhis and Baluchs, who are under-represented in the army and virtually absent from the higher echelons. This ethnic cohesion has, however, enhanced the military's efficacy in politics. Moreover, the military chiefs were given extensions which enabled them to further consolidate their hold over the armed forces. Field Marshal Ayub Khan, COAS from 1951 to 1958, was given two extensions; General Mohammad Musa, COAS from 1958 to 1966, had two full terms of four years each; and General A.M. Yahya Khan, COAS from 1966 to 1971, extended his tenure after assuming power in 1969, but had to resign after Pakistan's military debacle in East Pakistan in December 1971; General Zia ul Haq, who enjoyed the longest tenure of any COAS – from 1976 to 1988 – died in service in an aircrash in August 1988. Those who did not get extension included: Lt General Gul Hassan (December 1971 to April 1972, forced by the civilian government to resign), General Tikka Khan (1972 to 1976), and General Mirza Aslam Beg (1988 to 1991). They served under civilian governments. General Abdul Waheed (1993 to 1996) retired after completion of his normal tenure, although the civilian government offered to extend his tenure by one year.

Material Benefits to the Military

The military has become a ladder to lucrative jobs after retirement in almost all states that have witnessed the ascendancy of the military to power. Ayub Khan relied on this strategy after assuming power in 1958, and distributed the rewards of power to his colleagues in the military. General Zia ul Haq resorted to this strategy in a more consistent and extensive manner. It was during his rule that the higher echelons of the military emerged as the most privileged caste in Pakistan.

The Zia regime was quite generous towards its colleagues in the three services. The budgetary allocation for the defence services rose at a faster pace than during Zulfikar Ali Bhutto's period from 1972 to 1977. The army, especially its higher echelons, received a number of material benefits such as jobs before and after retirement, absorption in the Fauji Foundation (a welfare cum industrial organisation for the welfare of ex-servicemen), assignment in the Gulf states, allotment of agricultural land, and parcels of land for construction of houses in cantonments and urban centres, along with facilities for loans. A number of officers who had been given residential plots in various housing schemes at cheap rates sold them to civilians at exorbitant prices.

Still another material benefit the Zia regime offered to military personnel was the appointment of military officers to top civil jobs, leading to what Finer (1978: 84) describes as the 'military colonisation of other institutions' whereby 'the military acts as reservoir or core of personnel for the sensitive institutions of the state'. Military officers were assigned to the civil administration and to semi-government and autonomous corporations. A 10 per cent quota of civil jobs was reserved for military personnel and a system of regular induction into the elite group of the Central Superior Services was introduced. The groups most commonly selected for induction included the District Management Group (formerly the CSP), the Foreign Service of Pakistan, and the Police Service of Pakistan. This has caused bitterness among civilian counterparts who joined these services after tough competitive examination.

Such policies have enabled the military to penetrate important civilian sectors and expand their influence in the society. Material gains have also encouraged the senior commanders to maintain interest in politics so as to protect and increase these privileges. This has resulted in what Heeger (1977:242-262) describes as the 'de-mystification' of the military. The Pakistan military is no longer considered a neutral power broker among feuding political groups. It is now viewed as one of the contenders for power, a powerful actor deeply entangled in ongoing political controversies.

The Political Forces and Military Rule

Despite the military's repeated intervention in politics and the long spells of martial law, military rule has faced a crisis of legitimacy in Pakistan. However, if the military leadership could not obtain the much coveted legitimacy for its extended role, the political elite was unable to counterbalance the military's dominant role, and an adversarial relationship developed between the two. The political leaders, bitter at the loss of power, questioned the military's right to rule, while the military leadership regarded political leaders and parties as opportunist, corrupt and disruptive.

The bitterness in political circles intensified during Zia's rule because politicians were subjected to greater restriction during this period than during the two previous periods of military rule. Zia made no secret of his contempt for politicians and political parties, especially those who questioned his policies. He imposed a ban on political parties in 1979, although groups which supported his military regime, such as the Jamaat-e-Islami, the Muslim League (Pagaro Group), and some orthodox religious groups, were allowed to engage in low-key political activity.

The major goal of the Zia regime was to prevent dissident political groups from joining together to launch a national movement. The state apparatus was effectively used to contain political activities and to manipulate the weaknesses and differences between political parties. Whenever politicians attempted to establish coalitions, the central government would adopt measures to counteract them. The press was prevented from publishing the views of politicians in opposition to Zia. Restrictions were imposed on the movement of politicians; detention without trial, house arrest, and restrictions on travel outside the city or province of residence were quite common, and consequently discouraged leaders from interacting with each other. Political leaders were also often kept under surveillance by the intelligence agencies, which dissuaded many from establishing contact. Activists at the middle and lower levels were periodically arrested under martial law regulations.

The efficacy of the political forces was further undermined by their internal disharmony and organisational problems, which the government was able to manipulate to its advantage. Thus coalitions and united fronts created by the political parties to press their demands were often short-lived (Rizvi 1989:255-268).

Zia withdrew martial law on 30 December 1985 and restored a carefully tailored constitutional system that civilianised his regime, facilitated the co-option of a section of the civilian elite, and provided adequate guarantees for the entrenched position of the ruling generals. Zia continued to exercise the initiative in the political system through four major means. The military government did not revive the original 1973 constitution, but introduced amendments which drastically altered its character and greatly strengthened the position of the president vis-à-vis the prime minister and parliament. Further, the incorporation of martial law orders and policy decisions in the legal-constitutional structure of Pakistan under the Indemnity Law placed checks on the powers of the civilian courts and reinforced the position of the president. Also, the constitution was amended to allow President Zia ul Haq to continue to serve as chief of army staff after the restoration of civilian rule, making it possible for him to maintain the army as his exclusive preserve and giving him a relatively free hand to deal with military and defence affairs. And finally, Zia appointed as prime minister a little-known and weak leader, Mohammad Khan Junejo, whom he could control. While addressing the joint session of parliament on the eve of the withdrawal of martial law, Zia ul Haq declared that the 'new order' did not represent a departure from the policies of the martial law period: 'It is no rival or adversary of the outgoing system. It is, in fact, the extension of the system in existence for the past several years' (*Muslim* 31 December 1985).

Zia-ul-Haq jealously guarded his powers and wanted Junejo and other civilian leaders he co-opted simply to 'carry out orders' or undertake 'public relations jobs', rather than share power as equal partners. These leaders were often frustrated because of their inability to play an autonomous political role. Their frustration was accentuated by the fact that they needed the support and blessings of the president and the military to ward off challenges from the parties which stayed outside the civilianisation process and described the civilian government as a façade while Zia ul Haq continued to rule. As the civilian leadership of the post-martial law period discretely tried to distance itself from Zia to play an autonomous role, Zia dismissed the prime minister and dissolved the parliament in May 1988, thereby undoing the system he himself had created. His attempt to co-opt a new set of leaders came to an end when he died in August 1988.

The decision of the Pakistan Army not to assume power after Zia's death facilitated the holding of general elections in November 1988 which brought Benazir Bhutto to power. Several factors explain the military's decision to abide by the constitution. Despite the military's repeated intervention in politics, a sense of professionalism and discipline is still evident in the officer corps, although this would not prevent them seizing power if they perceived it to be necessary. Second, since Zia had already announced that general elections would be held in November 1988, a military takeover would have been difficult to justify in a politically charged environment. Any postponement of elections would have reinforced the impression that the military was the major obstacle to the restoration of a democratic system. Third, the senior commanders were conscious of the fact that the military's reputation had suffered through repeated involvement in politics, and especially because of Zia's eleven-year rule. Stories circulated about the acquisition of wealth and lucrative civilian assignments by senior active duty and retired officers. The failure to dislodge Indian troops from the disputed Siachen Glacier in Kashmir, and the April 1988 explosion at the ammunition depot in Rawalpindi were often cited as clear proof of the decline of professionalism in the army. With criticism clearly focused on their involvement in domestic politics, senior commanders felt that a decision to honour the constitution would help restore their reputation. Fourth, General Beg, as the new COAS, could not be sure of the support of the army's senior echelons. Although he had been vice COAS since March 1987, Zia, as COAS, had kept the army as his exclusive preserve by appointing his favorites to key positions. (Some of them died with Zia in the plane crash.) Beg, an Urdu-speaking 'Mohajir' immigrant from Uttar Pradesh, facing a majority of Punjabi and Pakhtun senior commanders, needed time to take stock of the situation and to consolidate his position. Fifth, the political situation in the aftermath of the plane crash was peaceful and stable; all major political parties and groups supported the constitutional transfer of power. The situation was thus not conducive to staging a coup. Any attempt to re-establish military rule at this stage would have been premature and would have encountered resistance from political circles.

The 1988 decision to allow a constitutional transfer of power to take place reflected a realistic assessment of the situation by the senior commanders. However, the military did not abandon interest in the political process as it impinged on its professional and corporate interests.

Post-Withdrawal Civil-Military Relations

The army chief continued to be a key figure in the power structure, who interacted with the civilian government headed by the prime minister directly or through the president. An extra-constitutional power triangle, locally known as the troika, developed. It comprised the president, the prime minister, and the army chief; they met frequently to discuss high policy on foreign affairs, security issues and domestic matters. The prime minister was the weakest in the triangle, for three major reasons. First, the constitutional amendments introduced by General Zia-ul-Haq in 1985, known as the 8th amendment, weakened the position of the prime minister and tilted the balance of power decisively in favour of the president, who was given discretionary power to dismiss the prime minister and dissolve the elected National Assembly if he felt that 'a situation has arisen in which the Government of the Federation cannot be carried on in accordance with the provisions of the Constitution and an appeal to the electorate is necessary' (Article 58(2)(b) of the Constitution). Second, the political forces continued to be weak and divided, which made the task of political management extremely difficult for the prime minister. Third, the army chief represented the most powerful and entrenched institution in the body politic. In January 1997, while the National Assembly was dissolved, the president created the National Security Council to formalise the 'advisory' role of the services chiefs and the chairman, Joint Chiefs of Staff Committee which placed an 'advisory' institutional constraint on the elected assembly and the civilian government. The military favoured retention of the power of the president to dismiss government because the senior commanders could persuade the president to do so, thus saving them from directly removing the government.

The military commanders are of the view that if their interests can be protected from the outside, there is no need for them to step in. Moreover, with growing ethnic, linguistic and religious polarisation, increasing civil violence, and socio-economic pressures, the direct assumption of power by the senior commanders could drag them into the ongoing controversies and undermine their reputation. The army's direct involvement in the maintenance of law and order in Sindh, especially in Karachi, during 1992-94, showed the hazard of such operations. The senior officers are thus reluctant to involve themselves directly in civilian affairs.

The military commanders attach such importance to their professional and corporate interests and make sure that the civilian leadership works towards their protection and advancement. They have a direct stake in foreign and defence policies, especially on Afghanistan, India and the nuclear issue, and want their perspectives to be accommodated; any major shift should be made in consultation with them. The military commanders do not want civilian interference in the internal affairs of the services. They jealously guard their autonomy pertaining to postings, transfers and promotions of service personnel, the disbursement of defence expenditure, training, and related affairs. Defence expenditure is another important interest. They are opposed to any unilateral cut in defence spending by the civilian government. Similarly, service privileges and perks, which have increased tremendously during the period of direct military rule, and absorption of ex-servicemen in civilian jobs are their permanent interests. They expect a civilian government to maintain a minimum measure of socio-economic stability and a functional participatory political order. Any serious crisis of governance on the part of the civilian government threatens the military's interests because a society in turmoil and crisis cannot sustain its professional and corporate interests. Therefore, the military cannot be expected to support a government that has lost credibility, for any reason, and is confronted with street agitation.

No civilian government of elected assembly since 1988 has completed its normal tenure of five years. Civilian governments have been dislodged by the president with the full backing of the top brass of the military when governments developed differences with the military and lost credibility at the popular level. Benazir Bhutto, who assumed power in December 1988 with the consent of the military top brass, soon developed differences with them in her enthusiasm to assert civilian primacy. This, coupled with her political and economic mismanagement, serious conflicts with the Punjab government led by her adversary, and mishandling of the ethnic problem in urban Sindh, weakened her popular base, making it possible for the president to remove her from office in August 1990. Her successor, Nawaz Sharif, known for his pro-military disposition, ran into difficulties with the military in a little over two years. The developments that really undermined his position included insufficient attention to socio-economic problems and serious charges of financial impropriety and economic mismanagement, not to speak of extremely strained interaction with political adversaries and the confrontation his government developed with the president. He was removed by the president in April 1993, in the same way Benazir Bhutto was dislodged. Later, the Supreme Court restored his government, declaring the president's dismissal order unconstitutional. However, the power struggle between the president and Nawaz Sharif, especially the latter's attempt to install a government of his own choice in the Punjab, created such confusion and uncertainty that the top brass forced him and the president out of office in July 1993. An interim civilian government was appointed and new elections were held, which brought Benazir Bhutto back to power in October. During her second term, Benazir Bhutto avoided conflict with the military, but her political and economic mismanagement, including complaints about corruption in the higher echelons of the government and misuse of state resources, surpassed that of her first term. The handling of the ethnic problem and confrontation with the superior judiciary undermined her rule. These factors alienated the military, which joined hands with the president to remove her from office in November 1996.

In all these dismissals, the president acted in consultation with the top brass of the military, and there is enough evidence to suggest that the latter had come to the conclusion that the time had come to get rid of the civilian government. On all these occasions, troops took control of all the major government installations, including the prime minister's office and residence, and radio and TV stations. In the case of the 1996 dismissal of Benazir Bhutto, the airports were closed and mobile phones were turned off. It was a coup-like operation on all these occasions, and the interim prime ministers were selected in 1993 and 1996 with the consent of the army.

The role of the Pakistan military has undergone major changes during the fifty years of independence. Its traditions emphasised aloofness from active politics and the primacy of the civilian leadership. The military gradually expanded its role, however, first by becoming an important actor in the decision-making process, and then by directly assuming power. It has, by now, become the most powerful political force in the political system. Its role has changed from direct governance to influencing the nature and direction of politics from the background.

The military prefers *role* over *rule*. If its professional and corporate interests can be protected adequately from a distance, it will not be tempted to step in directly and establish military rule once again. Much depends on how the political leaders perform the task of political and economic management. The civilian government faces two major constraints on its ability to assert its primacy. First, the regional security environment, marked by tension and conflict, increases the importance of the military in the decision-making process. Second, the political forces continue to be fragmented and weak, and often tend to disregard the democratic norms. The growing ethnic-linguistic divide and religious-sectarian cleavages, and the proliferation of sophisticated weapons in the society, have made governance an extremely delicate task. The civilian government needs the support and blessings of the military to stay afloat. The military's preponderant role in the polity is thus assured.

7

THE MILITARY AND DEMOCRACY IN BANGLADESH

Emajuddin Ahamed

Bangladesh is at a crossroads in its march towards democratic order. Though it started its political journey with a parliamentary system after independence, it failed to sustain it; slowly but steadily the parliamentary government degenerated into an authoritarian system. As Bangladesh completes its twenty years of independence it also completes thirteen years of military rule or governments dominated by the military.

In late 1990, however, the political situation altered dramatically. Autocratic rule was ultimately defeated by a popular uprising, and General Ershad had to resign. Under the close supervision of a caretaker government headed by Chief Justice Shahabuddin Ahmed, installed after the resignation of General Ershad, a free, fair and neutral general election was held on 27 February 1991. A truly representative *Jatiya Sangsad* (House of the Nation) thus came into being. In a bid to democratise the polity in Bangladesh the *Sangsad* substantially amended the constitution. A parliamentary system of government was proposed in the *Twelfth Amendment Act* in August and this was ratified by a constitutional referendum on 15 September 1991.

In sum, the institutional framework for parliamentary democracy has been set up in Bangladesh. The *Jatiya Sangsad*, comprising directly-elected representatives of the people, has been the centrepiece of national politics; a cabinet, consisting of the leaders of the majority party, has been made accountable to the *Sangsad*. The prime minister, the *primus inter pares*, is head of the government. The constitutional head of state is the president, who is elected by the *Sangsad*. Steps have also been taken to institutionalise an independent judicial system.

Is the institutional framework good enough for sustaining democratic order in Bangladesh? How will the military react? In the face of the highly politicised armed forces, what is the future of democracy in Bangladesh?

The Nature of the Political System at Independence

Bangladesh emerged as a sovereign state on 16 December 1971 after a bloodbath. The Awami League leaders, who led the independence movement, came to power. They had always favoured parliamentary democracy with real power vested in cabinet, collectively responsible to the legislature. A parliamentary form of government was introduced in Bangladesh according to the Provisional Constitution Order of 1972, and the political elite became the supreme policy makers. The 1972 constitution, which was passed by the Constituent Assembly on 4 November 1972, essentially continued the process. The major aspect of the 1972 constitution is the supremacy of the *Jatiya Sangsad,* comprising the directly elected representatives of the people, and a cabinet directly responsible to the *Sangsad* for its actions and policies.

The Awami League, which had massive popular support, became the ruling party. Although it was mainly a middle-class and urban-centred party, it had well-organised student and labour fronts, and within a short period a number of groups oriented to the Awami League, such as the Jatiya Krishak League (National Peasants League) and the Jatiya Jubo League (National Youth League), were organised. These groups canvassed and mobilised support for the party and supplied policy and program inputs (Ahamed 1980:148-156).

An important trend under the Awami League regime was the gradual strengthening of political infrastructure at the administrative level. The senior advisers of Sheikh Mujibur Rahman were all political leaders. Those who accompanied him on tours both within and outside the country were mostly from the Awami League and party-affiliated interest groups. In the government, the party tried to consolidate its position. The office of the prime minister became the most powerful one in the government. In addition to having head offices and ministries for which the prime minister had specific responsibility, the prime minister's secretariat comprised offices of the principal secretary, political secretary, economic secretary and 'invigilation director'. The overall coordination of government activities at the administrative level was left to the principal secretary. To cap it all, the prime minister was Sheikh Mujibur Rahman, the president of the Awami League, a great charismatic leader, the symbol of Bengali nationalism – a formidable '*Bangabandhu*' (Friend of Bengal). Many observers felt that real power would remain concentrated in the hands of the political elite for a long time to come in Bangladesh.

The Awami League, despite its political approach and the use of party channels of control and direction, failed to handle the problems of increasing economic crisis, social and political instability, and deteriorating security and order in the country. As its failure became manifest, the regime began to turn to the bureaucrats. The bureaucrats who seemed to have lost their position of influence and power between 1972 and 1974 came to the forefront in the early months of 1975 and emerged as the ruling elite after August.

During the first few years after independence, the Awami League regime performed fairly well. It was able to avert a major economic crisis, mainly with the help of massive relief operations carried out by the United Nations Relief Operations in Bangladesh and other international agencies. Compared to the anarchic conditions of 1971 and early 1972, the law and order situation improved considerably. Indian troops were withdrawn by March 1972. The constitution was passed by the Constituent Assembly within nine months of independence, and general elections were held after only six months, according to the provisions of the new constitution. The Planning Commission brought out the First Five Year Plan within a year and a half. In all these matters the legend and charisma of Sheikh Mujib played a vital role (Ahamed 1980:149).

From January 1974, however, the economic situation in the country became critical. This was due partly to global inflation in 1972, and partly to the inefficiency and corruption of the leaders of the ruling party. Though 86 per cent of industries and 87 per cent of foreign trade were nationalised, distribution was conducted by private traders who were issued permits and licences. A substantial number of these permits and licences were issued to Awami League workers, who, in turn, sold them to traders, and consequently became the owners of large sums of 'unearned income'. Most of the administrators of the nationalised industries were recruited from amongst party leaders and workers who had very little knowledge of management or administration. Production, as a result, declined to an unusually low level. While production declined, the smuggling of jute and food grains to India reached alarming proportions, thus draining agricultural products out of the country. In the process, the economy was virtually in a state of collapse, and the situation was aggravated by the worst floods in Bangladesh history in July and August 1974. During the floods the price of consumer goods rose rapidly, and by September 1974 the rise was about 600 per cent over the 1969-70 price level. Sheikh Mujib declared that there was a 'near famine condition' in the country (Ahamed 1980:151-52).

The economic crisis in Bangladesh was compounded by political problems. Class conflicts, which had for so long been subjugated by the demand for regional autonomy, emerged as the crucial problem. The real threat to political and social stability in Bangladesh during the Awami League regime came from the radical forces. They attempted to bring about a 'second revolution' through armed struggle. There were several radical revolutionary parties in Bangladesh; most of these had been working as underground organisations during the Ayub era (1958-1969). Some surfaced after independence.

They argued that the Bangladesh Revolution of 1971 was an 'unfinished one'. When the War of Independence was being transformed into a truly people's liberation war and the radical forces were coming to the forefront, the 'land-based bourgeois government of India' in league with the 'Soviet Social Imperialist Power' interfered, and the Awami League leadership, which represented the exploiting classes in Bangladesh, came to power. Their strategy was to replace the puppet regime by force (Maniruzzaman 1976).

The revolutionary parties trained armed cadres to overthrow the Awami League regime through guerrilla warfare, and started sabotaging communication links and killing Awami League leaders and other 'enemies' of the revolution. The exact number of secret political killings during that period is not known. One government estimate put the figure at over 6000, including four Awami League MPs. Along with secret killings, there was a sharp rise in armed robberies from private houses, looting of banks and shops, and attacks on police stations (Ahamed 1980:157).

The regime's initial response to the increasing violence consisted of threats, appeals and normal police action. In its attempts to combat radical political parties the Awami League relied mainly on party channels of control and direction, but this had limited success because the Awami League itself was plagued by faction-al strife. Soon after independence the Awami League's student and labour fronts were divided over the question of whether to introduce 'pure socialism' or a mixed economy. Senior leaders also became involved in the controversy, and the effectiveness of the party suffered greatly.

The factional strife was exacerbated first by Mujib's political approach to eco-nomic management, which led to the speedy growth of a new class of rich com-pradors, who were divorced from the forces of production. Further, Mujib's prag-matic approach to socialistic principles practically immobilised the party. To overcome this ineffectiveness, the Awami League formed an alliance with such less-radical parties as the National Awami Party (M) and the Pro-Soviet Bangla-desh Communist Party. This alliance too proved ineffective, and Bangladesh slowly but steadily turned into a praetorian polity (Nordlinger 1977:7-8, 75-76).

The revolutionary forces could have been confronted by ideological clarity at the political level and by governmental performance at the societal level. The Awami League regime, however, failed on both counts: the political ideology of

---

[1]   Formulated by Sheikh Mujib's nephew, Sheikh Fazlul Huq Moni, Mujibism im-
         plied a variant of socialism with anti-imperialist but democratic overtones.

Mujibism,[1] which was initiated to counteract the radical forces, was not intellectually refreshing; its performance, especially after the famine of 1974, fell below expectations. For survival, the regime had to resort to repressive measures; that, however, proved counterproductive. As a last resort, the government declared a state of emergency on 28 December 1974 and suspended the fundamental rights granted by the constitution for an indefinite period. The emergency provided for special powers of arrest, curtailed the powers of the judiciary, and muzzled the press. In January 1975, on the initiative of Sheikh Mujib and reportedly against the wishes of most of the members of the *Jatiya Sangsad*, the constitution was amended to provide for a presidential form of government. Sheikh Mujib was subsequently vested with executive powers and authorised to declare Bangladesh a one-party state. Later Sheikh Mujib closed all but four newspapers, two English language and two Bengali. He also founded the national party, the Bangladesh Krishak Sramik Awami League (BAKSAL), patterned on Nyerere's *Ujama* (African Socialism).

   In fact, this final act not only considerably reduced the support base of Mujib in Bangladesh but removed much of the legitimacy of his rule. The banning of the communal parties such as the Muslim League, Nizam-i-Islam, and Jamat-i-Islam for their negative and anti-people role during the War of Independence alienated the rightist elements. The liberals favoured a Western-style parliamentary democracy; they were alienated when the Awami League regime adopted socialistic principles. When in the face of an acute economic crisis Mujib adopted a pragmatic approach, which considerably watered down his brand of socialism, the radical forces became antagonised. Even the young radicals of his own party left and formed a new party. The formation of BAKSAL was resented by both the liberals and radicals.

   The precipitating factor for military intervention was, as suggested by several scholars, the personal grievances of the coup leaders, some of whom were dismissed by Mujib for performing duties ordered by him. The pre-dawn coup, which was staged on 15 August 1975 and eliminated most members of Mujib's family, except his two daughters, was masterminded by three majors who had developed bitter personal enmity against him. They captured power and declared on national radio 'the end of an era of tyranny' (Ahamed 1990).

The Emergence of the Military as the Ruling Elite

In a post-colonial state like Bangladesh the military tends to be dominant not only because these states have inherited an overdeveloped bureaucratic structure and its institutionalised practices, but also because of the nature of its institutional framework (Ahamed 1988:49-50). Organisation provides the armed forces with discipline and cohesion, hierarchy and centralised command; the institutional structure gives them power. It is no wonder therefore that the military became a dominant force in Bangladesh.

The armed forces of Bangladesh were not a well-knit establishment in the beginning, however, and could not emerge as a decisive factor in Bangladesh politics during the early years. This was due partly to the socio-political environment after independence and partly to internal schism and cleavages among the officer corps, which were effects of the bloody Independence War that continued from March to December 1971. The bureaucratic elite, both civil and military, was not held in high esteem in the society because of its association with military rule in Pakistan during the previous twelve years. Bureaucracy was in fact a much hated word in the political lexicon of Bangladesh. Sheikh Mujib often became livid with anger when he denounced bureaucracy. Moulana Bhasani, another prominent Bengali leader, did not complete a public speech without making a stinging attack on the bureaucracy.

Yet a large number of civil servants and military officers played a key role in the political struggle in the 1960s and in the Independence War. Many of them were aligned with the Awami League and personally remained on good terms with Sheikh Mujib during the Ayub era. Some of them supplied secret information to the Awami League leadership and provided data which helped Mujib to sharpen his case for regional autonomy. The Agartala Case,[2] which was believed to have been staged in 1968 mainly to defame Mujib, implicated a number of civil servants and military officers.

Civil servants and military officers willingly lent their full support to Mujib's call for civil disobedience and non-cooperation, which paralysed the entire administration in East Pakistan in March 1971. When the Pakistan army launched its brutal attack on the night of 25 March, the Bengali military officer corps became one of the targets. During the Independence War military officers took responsibility for training the *Mukti Bahini* (Freedom Fighters) at various training centres both within and outside Bangladesh, and they themselves fought against the Pakistan army.

Despite this political role, the military could not consolidate its position after independence and did not emerge as a cohesive force for several reasons. In the

---

2   The Agartala Conspiracy Case, in which Sheikh Mujibur Rahman was charged along with thirty-four other Bengali politicians, civil servants and military officers with conspiring to bring about East Pakistan's secession in collusion with India, was initiated by the Pakistan Home Ministry on 6 January 1968.

first place, the size of the armed forces was quite small. In 1975 there were about 36000 men in the defence services in Bangladesh, of whom 30000 were in the army, 500 in the navy and 5500 in the air force. In addition, there were 30000 men in the Bangladesh Rifles and 16000 in the *Jatiya Rakkhi Bahini* (National Security Force), which were paramilitary forces. Of those 36000 men, about 28000 (including 1000 officers) were 'repatriates' from West Pakistan; the remainder belonged to the former East Bengal Regiment and the new group recruited from amongst the *Mukti Bahini*. Though the number of officers was above 1200 in 1975, the number of officers above the rank of major was not more than 250 (Ahamed 1980:141).

While the size of the armed forces was small, the level of internal rivalry and cleavage was high. Conflicts between the Bangladesh Rifles and regular defence forces (former East Bengal Regiment) had continued since independence, and it assumed alarming proportions in 1972. Even the regular forces became involved in internecine conflicts. Some of the repatriate officers were either unceremoniously retired, or were placed under officers who were junior to them in the Pakistan defence forces but had been promoted for participating in the Independence War. The officers who took part in the Independence War were offered two years' seniority and treated preferentially. This differential treatment caused animosity among the freedom fighters and repatriates.

The repatriates regarded most of the freedom fighters as basically secularists, socialists and Pro-Indian, while the freedom fighters stereotyped the repatriates as opportunists and pro-Pakistanis. To the repatriates the War of Independence was fought with Indian resources and the victory was served by Indians to the Bengalis on a silver platter; to the freedom fighters, the repatriates basked in the Pakistani sun while the whole Bengali nation was locked in a life and death struggle. The freedom fighters, on the other hand, complained that repatriates were greedy enough to enjoy the fruits of independence without suffering for and contributing to it (Ahamed 1988:52-56).

The numerical superiority of the repatriates also made the freedom fighters feel insecure. The repatriates complained that they were not given full pay for the twenty-month period that they had to remain in the Pakistan concentration camp before being repatriated to Bangladesh in September 1973. This feeling of being discriminated against on the part of the repatriates, and consequent acrimony between the two groups, badly affected the morale of the military officers, accelerated the process of polarisation, and strained the command structure of the defence services. The armed forces in Bangladesh were also divided at the initial stage in terms of ideology. The repatriates retained much of the conservative outlook that characterised the armed forces in Pakistan, while the bulk of the freedom fighters were highly politicised and somewhat radical in their views. The two groups also held distinct views with regard to the institutional framework the armed forces should take in the future. One group favoured the retention of the conventional army on the pattern of British India or the Pakistan armed forces. The other group advocated that the armed forces be transformed into a kind of productive army on the pattern of the Chinese People's Army. A few officers, advocating this view, joined the underground wing of a political party, the *Jatiya Samajtantrik Dal* (JSD) and organised cells of the *Biplobi Shainik Sangstha* (the Revolutionary Soldiers Association) on the model of the Soviet of Soldiers which developed in the Tsarist army before the Communist Revolution in 1917. The two best-known advocates of the concept of productive army were the two valiant freedom fighters, Colonel Abu Taher and Colonel Ziauddin. These factors suggest that the armed forces in Bangladesh could not emerge as a decisive factor in politics at the beginning because of internal rivalry, ideological conflicts and intra-group feuds (Lifschulz 1979:85-88).

While the armed forces could not take advantage of their organisational strength, they could clearly perceive that their corporate interests were not safe in the hands of Awami League regime. The military elite resented the fact that the government did not take quick and effective measures for the reconstruction of the training institutes and cantonments destroyed during the Independence War. Consequently the defence services remained poorly equipped. Expenditure on defence services was not only minimal but was gradually reduced. In the 1973-74 budget, expenditure on defence was little more than 16 per cent; in 1974-75 it was reduced to 15 per cent, and in 1975-76 it was less than 13 per cent.

The establishment of a new militia, the *Jatiya Rakkhi Bahini* (National Security Force), organised under the direction of the prime minister's office and attached to the Awami League, introduced a parallel organisation to the regular armed forces. The government seemed to be more interested in the development of the militia than in the armed forces. It was planned that this militia would be increased annually so that by the end of 1980 its strength would be 20000. It was also planned that one regiment of the *Jatiya Rakkhi Bahini* would be placed under the command of each district governor.

Most of the groups in the defence services in Bangladesh shared a common anti-Indian orientation. This was so for several reasons. First, most of the members of the armed forces who fought during the War of Independence strongly believed that the Indian Army just walked in when the war was nearly over at the end of 1971, thereby robbing the Bangladesh military of the glory of liberating their motherland. Second, many senior military officers believed that the government-in-exile at Mujibnagar signed a secret treaty with the Indian government, which was detrimental to the sovereignty of Bangladesh. They also believed that Sheikh Mujib became less interested in the development of the defence forces because of that treaty. Third, many senior army personnel felt that the *Jatiya Rakkhi Bahini* was planned and designed by the Indian Army for the safety of the Awami League regime. The poorly-equipped defence services were also bitter about the fact that the Indian Army took away all the sophisticated weapons left by the Pakistan Army. This anti-Indian feeling gradually developed into an anti-Mujib feeling because of Mujib's pro-Indian foreign policy.

Despite their grievances against the Awami League regime, the defence services in Bangladesh remained practically immobilised because of the schism and cleavages that affected them during the early years. When they were asked by the prime minister to go to the aid of the civil authorities, and conducted a number of successful operations, they not only regained their sense of unity and cohesion but also came to believe that their services were indispensable. From July 1973 to July 1974 there was a number of combined military operations between the *Rakkhi Bahini* and the police, such as checking for smuggling at the border, handling 'extremists', and maintaining law and order. As internal threats mounted, and were successfully managed, the military officers began to believe that only the Bangladesh Army could save the country. Officers' growing participation in the day-to-day affairs of the state made them not only sensitive to political power but also aware of the basic weaknesses of the regime, particularly the corrupt practices of some top ranking leaders, and of their unpopularity. Thus when a pre-dawn coup was staged on 15 August 1975 by a handful of junior officers (twenty to twenty-five majors and captains) with the help of two battalions of the armored corps and 1500 soldiers, it came as no great surprise.

The August 1975 coup paved the way for the emergence of the military as the ruling elite. The Zia regime (1975-1981) helped them, albeit unwittingly, to attain a new height of maturity; the Ershad regime turned out to be a period of consolidation. The August coup may be regarded as a pacesetter in that it was closely followed by a series of counter coups or coup attempts. The seeds of all those were sown in the August putsch.

The 3 November coup was essentially a pre-emptive bid to prevent the radical forces from taking over control of the armed forces. It, however, failed to take roots. Khaled Mosharraf and the other ringleaders were overwhelmed by the 7 November Soldiers' Uprising, which in effect catapulted Major General Ziaur Rahman to political power.

General Zia, having assumed power by default rather than by design, was confronted by serious problems from his own constituency: the highly politicised army. Though before the 7 November uprising Zia was the recognised leader of the freedom fighters and as such was highly respected and loved by his comrades-in-arms, he had something of a falling out with them after the death of Colonel Taher (who was arrested, subjected to a prison trial and hanged on Zia's orders), because Taher was mainly instrumental in organising what happened on 7 November. Then Zia turned to the repatriates and managed to strike a balance between the freedom fighters and repatriate officers of the defence services.

As a soldier, Zia's loyalty to and reliance on the military was deep. Unlike his predecessor, Sheikh Mujibur Rahman, who kept political elements separate from the military, Zia pursued a policy of welding these together and tried to incorporate military personnel into different sectors of national life. The salary of both the *jawans* (privates) and officers was enhanced; the system of rent payment for accommodation was modified to their benefit; and Zia created openings for the assignment of retired military officers to lucrative jobs in other sectors.

On 1 March 1979, 25 of the 625 officers in the senior policy pool, responsible for policy-making in the secretariat, were military officers. Of 101 chairmen or managing directors of public corporations in June 1980, 42 were military officers or retired serviceman. In January 1981, 22 of the 40 district superintendents and additional superintendents of police were army officers. Moreover, 500 retired military officers were employed in industry, indenting business, foreign trade, and supply and contracts under the patronage of the government. Quite a few military officers were allotted residential plots in the developed areas of the city, and were even granted liberal loans for building houses by the House Building Finance Corporation. With all of these actions, Zia's critics argued, he was consciously following the Indonesian model of partnership between the military and civilian sectors: civilians being the junior partners (Ahamed 1988:124-25).

General Zia laid the foundations of a number of civilian institutions such as the Bangladesh Nationalist Party (BNP), and *Gram Sarker* (village government). He also initiated a number of participatory programs such as canal digging and eradicating illiteracy through literacy squads which were established in early 1979. He introduced a multi-party system in the country, and before the presidential elections in June 1978, when he was elected president of the country, Zia resigned from the post of the chief of army staff. During his time, general elections were held in February 1979 to form the *Jatiya Sangsad*. A process of civilianisation was launched by President Zia in late 1977. One can, however, argue that the civilianisation process culminated in the primacy of the military. One of the reasons why Zia was killed in the abortive coup of 30 May 1981, some scholars have argued, was his 'over-democratising' of the political system. The measures taken by Zia not only raised the expectations of the military, but gave them a stake in the polity. The military thus emerged in the 1980s as a powerful socio-economic group, much more confident than any other sector in Bangladesh society.

This political consciousness of the military began to take shape at two levels during the Ershad regime. Deeply entrenched at the centre of power, they could not afford to be indifferent to the forces shaping politico-economic decisions at the highest level, and thus became positively involved in a process which was expressly political. Second, from the early 1980s they began demanding a con-stitutionally-incorporated active role in the governance of the country (*New York Times* 14 November 1981).

The military, if it had wanted, could have seized political power in the wake of the Chittagong coup of 30 May; however it refrained from doing so for good reasons. The senseless and dastardly assassination of Zia by a section of the armed forces not only endeared Zia to the nation but also created a kind of abhorrence towards men-in-uniform. The repatriate generals under the leadership of General H.M. Ershad weighed this carefully, and by way of buying time lent support to the constitutional change of government. The generals also knew that the viability of the successor government during a period of uncertainty could be ensured largely through their support. Thus they extended liberal support to the Sattar government, ensuring continued military domination over the policy-making structure.

Justice Abdus Sattar, the 75-year old successor to Zia, in his campaign speeches for the November 1981 presidential elections, emphasised among other things his close association with the late president and as such his enjoyment of the trust and respect of the country's armed forces (Ahamed 1988:132). The military elite thus threw their weight behind Justice Sattar's candidature. Zia's policy of fusing the upper echelons of the bureaucracy and the military into the bedrock of a stable political system was endorsed by the military. Moreover, the structural weaknesses of the Bangladesh Nationalist Party (BNP), an outcome of Zia's 'open arms policy' of welcoming divergent political elements ranging from the progressive left to the fundamentalist right, were also perceived by the military as advantageous to their corporate interests. The BNP, which had been held together mainly by Zia's charismatic personality and political power, was likely to yield wider scope for bargaining to the military after the death of its leader.

Though the corporate interests of the military remained the crucial factor, internal dissension and factional cleavages within the ruling party provided the sought-after occasion for the generals. The BNP was developed rapidly by its leader, General Zia, mainly with a view to extending his power base beyond the cantonments. While he was alive, factional cleavages did not surface. His sad demise, however, seemed to have lifted the lid, leading to a sudden outburst of conflicting views and interests, and the proliferation of antagonism and dissidence within the BNP. Thus, within a year of Zia's death, the Bangladesh polity verged on the brink of praetorianism (Perlmutter 1977:104-107). It was anybody's guess whether the military, which emerged as a well-knit and self-confident force after the Chittagong incident, would assume political power at an opportune moment. The generals did not have to wait long; only four months after the landslide victory of Justice Sattar in the presidential elections of 1981, Bangladesh experienced a bloodless coup. The military, under General H.M. Ershad, wielded political power from then until 6 December 1990, when a violent popular uprising forced Ershad to resign.

Politicisation of the Armed Forces

A high level of politicisation of the armed forces is evident in Bangladesh. The 15 August 1975 coup, by a handful of junior officers with the help of two bat-talions of armoured corps, was the first indication of the armed forces' overt intention to play a political role. It was followed by a series of coups and counter-coups until 30 May 1981 when General Zia was brutally killed by a group of about twenty mid-level officers at Chittagong in another abortive coup. Bangladesh was placed under martial law for the second time under Lieutenant General H.M. Ershad from March 1982 to November 1986. The military-dominated civilian regime remained in power until December 1990.

The military ruled Bangladesh for more than nine of the twenty years of its independent existence; another four years were under the shadow of martial law, with men-in-uniform in the background. What is more significant is that the mili-tary not only assumed a political role, but claimed that they had a right to do so. Before the assumption of power in March 1982, Major General Ershad demanded that the military be accorded a constitutional role to ensure the protection of the political system (Ershad 1981:12; *New York Times* 14 November 1981).

The process of politicisation of the armed forces in the post-colonial state of Bangladesh is linked with the organisational framework of the military in British India and the orientation of its officer corps. In Western countries the concept of the military as a more or less politically neutral body has emerged mainly because democratic institutions have evolved over a longer period of time with little involvement of the military. Moreover, as an apparatus of the state, military organisations were designed mainly to handle external defence. The British Indian Army, which was the predecessor of the armed forces of all the South Asian states, was by contrast trained from its very inception to be 'the custodian of law and order' with a view to promoting imperial interests. It was thus essentially in opposition to the national interest and demands, and its organisation was always subject to political considerations. The roots of politicisation of the armed forces can therefore be traced to this peculiar conception of its role.

For the supreme purpose of securing and perpetuating colonial interests in India, the British army's policy had been to capitalise on existing religious antagonisms between the minorities through a policy of 'divide and rule'. The British Indian military's deployment strategy was based on the dictum: 'Keep your Sikh regiments in the Punjab, and they will be ready to act against the Hindoos; keep your Hindoos out of the Punjab and they will be ready to act against the Sikhs' (Philip 1962: 508).

With the nationalist movement gaining ground increasingly in India from the latter part of the 19th century, an intense effort was made by the colonial government to indoctrinate Indian troops in general and the officer corps in particular with an anti-political and anti-democratic orientation. They were taught that politicians were no more than 'rabble rousers' and 'disruptionists', and that their activities merely undermined the social order and systemic solidarity. Thus the British Indian military officers in the course of time were not only thoroughly anglicised but also rendered anti-national, anti-political and anti-democratic.

Analysing this aspect of the British Indian military, many scholars came to believe that among military officers assimilation displayed itself not merely in 'the exquisitely tailored lounge suits of officers in mufti, in a penchant for understatement, for beautiful silver, and for cavalry moustaches', but also in their belief that politicians were no more than 'scallywags' (Rudolph and Rudolph 1964).

After independence, the organisation of the armed forces in India, and their systems of training and recruitment, underwent profound changes; but the armed forces in Pakistan continued to be organised and trained on basically the same lines as in British India (Khan 1963:220-235). A general headquarters (GHQ) was set up as the central agency responsible for the administrative affairs of the various defence services. Training institutions such as the Pakistan Military Academy or Air Force Academy were established on the same lines as at Sandhurst in Britain and Dehradun in India. The new military leaders continued to be recruited from the same bases; the armed services personnel continued to remain in the cantonments, which were physically and culturally distanced from the civilian sectors, having a sense of being a part and yet apart from the society in which they lived (Alavi 1966). This duality in attitudes of the soldiers towards their society and their professional expertise created an ambivalence in their attitude towards the political institutions in Pakistan. The root causes of the martial law clamp-down in Pakistan in 1958 can be traced to the dynamics which were generated in the Pakistan Army because of training, organisation and the orientation of its officer corps.

After the conclusion of the Mutual Defence Assistance Agreement with the US in 1954, the Pakistan Army acquired sophisticated American military technology. Acquisition of new technology enhanced not only the Pakistan military's striking power but also its bargaining strength. Soon after, it began to penetrate the civilian government of Pakistan. Thus, ultimately by staging a coup and assuming dictatorial powers in 1958, General Ayub Khan established the supremacy of the men-in-uniform in Pakistan.

Most of the Bengali military officers, who played crucial roles in seizing political power in Bangladesh in the 1970s, were recruited during this period and were trained and socialised under the shadow of Ayub Khan's martial law regime. The proclamation of martial law in 1958 had far-reaching effects on the Bengali military officers in many ways. Officers became conscious of the role the military could play in the political system; they also became sensitive to political power. They became conscious of the regional imbalance in the armed forces, too, and they began to realise that the Bengali officers in the Pakistan Army were not accorded equal treatment. Bengali officers also felt that a policy of discrimination was practised against them in matters of pay, promotion and other perquisites. These discriminatory policies made the Bengali officers not only resentful, but also vociferous in their complaints against the West Pakistani ruling elite. In the 1960s their complaints became louder when by default Bengali bureaucrats, both civil and military, became the chief spokesmen for Bengali interests in the absence of free political processes. This role politicised them further. The Agartala conspiracy case bears ample testimony (Ahmed 1991:91-110).

The most important factor in the intense politicisation of the Bangladesh armed forces was the War of Independence of 1971. The fact that a large number of officers and *jawans*, throwing aside their professional norms and indignantly breaking the canons of military discipline and chain of command, rose against the establishment and joined the war, was itself a revolutionary step. Under normal circumstances, all of them would have been court-martialed, but after independence they became war heroes and were greeted with warm-hearted glee and pride by the nation. Moreover, the new strategy of guerrilla warfare, devised in a conference of sector commanders at Teliapara in July 1971, had the double effect of further politicising the armed forces and radicalising them to a great extent (Ahamed 1988 :43-45).

In sum, the Bangladesh Army, which was the lineal descendant of the British Indian and Pakistan Army, inherited not only the institutional framework of its predecessors but also their orientation against civilian rule and their sensitivity to political power. The War of Independence removed the distance between the civilians and armed forces personnel, and made them aware of the nature of weak political leadership and fragile political institutions.

Popular Attitudes to Democracy

Though the armed forces in Bangladesh have been highly politicised, the people of South Asia have been deeply committed to democratic order. During the British rule in India, Bengalis were in the forefront of democratic movements in the 1920s and 1930s. The All-India National Congress and the Muslim League, which had been mainly responsible for the partition of India and Pakistan, were led by Bengali political leaders in the formative phases. The freedom movement in British India, in a sense, was a movement for a democratic polity and was deeply rooted in the democratic ethos.

The Lahore Resolution of 1940 appealed to the people of East Bengal mainly because of its democratic overtones: it espoused the principle of national self-determination; it also laid stress on internal autonomy. Pakistan came into being in 1947 on the basis of the Lahore Resolution. The continuance and full flowering of parliamentary democracy became the pet demands of the East Pakistanis after that, and most of their movements were firmly grounded in democratic ideals. Seven of the historic twenty-one points of the United Front, a grand coalition of the opposition political parties in East Pakistan organised with a view to focusing their demands and fighting the ruling Muslim League in the 1954 provincial elections, were closely related to the proper functioning of the parliamentary system in East Pakistan (Jahan 1972:45-47).

The famous Six-Point Program, which ultimately led to a full-fledged nationalist movement among Bengalis in the late 1960s, began with a call for the establishment of a federation in Pakistan on the basis of the Lahore Resolution; it also demanded a parliamentary form of government with the supremacy of the national assembly, directly elected by the people on the basis of universal adult suffrage (Ahamed 1989:32-43). The main motivating force for Bengali involvement in the War of Independence in 1971 was their desire for a democratic system, a desire blatantly denied by the Pakistani ruling elite during the post-election years.

But while the people of Bangladesh are committed to a democratic order, the political parties, which are the positive instruments for a working democratic system, are not yet properly prepared for the job. Though Bangladesh has scores of political parties, only a handful of these are institutionalised, well-knit and organised at the grassroots level, and having definite policies and programs of action. This is due partly to political history and tradition and partly to the socio-economic structure of the country.

In South Asia political parties have never been decisive instruments for framing public policy or for projecting alternatives. Except for short interludes, moreover, political parties have had few opportunities for functioning openly since competitive politics has been restricted. During the colonial period political structures were merely embryonic, and their operations were mostly extra-legal. Even after independence in 1947 the ruling elite continued to maintain many of the restrictions which had been imposed on the free flow of political activities during the colonial period. During military rule, political parties and party activities were usually the first casualties.

Democracy is essentially a system of alternative programs and policies propagated by political parties. When a particular set of programs and policies fails to command the support of the people alternative programs and policies are tried. Elections are formal procedures to choose programs and policies at a particular point in time. Bangladesh has, however, inherited a political tradition where mass movements and elections are entwined. During the last four decades there were a number of political movements, which crystallised certain issues and mobilised political forces. Elections were then held, not to choose between the alternative programs and policies, but merely to pick the winning political forces.

Though a vast majority of voters participated in these elections, they took sides not merely as party supporters but also as supporters of the crucial political movements; some of these took the form of national movements. These elections, strictly speaking, became plebiscites. The election of 1946 on the Pakistan issue, the 1954 elections on the autonomy question, the elections of 1970 on the basis of the Six-Point Program, and those of 1991 under the caretaker government were meant to serve other functions; they were more legitimising plebiscites than elections. Each was unique, and had distinct appeals to the voters.

Not only is the political history and tradition not congenial to the growth of a stable party system in Bangladesh, but neither are the socio-economic conditions. The endemic poverty of the people, intense factionalism among the various social groups and classes, and a network of patron-client relationships reaching from the grassroots to the central politico-bureaucratic elites at the national level, have resulted not only in organisational weakness and a very low level of institutionalisation in the polity, but also in institutional fragmentation.

Under such circumstances no political party can serve as the effective allocator of values or platforms for conflict resolution or a meaningful focus of civic loyalty. Political loyalty has been directed to persons, to the loci of patronage. Since political loyalty has been channelled towards patrons or centres of patronage, persons who can seize the principal patron roles and sustain the flow of material benefits to the clients are likely to receive the conditional allegiance and support of the client network. That explains why some of the opposition leaders change their position overnight and become staunch supporters even of a regime dominated by the military. A political party cannot retain the support of a substantial portion of the voters and remain underdeveloped.

Prospects for Democracy and the Role of the Military

Analysing all these factors, some scholars at home and abroad have suggested that the Bangladesh polity might well be on the road to persistent praetorianism with an occasional civilian-military façade (Baxter and Rahman 1991:59). The popular uprising of 1990, with the direct participation of most of the political parties in Bangladesh, and subsequent events, however, give grounds for optimism. Though Bangladesh has yet to build a political system based on consensus and compromise, it has come a long distance in that direction.

The political parties, despite their stunted growth and lack of institutionalisation, have now arrived at a consensus on the nature of the political system in the country. Nothing short of a representative parliament is acceptable. The government must be accountable to the parliament. The judicial branch must be independent as the bulwark of basic human rights. The press must be free. The consensus has been evident in the rejection of seven-party and five-party alliances to participate in either of the *Sangsad* elections under Ershad and also in the eight-party alliance's refusal to take part in the 1988 *Sangsad* election.[3]

These demands, having been repeatedly voiced from different party platforms during the last decade, became the core of the consensual agreement reached by the three political alliances on 19 November 1990. These alliances, working as the motivational force behind the popular uprising, were instrumental in bringing it to its logical conclusion on 6 December 1990. In a society characterised by endemic violence and intense factionalism, thanks to the willing co-

---

[3] Most of the political parties which were opposed to General Ershad's usurpation of political power and his autocratic rule formed two alliances in 1983: a fifteen-party alliance centred on the Awami League, and a seven-party alliance centred on the Bangladesh Nationalist Party (BNP). On the issue of participation in the 1986 general election the fifteen-party alliance broke up, forming an eight-party alliance centred on the Awami League, and a left-leaning five-party alliance. These three alliances played a crucial role in ousting General Ershad from power in December 1990.

operation of all the political parties the general election of February 1991 turned out to be absolutely free, fair, neutral and peaceful. *The Twelfth Amendment Act*, reintroducing the parliamentary system of government, was enacted in an environment of unprecedented cordiality among the political parties on 6 August 1991. The parliamentary committees of the fifth *Sangsad*, designed to institutionalise parliamentary control over the different ministries, have started functioning.

The orientation of the armed forces in Bangladesh also seems to have undergone some change. They treated the movement against Ershad from October to December 1990 as a political problem and wanted it to be solved politically, General Ershad's insinuation of a more active role for them notwithstanding. Most coups are internally generated by local cleavages and power conflicts, but external encouragement or discouragement can be crucial to their success or failure. In Bangladesh, American assistance has been of crucial importance to the success of the post- Mujib regimes, and the 15 August 1975 coup was a turning point in the warming of Bangladesh-US relations. The triumph of democratic order globally, and especially in South Asia, may help further deepen the changing orientation of the armed forces in Bangladesh.

An alternation of military and military-dominated civilian regimes in Bangladesh thus may not be the only prospect. A democratic order is more likely to strike its roots into the political soil of Bangladesh if the political parties can maintain the emerging consensus and politics of compromise.

8

PATTERNS OF MILITARY RULE AND PROSPECTS FOR DEMOCRACY IN SOUTH KOREA

Yung Myung Kim

The role of the military in South Korean politics poses some interesting questions for the study of civil-military relations in developing societies. The military has dominated Korean politics for an unusually long period of time – nearly thirty years. On the other hand, recent trends towards democracy in Korea appear to be more deeply entrenched historically than in many other recently democratised polities, especially those in Latin America. This chapter attempts to clarify some more obvious issues related to these characteristics of civil-military relations and democratic transition in South Korea (hereafter Korea). Specific issues to be addressed include: the nature of the political system after independence which provided a structural framework for the military's political dominance; the internal characteristics of the military, reflecting and interacting with the overall political structure, which induced military officers to assume supreme power in Korean political economy; the reasons for the eventual demise of military rule and the beginning of civilian control of the military; and future prospects for democracy in Korea and the military's role in it.

Methodologically, a distinction may be drawn between structural and motivational factors in explaining the complex phenomenon of civil-military relations. The former help explain overall trends in civil-military relations; the latter are relevant to the more specific behavior of political actors. In this chapter, we will concentrate on structural factors, especially those affecting the balance of power between the military and civilian sectors, because our interest is in overall patterns of civil-military relations rather than specific political events.

The Emergence of Military Rule

There is no shortage of academic studies of the causes of military *coups d'état* which identify various factors at different levels of analysis – intra-military, societal, and international (Finer 1962; Huntington 1968; Janowitz 1964; Decalo 1976; Y.M. Kim 1985). However, the basic reason why the military not only intervenes in but dominates the politics of developing societies for considerable periods of time should be found primarily in the structure of relationships between the military and civilian sectors. Military rule in Korea illustrates clearly the almost inevitable consequence of unbalanced power relations between the military and civilian sectors following the creation of a newly independent state; with the division of the Korean Peninsula, the military was developed disproportionately to the civilian sectors.

It should thus be noted at the outset that the military was overdeveloped compared to any other sector in Korea at the time of the coup of 16 May 1961. The Korean military started as the Korean Constabulary, established by the American military government (1945-1948) for the purpose of maintaining domestic stability mainly against agitation by leftist groups. The military gained increased socio-political importance because of the division of the nation during the Occupation period. The Korean War (1950-1953) provided an important background to the military's dominance of Korean politics, although its intervention in politics did not take place until several years after the end of the war. A major reason for this was the time-lag between the creation of the Republic and the military on the one hand and the politicisation of military officers on the other. As a result of the war, the size of the military grew to a spectacular extent (from 100000 in 1950 to 700000 in 1956, although it was reduced by 100000 in 1957), but its institutional, technological, and organisational development was even more significant. Assisted by massive US aid, the military developed into the most modernised and Westernised sector in Korea during the 1950s. The civilian sectors, especially universities and the bureaucracy, were also experiencing modernisation, but they were less organised and less modern in outlook, smaller in size, and limited in political and economic participation (Lee 1968:150). Later, with rapid industrialisation, the civilian sectors modernised more rapidly than the military, but reversing the military's political dominance, once it had taken root, proved complicated and time-consuming, as was tragically manifested in the Kwangju Uprising of 1980.

At a societal level, the political situation created the structural conditions for long-term military rule in Korea: the Republic was founded upon an imported ideology of liberal democracy, but Korea's political tradition lacked experience of this Western system; as a result, liberal democracy quickly degenerated into the authoritarianism of Rhee Syngman's 1948-1960 patrimonial rule. The effort of the succeeding Chang Myon government to re-establish a democratic system was bound to fail because its leadership could not control the political turbulence created by the April Uprising of 1960 which toppled the Rhee regime. Imposing liberal democracy upon an unprepared nation simply did not work. What it did was to provide the basis for the emergence of military rule, initiated by younger officers who denied the idea of liberal democracy entirely and instead sought single-mindedly the objectives of economic growth and effective leadership. The coup which took place on 16 May 1961 cannot be fully understood without considering the coup leaders' motivations, which stemmed from the political discontent over the lack of opportunities for promotion and specific political circumstances created after the April Uprising. However, even if those conditions had not occurred, it seems likely that the Korean military would have taken a major role in politics at some time.

In a sense, the coup of 1961 proved to be an historical turning point which temporarily put an end to political struggles amongst the diverse forces which sought to fulfil different objectives of 'nation building' in the newly independent country. In this struggle, the military's alternative – capitalist industrialisation combined with authoritarian control – gained supremacy and dominated Korean society for some time.

Changes in Military Rule: The Park Chung Hee and Chun Doo Hwan Regimes

After the 1961 coup, officers governed South Korea for two years under the Supreme Council for National Reconstruction. They eventually turned the system into a kind of quasi-civilian one, providing party politics in which coup-leaders-turned-civilians occupied supreme positions. But this quasi-civilianised party politics became increasingly a device for Park's personal accumulation of power. The personalisation of power came to define the characteristics of Korean military rule in the 1960s, culminating in the promulgation of the Yushin Constitution in October 1972.

Why did Korea's military rule turn out to be quasi-civilian and personal, rather than direct and institutional, as was the case with its Latin American counterparts? Answers are to be found in the internal characteristics of the Korean military at the time of the coup: the Korean military was not sufficiently institutionalised to put its political domination on a formal basis; the coup was executed by factions centred on the eighth class of the Korean Military Academy, and the infighting among the coup leaders was substantial (S.J. Kim 1971:112-118; Lovell 1975:183-188). Factional disputes during the years of direct rule were essentially struggles for more power sharing, but they also reflected different conceptions of the coup leaders' role in politics. At the time of the coup, the officers, although having to a considerable degree a ruler mentality, did not have a clear ideology or set of policy programs to implement after seizing power. In other words, they had not yet developed the kind of 'new professionalism' which Latin American officers developed from the late 1950s (Stepan 1973); all they possessed was unequivocal anti-communism and vague conceptions of reform, intra-military and societal. The younger officers who planned and executed the coup were more of a 'ruler' type (Nordlinger 1977: 26-27) and, thus, intended to stay in power indefinitely. Senior officers, who were involved at later stages of the coup, were 'moderators' (ibid.: 22-24) who wanted to return to the barracks after 'cleaning' the polity. Because of internal struggles among coup leaders, the regime's characteristics turned out to be eclectic; it was, after a considerable period of direct military rule, a quasi-civilian regime.

Quasi-civilianisation and factionalism provided the conditions for Park's accumulation of personal power. Quasi-civilianisation came with the inauguration of Park Chung Hee as president after his narrow electoral victory against Yun Po Sun, former symbolic president in the Chang administration. It generated party politics around the ruling Democratic Republican Party and divided opposition parties, which merged in 1967 to form the New Democratic Party. Over a long period, however, party politics became a device for prolonging and concentrating the president's political power. The political role of parties decreased and the ever-strengthening bureaucracy and security forces took over their role.

The weakening of party politics and strengthening of the bureaucracy was directly related to the concentration of power in the hands of the president. Park lacked Rhee's personal charisma and failed to consolidate his power base from the outset. But he possessed the rare capacity to tilt the power balance toward himself in entanglements within the ruling group. He removed the possibility of revolt from within the military and utilised party politics for his own ends. After seizing supreme power, he removed any possibility of an independent power base being formed by using his classic tactics of 'divide and rule' within the military and the party (S.J. Kim 1971).

A turning point in Park's consolidation of personal power came with the constitutional revision of 1969, which was executed despite considerable resistance, not only from opposition politicians and students/intellectuals (who represented the political opposition at the time) but also from within the ruling group, especially from Kim Jong Pil. The constitutional revision allowed Park a third term as president and signalled much more systematic and formidable institutional arrangements aimed at giving Park indefinite control of power – the proclamation of the Yushin system. With this, the façade of party politics introduced after the 1961 coup virtually disappeared and Park's life-time authoritarian rule was guaranteed. Authoritarian control was strengthened and power became highly personalised. Park justified the authoritarianism by emphasising administrative efficiency which he deemed indispensable for reunification and economic growth.

Competing explanations have been given for the emergence of the Yushin system, which was similar to the bureaucratic authoritarian system in Latin America (Kang 1983; Im 1987; Y.M. Kim 1986). Clearly, however, it represented a culmination of the personalisation of power which developed after the inauguration of Park. With the advent of the Yushin system, a military-authoritarian regime changed into a more personalised authoritarian one. This change required massive political repression of civil society and of elite politicians. In order to maintain political control, as well as using outright repression, the president employed the 'ideology of security', referring to the threat of North Korea. Personal control, combined with quasi-military-mobilisation, made possible his (and the military's) long-term domination of Korean society, a condition which was absent in most other developing countries.

The Yushin system eventually collapsed with the assassination of Park Chung Hee by one of his close associates, Kim Jae Kyu, the chief of the Korean Central Intelligence Agency (another institutional device created for quasi-civilian rule). Yet, the demise of the personal ruler did not result in the demise of military rule; rather, another military group, often called the New Military Group, occupied the power vacuum created by Park's death. To understand why this happened we should first look into the causes of the breakdown of the Yushin system.

The Yushin system resembled the bureaucratic authoritarian (BA) system in Latin America, but its power base was more personal than the latter. At the same time, it shared characteristics with the pre-war militarist system of Japan, in that the state systematically employed the security threat, real or perceived, as a means of mobilising and controlling civil society.

The 'Total Security System', the term coined by the military regime, was another aspect which distinguished the Yushin system from the Latin American BA regimes. The regime's rationale for the proclamation of the Yushin system was in terms of national security and economic growth, as well as the administrative efficiency deemed indispensable to accomplishing the first two objectives. During the Yushin years, from 1972 to 1979, the whole country was systematically organised into a kind of garrison state, which ultimately contributed to strengthening the authoritarian ruler's political power. It is true the Korean peninsula was at the time on military alert, and many Koreans shared the government's threat perception in the mid 1970s when a large part of the Indochina peninsula was under communist control. This not only facilitated the state's control over the society, but effectively weakened the opposition (Sohn 1989:82-83).

Combining personalisation of political power and militarisation of the society, Park Chung Hee stifled any semblance of liberal democracy, the façade of which was created after the 1961 coup. He denounced the 'Western system of democracy' as inappropriate to Korea's 'emergency' situation and instead presented 'Korean-style democracy' which emphasised efficiency and national harmony under a great leader (Park 1978). Needless to say, the Korean-style democracy was an antithesis of genuine democracy, and was directed toward perpetuation of Park's personal power.

However, this coercive system could not be imposed upon civil society indefinitely. In addition to the general problems of BA regimes, such as the inefficacy of coercion as a basis for long-term political control, and the breakdown of the ruling coalition in the midst of political-economic crisis (O'Donnell 1979), personalisation of power produced a political problem more salient than in more institutionalised Latin American BA regimes, namely the problem of political succession. Because the consolidation of personal power prevented the regime from preparing for post-Park transition, Park's political options were much too limited when popular revolt erupted in 1979; he could not find an effective political successor who would maintain the existing political and economic structures while easing the pressures of popular discontent. The regime was unable to respond effectively to growing political challenges from the combined forces of students, intellectuals, workers, and opposition politicians. The situation was further aggravated by personal animosities between close associates of the president, his chief body guard, Cha Ji Chul, and Kim Jae Kyu, his assassin. It was aggravated by a dispute about which option to take to resolve the political crisis. The hardliner Cha's option of brutal suppression was gaining presidential approval when both of them were murdered by Kim, who was considered the moderate.

Despite the passing of personal rule, the basic structures of the polity, the society, and the economy remained the same; if there was any change, it was toward a deepening of the existing system, although there were naturally changes in political recruitment. The basic reason for this was that Park's death and the breakdown of the Yushin system did not come about by popular uprising but from within the power bloc. What was toppled was an individual ruler, and not the system itself. This was mainly because the opposition forces lacked sufficient power resources to use the death of the ruler to change the regime. The Yushin system had become outdated and was losing its dynamism, but the socio-political and, above all, military structures which defined the system remained intact. In a way, it proved the resilience of the Korean style 'Total Security System'.

After brutal struggles between military-authoritarian and civilian-democratic forces during 1979-1980, the eventual victor turned out to be the New Military

Group centreed around Chun Doo Hwan and Roh Tae Woo, who were to become the next two presidents. What was this group? During his one-man rule, Park Chung Hee, while firmly controlling the military with a combination of 'stick and carrot', had allowed a selective group of senior officers to accumulate power as long as they were loyal to him. This politicised a segment of the officer corps and provided them with a basis for resuming power after Park's assassination by the military. The locus of power resided in a group named *Hanahoe*, of which both Chun Doo Hwan and Roh Tae Woo were leading members. Members of the group were graduates of the Korean Military Academy and were from North Kyongsang Province. It was supposed to be an informal fraternity society but, under tacit permission of the president, it accumulated political power and finally emerged as the most powerful group after Park's death.

Officers' ideological orientations were also undergoing change during Park's rule. Within the military there emerged growing interest in non-military political and social issues. Through curriculum changes in the institutions of higher military education, such as the National Defence College, military officers systematically studied political and social issues (J.H. Kim 1978). For them, the concept of national security should be expanded to include defence against internal enemies such as communist agitators. Although the officers' major concerns lay still in the area of national defence against possible invasion from North Korea, they were developing aspects of the 'new professionalism' found in their Latin American counterparts. As a result, they strengthened and systemised a ruler mentality which provided an ideological basis for reintervention in politics.

Compared to the military's ideological, organisational, and physical strength, democratic forces lacked the organisational cohesion necessary to force the military to remain in the barracks. Students, workers, and intellectuals were incapable of accomplishing what they wanted, namely political democratisation and a more equitable distribution of wealth, because they lacked organisation and effective leadership. Added to this was the division in the leadership of the opposition party between Kim Dae Jung and Kim Young Sam. Power imbalance between the military and democratic forces was further widened by the withdrawal of support for the democratic movement by the middle class, which had more interest in political stability and economic growth than in democratisation. As a result, the breakdown of the Yushin system did not develop into more than a violent transfer of power from one authoritarian regime to another. The Chun regime retained essential characteristics of the Yushin regime, though there were also significant differences between the two.

While the 1961 coup was accepted by the general populace as an almost inevitable result of political crisis, Chun's seizure of power was simply not accepted by everyone in Korea, for reasons discussed below. The immense political cost of Chun's rule was manifested in the bloodshed in Kwangju. He tried to compensate for weak political support by coercion (and lip service to social reform). Thus, the degree of political repression was considerably higher after his assumption of power than immediately after the 1961 coup (although somewhat lower than under the Yushin system).

However, Chun's coercive rule was met by strengthened opposition, which grew in size and was better organised and ideologically radicalised. This was an inevitable consequence of social diversification and a long history of political opposition but, more directly, a result of the brutal suppression of the democratic movement in Kwangju and of growing anti-Americanism derived from the alleged role of the US there. Consequently, democratic challenges to the Chun regime grew much stronger than those to the Park regime.

Regime characteristics were also different. Park Chung Hee consolidated personal control over the state apparatus and political society which Chun could not emulate. Chun, for his part, accumulated some degree of personal power over the ruling bloc, but the possibility of his long-term rule was effectively blocked from the very beginning because he argued that a single term president presented possibly the only source of political legitimacy. In addition, the institutional development of the military by then rendered one-man rule extremely difficult. As a result, soon after Chun's inauguration the issue of political succession became prominent within both the ruling and opposition camps.

Although Chun's control of the military was relatively firm, it cannot be said that he established personal control over it. Rather, the New Military Group constituted a collective leadership around the senior leader, Chun, again reflecting the military's institutional development as compared to 1961. Although it could not, either, be regarded as an institutional military regime, in which the military's institutional norms and procedures dominated the regime structure, the Chun regime certainly possessed some of the characteristics of such a regime. This fact was significant in the transition from Chun's rule; Chun's fall did not require the sort of violence which was necessary in the transition from Rhee and Park because under his rule power was not entrenched exclusively in a personal dictator. Especially toward the end of Chun's rule power was more or less divided among the ruling group, and internal friction within the ruling group played a significant role in determining the direction of political transition.

The most significant difference between the two regimes probably lay in the historical functions each was bound to perform. While Park's regime, for all its contradictions, played positive roles in economic development and political stability at an earlier stage of nation building, Chun's rule was essentially redundant in that the historical function of military-authoritarian rule had virtually evaporated. Chun tried to reverse the historical flow toward a more open political and economic system and, in so doing, paid the price with the lives of hundreds of citizens. As a result, the Chun regime lost its political legitimacy. This was not compensated for by government's efficacy in policy implementation; in fact, a powerful democratic movement erupted in spite of the economic boom in the latter half of Chun's term. Lack of political legitimacy produced constant and severe opposition during Chun's rule.

Democratisation and the End to Military Rule?

With the inauguration of Roh Tae Woo as president in 1988, Korean politics appear to have entered a new era of democratic transition. This transition is not just a result of the transfer of power from Chun to Roh but a consequence of long-term structural changes in the relationship between the military and civilian sectors.

During the course of almost thirty years of military rule, the Korean economy and society were fundamentally transformed; society became diversified, class forces grew and became better organised, and the democratic orientation of the general populace strengthened. With these changes, the military was no longer the most advanced sector of Korean society. Structural changes were already evident when a massive struggle erupted between the military and civilian forces in 1980, but the New Military Group appears not to have been aware of this change, believing that it could still lead and dominate Korean society. The year 1987 was different from 1980; Chun's term was about to terminate, although rumors lingered that he would seek to stay in power. The remaining problem was how to reorganise the political structure for the post-Chun period. Harsh authoritarian rule was out of the question from the beginning; the democratic movement had strengthened, and the military certainly wished to avoid brutal struggles such as the Kwangju Uprising.

The result was a combination of democratic pressures from the opposition camp (basically the same members as in 1980, but better organised and far more radicalised) and the political tactics of the ruling group, which made for limited democratisation. Democratic forces issued a powerful challenge but the ruling group did not employ the armed forces to put down the challenge, because senior officers as well as the president were not willing to risk such action and the US government was putting pressure on the regime for a peaceful transition of power. Roh Tae Woo, representing a moderate faction of the ruling party, used the situation to turn the tide toward his group. Roh proclaimed that he would agree to presidential elections, which the opposition had long demanded, and promised the release of Kim Dae Jung and other opposition leaders. (It was recently reveal-ed that this political concession was initiated by Chun rather than Roh. See S.I. Kim 1992.) As a result, the struggle for democratic transition moved from the streets to the political parties. In subsequent presidential elections the opposition was once again hopelessly divided between archrivals Kim Young Sam and Kim Dae Jung. In a factionalised contest Roh earned electoral victory with only 36.6 per cent of total votes. His victory was only possible because of the division of the opposition and, thus, his political legitimacy was shallow from the beginning.

Democratisation in Korea displays some features unique among recently democratised countries. Most obviously, while in other countries the ruling party lost power for a variety of reasons, in Korea it retains power as democratisation was achieved by one faction, a moderate faction, of the ruling group.

How, then, can the ruling bloc still hold power in Korea despite massive chal-lenges from the majority of the electorate, and why does the Roh government try to convince people that it represents their democratic wishes? The answer to the first question can be found in the weakness of the opposition. Even when the military is willing to give up power, its withdrawal from politics cannot be completed unless there are political institutions, notably political parties, capable of assuming power (Finer 1985:75-76). In Korea, the opposition party has lacked this capacity mainly because it has been divided into two intransigent rival camps. In the case of the second question the answer lies in what was discussed previously, the evaporation of historical functions of authoritarian rule. Roh Tae Woo appears to understand that it is now impossible for any group in Korea to continue authoritarian rule. He tries to consolidate political support with plans for democratic reform, although it is hard to initiate because the veto power of entrenched interests, including the president's own, is still very strong. The passing of authoritarian rule, combined with lack of alternative democratic leadership, ultimately led the process of political transition in Korea into a kind of compromise (a compromise by default), a limited democratisation initiated by opposition forces but soon taken over by the existing power bloc.

After inauguration, Roh consolidated his grip on the military by a series of changes in key positions. Officers' political attitudes also seem to have been changing. There were instances of discontent about decreased political status among officers, inevitable in the democratisation process; but they were over-come and the president's control of the military now seems to be stable enough. Korean officers appear to understand that another intervention in politics would be futile. They vividly remember what happened to Chun's brutal takeover of power and, more fundamentally, they perceive irreversible changes in the relationship between the military and the civilian sectors.

Within the military itself there also seems to be less inclination towards political intervention; disharmony between age and rank, premature promotions, and factional struggles, which were the essential causes of the officers' political discontent, seem to have virtually disappeared (Hong 1990:136-138). Officers still find some sources of discontent, such as narrow opportunities for promotion, but this is not likely to lead to direct intervention in politics.

However, while the structural conditions which would facilitate military rule have now disappeared and officers' motives for direct political action have also significantly diminished, it is still doubtful whether the democratic polity in Korea is securely institutionalised.

To be able to answer this we need to understand exactly what are the characteristics of the Roh regime. Roh Tae Woo was clearly a leading member of the New Military Group which staged the coup against the formal military authority, and brutally suppressed people demanding democracy. The military is still a powerful force in Korean society; it wields strong influence in Korean politics and ex-officers still dominate key areas of politics and society. It is thus difficult to consider the Roh government genuinely civilian. But, on the other hand, it can scarcely be described as a military regime (even a quasi-civilian military regime) either, because it does not depend primarily on the physical force of the military for its political control. Politics in Korea is now managed through a kind of civilian-led liberal democratic procedure in which elections and public opinion are significant. Seen in this light, the present regime stands somewhere between military-authoritarian and civilian-democratic (and hopefully developing from the former to the latter).

Prospects and Conclusions: Toward a Democratic Polity with Civilian Control of the Military?

As has already been argued, the basic reason for the unusually long term of military rule in South Korea lies in an unusually spectacular gap in power resources between civilian forces and the military. Overdeveloped state apparatus, including the military as well as police and bureaucracy, consolidated a preemptive control over the underdeveloped civil society. This phenomenon is not uncommon in post-colonial societies (Alavi 1979), but it was especially evident in Korea because the South has been in constant military tension with the North, and the military has thus occupied a more critical position than in other post-colonial societies.

Nevertheless, it is paradoxical that once the democratisation process began, the chances for the military's reintervention in politics appear to have become more remote in Korea than in, say, Latin America, where the military was forced out of political power but society is still conflict-ridden. Certainly, since Roh's inauguration, Korean politics is in disarray with factional struggles and unfulfilled democratic dreams, while the economy is also in considerable difficulties with a growing trade imbalance, inflation, and class conflicts. Yet, these issues do not appear likely to bring the military back into politics in the foreseeable future. The structure of the relationship between the military and civilian sectors has been reversed; now the military is underdeveloped in comparison to the civilian sectors, and political power will never again be derived primarily from naked physical force.

In this regard, the Korean cycle of authoritarianism and democracy appears to be longer than in most developing countries (though resembling Spain and Portugal where democracy is more or less consolidated after long periods of dictatorship by personal rulers). Korea now seems to have entered the first stage of democratisation after a long period of authoritarian rule. But whether democracy will be institutionalised and civilian control of the military consolidated in the short run is another question; short-term reversals of events (which may be derived from conjunctural and motivational factors) are always possiblities in a long-term cycle (which is determined by structural factors).

For the foreseeable future, Korean politics will demonstrate democratic tendencies, with a clear limit to the participation of diverse interests (especially those of the have-nots) in the political process. Limited democratisation may well be a worse alternative, because it will incite discontent among radical and reactionary forces at the same time. What is important in this situation is effective political leadership to control demands by the diverse forces to a degree acceptable for the maintenance of the nascent civilian political structure, and at the same time pursue democratic reform and more equitable social transformation. When political leadership lacks this capacity, the military, and other discontented forces as well, will impose political pressure in one way or another, even if an outright coup is not plausible.

Civilian control of the military, a minimum requirement of consolidation of democracy, depends upon the internalisation of 'democratic professionalism' among officers, according to which the military accepts 'not only the political subordination of the armed forces to the democratically determined will of the nation, but also their professional subordination to constitutionally designated state authorities' (Fitch 1989:134). It is too early to determine whether Korean military officers have internalised democratic professionalism. Political orientations of Korean officers are hard to clarify because there are deficiencies in empirical analysis, but the opinions and actions of several senior officers during democratic transition showed that they still retained the essential features of the new professionalism. It would be unreasonable to expect that Korean military officers will abandon this political attitude in the short term. Their political attitudes are rapidly changing, but this change was imposed upon them by democratic transition. To achieve a more positive acceptance of democratic civilian authority by the military, changes must occur not only in officers' political orientations but also in political institutions and overall social structure as well.

9

THE MILITARY VERSUS DEMOCRACY IN FIJI: PROBLEMS FOR CONTEMPORARY POLITICAL DEVELOPMENT

Stephanie Lawson

Like many former British colonies, Fiji inherited a form of Westminster parliamentary government. The 'parent model' was modified to the extent that it incorporated a number of provisions designed to secure a special position for indigenous Fijians vis-à-vis the Fiji Indian community. This deviation from modern democratic norms was meant to stabilise Fiji's 'plural society' by ensuring equal representation in the House of Representatives for the two major ethnic groups. For the first seventeen years following independence it seemed that this model had achieved broad acceptance by most parts of the polity. During this time, the office of government was held continuously by the Fijian-dominated Alliance Party led by one of Fiji's paramount chiefs, Ratu Sir Kamisese Mara. In April 1987, however, the Alliance Party was defeated at the polls by a coalition, led by Timoci Bavadra, comprising the relatively new multiracial Labour Party and Fiji's oldest political party, the National Federation Party, which had always attracted the bulk of Fiji Indian support. Less than six weeks after the elections, the new government was overthrown by a military coup and Fiji's form of parliamentary democracy followed the path of failure experienced by so many postcolonial states. Both democracy and its corollary model of civil-military relations were shown to have been acceptable to Alliance leaders and supporters, as well as key elements in the military, only so long as the Alliance retained office as government. In other words, those democratic norms associated with the doctrine of constitutionalism and the principle of alternation in government lacked a secure foundation.

The military intervened again some six months later when coup-leader Rabuka[1]

---

[1]   As a lieutenant-colonel, Sitiveni Rabuka was then the third-ranking officer in the Royal Fiji Military Forces. He became commander of the Fiji Military Forces and was promoted to the rank of major-general.

accused civilian leaders, including his own traditional paramount chiefs, of failing to follow through his initial 'objectives', namely, the absolute entrenchment of 'indigenous rights'. In subsequent developments the 1970 constitution was abrogated, Fiji declared a Republic, a civilian administration installed, and a new constitution promulgated in the name of the 'Sovereign Democratic Republic of Fiji'. The first general elections following these events were held in 1992, and the rigid discriminatory electoral and parliamentary provisions ensured the return of a government sympathetic to the stated objectives of Rabuka's coup. Given this scenario, it might be thought that the conditions for future civilian supremacy – albeit within a traditionalist/nationalist Fijian framework – have been firmly re-established while, conversely, those conditions most conducive to praetorianism have weakened considerably. But this depends ultimately on the strength of the new civilian institutions. These purport to rest on a 'traditional' Fijian foundation of authority, and chiefly leaders have the advantage of being able to evoke powerful symbols of legitimacy. But the appeal of these symbols and the institutions they now support is limited to a minority of the population. Furthermore, the recent history of Fiji suggests that, at the very least, the future role of the Fiji Military Forces will be to act as covert guardian of the 'national interest'. In the terms ordained by Rabuka's 'objectives', this national interest necessarily precludes a return to more democratic constitutional forms which would allow adequate participation in politics by the entire body of citizens – both Fijian and Fiji Indian.

This study takes as its primary focus the notion of 'regime vulnerability' as applied to the civil institutions of government in Fiji both before and after the coup. In adopting this approach we shall of course consider the past, present, and future role of the military with particular emphasis on its relationship with civilian authority. As a necessary preface to this study, we must clarify first what is meant by 'regime vulnerability', especially in terms of the comparative strength or weakness of civil institutions.

Regime Vulnerability

Following its early articulation by Finer (1962), the idea that the level of political culture in a given society (and the concomitant strength of its civil institutions) is decisive for the regime's vulnerability to military intervention has underscored a host of later studies (for example, Huntington 1968; Perlmutter 1981; Rapoport 1982; Luckham 1971; Eide and Thee 1980). And although the general notion has no necessary or exclusive link with the collapse of post-colonial democratic regimes in the Third World, many of the case studies undertaken within this context address precisely the 'failure of democracy' problem. Further, Finer's conceptual framework clearly supports the assumption that Western democracies have achieved a 'mature political culture' through which civilian institutions are strongly legitimated, whereas political and social institutions elsewhere are relatively weak and lacking in legitimacy (see Berghahn 1981:69). In much of the literature on Fiji that has burgeoned since the coup, the assumptions underlying Finer's basic proposition have received implicit support. Various justifications offered by Fiji's military leader, and many supporters of his initial intervention and subsequent role in the process of constitutional change, have also served to reinforce the images projected by Finer's claims.

The utility of the concept of regime vulnerability has attracted some criticism, especially in terms of its explanatory and predictive force. Luckham (1971:10), for example, points out that the criteria for determining the strength of civilian institutions assumes, in many cases, precisely that which needs to be explained. He refers to several of the criteria proposed by Finer, and especially to the requirement that there must be 'publicly agreed procedures for the transfer of power' (ibid.:11). Luckham suggests that the coup itself may, in some circumstances, 'become a publicly recognised and quasi-legitimate means for the transfer of power' (1971:11). One implication of this is that the presence of publicly agreed procedures per se does not serve adequately to distinguish 'weak' civil institutions from 'strong' civil institutions. But Finer's basic criterion is rescued from any ambiguity in its application if we simply add the premise that publicly agreed procedures for transferring power from one government to another must exclude any form of military intervention (and this is undoubtedly what Finer meant). It is certainly the case that any democratic method devised for the transfer of power must, by definition, preclude military intervention, for modern democratic theory and practice is founded, *inter alia,* on strictly constitutionalist principles which deny the legitimacy of force, or the threat of force, in determining succession of government.

Another critic of orthodox regime vulnerability theory, Thompson (1975:459, 466), suggests that hypotheses subscribing to the weakness of governmental institutions as a standing invitation to domestic military intervention are virtually tautological and, further, that overemphasis on the themes which support such hypotheses has obscured the role of the military as a *homus politicus* in its own right. Four themes are identified by Thompson (1975:460-64). One is that the study of unique historical and cultural legacies provides an essential explanation for present behavior. A second concerns the 'failure of democracy' which is predicated on excessive diversity within the polity, a lack of democratic preconditions, and a general disillusionment when economic improvements lag well behind expectations. Another theme extends the second by employing the notion of a political void. This void is created by the absence of traditional loyalties to constitutionalist forms which leads in turn to institutional atrophy. The military, acting as a Hobbesian trump, is drawn into the void. Finally, the 'disjointed system' theme concentrates on the lack of authoritative formulae for the resolution of conflict. In this situation, rival groups seeking to establish their own primacy continually undermine that sense of community essential to the structural development of central, legitimate institutions. In the absence of such institutional development – and depending on the evolutionary stage of class relations – the military may be pulled into a praetorian role of conservative guardianship. Thompson (1975:466) comes to the unremarkable conclusion that all these themes 'share a common image of the military coup: weak political systems pull the military into action'. A key purpose of Thompson's review of these themes, however, is not to demonstrate the obvious, but to construct an alternative image of the location of the military within the state. This location is described by Thompson (1975:486-87) from a praetorian perspective insofar as the military is perceived to be an integral part of the political system rather than an entity which operates outside it. This has some important implications for the present study, to which we shall return at a later point. For the present it is necessary to clarify the conceptual issues further by examining the notion of 'regime' itself.

In most of the literature on military intervention, the terms 'regime' and 'government' are used interchangeably. This is perhaps because the overthrow of a government generally entails, *ipso facto,* the overthrow of the regime. Furthermore, most writers in the area are content to utilise the concept of 'regime' simply as a term to attach to 'civil' or 'military'. But although regime and government are closely related, they are not the same thing, and it is important to understand the basic analytical distinctions between them. This is especially so in the case of Fiji when we come to consider the notion of legitimacy and how it operates at different levels. Also vital to the study of political structures and their legitimacy is, rather obviously, the state. Control of the state apparatus is the focal issue in cases of military intervention, and associated ideological contestations revolving around nationalism are usually linked directly with this quest for control. The relationships between state, regime, and government are complex, and to deal with these properly would require much more scope than is available here. In order to at least differentiate these structures for the purpose of the present discussion, it must suffice to say that the state itself is the locus of political power while the concept of regime is concerned with how, and by whom, that power is exercised. In other words, 'regime' is concerned with the form of rule (see Chazan et al. 1988; Lawson 1993).

Governments are awarded management or control of the state apparatus in accordance with the norms and principles of the regime which are embodied, for practical purposes, in certain rules and procedures. Governments derive much of their legitimacy as controllers or managers of the state apparatus from the norms and rules of the regime. These are generally embodied in a constitution which sets out those 'publicly agreed procedures for the transfer of power'. All this is implicit in the democratic doctrine of constitutionalism. At another level, however, the regime itself requires legitimacy. And where this is weakly support- ed, it follows that the regime – and governments formed under it – are vulnerable to challenges which, in the particular case we are dealing with here, came in the form of military intervention. The point in setting up this rather formalised schema here is to clarify the point that 'regime vulnerability' entails more than just 'government vulnerability'.

In the case of Fiji, both the government that was overthrown, and the regime under which it was formed, were regarded by the military and other opponents of the government as lacking an essential legitimacy. This is clearly evident in the justifications surrounding the coup and the subsequent process of constitu- tional change. But to understand the problems associated with political legiti- macy, it is important to investigate the historical context which gave rise to the civil institutions of post-colonial Fiji, and the specific factors which contributed to their essential 'weakness'. Through this it will be seen that the various hypo- theses concerning regime vulnerability are indeed relevant, not only to the analysis of the original coup in Fiji, but to the future of civil-military relations there.

Fiji's Colonial Legacy [2]

British colonial rule was established in Fiji in 1874 following a period of internal strife occasioned partly by the activities of European settlers and traders in the eastern regions of the island group. It was in this region, too, that the most power- ful of the Fijian confederacies were located and rivalries between leading chiefs there exacerbated the general deterioration in domestic politics that followed European contact. The British government was to some extent a reluctant colo- niser at this time. The further extension of empire in the remote Pacific promised little in the way of economic rewards and only the potential for strategic advan- tage offered any return on their 'investment'. The general policy towards the new colony of Fiji, then, was that its administration should pose as small a financial burden to Whitehall as possible and, ideally, that it should be economically

---

[2]   This section is based on a much more detailed account set out in Lawson (1991).

self-sufficient. Fiji's first substantive governor, Sir Arthur Hamilton Gordon, therefore set about implementing a set of policies which were directed not only towards establishing a solid financial base for the new colony, but which reflected also a relatively new approach to the 'management' of colonial subjects. The strategies adopted by Gordon to secure these objectives were decisive for the later development of politics in Fiji.

The first of these strategies concerned 'native policy' and this was aimed partly at making the colonial experience for Fijians an exception to the dismal history of colonised people in other parts of the empire. One of the measures introduced was the reservation of those Fijian lands not already 'legally' alienated to white settlers, and the prohibition of any further land alienation. Although this measure was sound in principle, the method by which land tenure was assigned on the basis of certain kinship groups, and which remains in place to this day, imposed a uniformity and inflexibility that bore little resemblance to pre-colonial Fijian practices. The land tenure system has since served as a serious impediment to the efficient and equitable utilisation of land resources amongst Fijians. In addition, the bureaucratic structures relating to the administration of land, including the leasing of agricultural land to both Fijian and Fiji Indian tenants, have creamed off much of the income from leases. A substantial proportion of the remaining funds is distributed to chiefs. Fijian 'commoners' receive few direct benefits from the leasing of their lands, and this was one of the issues that the Labour/NFP coalition government had placed on the political agenda. Concern for the security of indigenous land rights was made a focal issue by the Alliance Party during the 1987 elections and figured prominently in the rhetoric surrounding justification of the coup. It is therefore important to note that the 1970 constitution of independent Fiji provided triple entrenchment of Fijian rights with respect to land and other customary entitlements.

A second strategy for securing the principles of the new enlightened native policy was the establishment of a system of indirect rule. This was achieved by taking the relatively authoritarian chiefly structures of control which characterised socio-political organisation in the eastern regions as the basis for the system, and imposing these uniformly over the entire island group. In addition, selective recruitment to the colonial bureaucracy from amongst easterners served to marginalise Fijians from other regions. One consequence of this was that eastern chiefs achieved much greater prominence within the colonial regime. As political institutions evolved from an initially rigid crown colony system to something resembling responsible government in the pre-independence period, eastern chiefs retained their political prominence and reinforced their prospects for future control through the formation of the Alliance Party. This underscored exclusive claims to political legitimacy by eastern chiefs vis-à-vis any other political group in Fiji.

The third strategy employed by the colonial administration involved balancing the policy of 'native protection' with the requirement of financial self-sufficiency. The use of Fijian labour in the emerging plantation economy was viewed as detrimental to the traditional Fijian way of life and Governor Gordon looked immediately to the Indian sub-continent from which other British colonies had successfully recruited their 'helots of empire'. The first Indian indentured laborers arrived in Fiji in 1879 and by the time the system was abolished in 1916, Fiji had acquired a substantial, and permanent, population of Fiji Indians whose descendants now comprise around 46 per cent of the total population. This created what is commonly described as Fiji's 'plural society' in which the two major ethnic groups are perceived as constituting monolithic entities in a two-sided contest for political power. This perception is largely responsible for popular conceptions concerning the essentially 'racial' cause of the May 1987 coup. And although most academic commentators – with the notable exception of Scarr (1988) – have evinced a complex array of causes which point to the salience of other decisive factors (see, for example, Lawson 1991; Ewins 1993), the general perception of contemporary developments in Fiji remains fixed firmly within a racially-oriented paradigm.

Another aspect of Fiji's colonial legacy which is closely related to the developments outlined above, and with the issue of eastern chiefly legitimacy, concerns the doctrine of Fijian 'paramountcy of interests'. This doctrine upholds the supremacy of Fijian interests over and above the interests of any other racial or ethnic group in Fiji. It developed as a colonial version of an indigenous rights charter which, although never formally codified, developed into a powerful orthodoxy. The doctrine's initial purpose was to underscore the early policies instituted by Gordon. As we have seen, these had been designed largely to protect Fijians from European settler exploitation. But as the Fiji Indian community grew, the doctrine was employed by European and Fijian leaders alike as a counter to the Fiji Indians' quest for social, political, and economic rights. It became, in effect, a forceful rhetorical weapon in a war of subjugation which was at first prosecuted most vigorously by the small but influential European commercial elite concerned to retain their own privileged position in the colony. This enabled Europeans, *inter alia,* to represent themselves as champions of the Fijian people and guardians of their interests. For their part, Fijian political leaders, who were drawn almost exclusively from chiefly ranks (with easterners predominating), took up the same rhetorical stance and denounced Fiji Indian claims for equal political rights as anathema to the interests of the Fijians as a whole.

This of course raises questions as to the precise nature of the interests of each 'group', and especially whether the interests of Fijian chiefs are automatically consonant with those of commoners. One must question also the notion that any interests espoused by the eastern chiefly elite necessarily accord with the interests of Fijians in other regions. These issues will be considered later in the context of contemporary politics. For the moment it is important to note that the doctrine of Fijian paramountcy developed a political salience which went far beyond its original utility. We have seen already that Fijian rights relating to land and other resources were well established in the early colonial period and firmly secured through the 1970 constitution. But the general themes of the doctrine, combined with the spectre of an 'Indian land-grab', continued to be pursued by Alliance and other nationalist leaders at the level of political rhetoric (and invective) in post-independence electoral campaigns. With respect to the Alliance and the eastern chiefly elite, this served the instrumental purpose of uniting the bulk of the Fijian electorate behind their leadership in direct opposition to Fiji Indians. Furthermore, the Alliance presented its leadership as the embodiment of all that is distinctively, traditionally, and legitimately 'Fijian'.

Both the formal political institutions and the party system that emerged in the late colonial period reflected these earlier developments, as did the 1970 constitution of independent Fiji. Apart from recognising and securing the special rights and interests of indigenous Fijians, the constitution provided for a complex system of communal representation through which equal numbers of Fiji Indians and Fijians were returned as members of the House of Representatives. In addition, eight 'general' members were to be returned as representatives of 'other races'. Most of these were of European descent and were aligned politically with the Alliance Party. This meant that despite formal parity of representation for Fiji Indians, the racial allocation of seats gave an immediate electoral advantage to the Alliance and, indeed, seemed designed to ensure that the Alliance would continue indefinitely in office. Viewed in this light, the 1970 constitution cannot be seen as an instrument for securing the practice of democratic politics beyond the formal superficialities of parliamentary government. More specifically, the principle of alternation in government, which is an essential hallmark of modern representative democracy, was undermined to the extent that the legitimacy of the opposition party as a potential or actual government was not recognised by the Alliance leadership.

Continued Alliance dominance, however, depended on their maintaining a solid electoral base amongst Fijians. Any intra-Fijian disunity would necessarily erode this base and leave the Alliance vulnerable to electoral defeat, and this is precisely what happened in the elections of 1987. Although the Labour/NFP coalition was unable to attract more than around 10 per cent of the overall Fijian vote, it was able to muster sufficient Fijian and 'other races' support in several crucial urban and peri-urban constituencies. This, combined with a further slippage of Alliance support to minor parties and independents as well as a significant level of Fijian abstention from voting, gave the coalition a majority of seats. But the events which followed the formation of the new government indicated clearly the extent to which it lacked that widespread legitimacy essential to the principle of alternation in government. Despite Ratu Mara's formal concession of defeat, Alliance members boycotted the opening of parliament and several became involved in the activities of the extremist Taukei movement – a nationalist Fijian group which emerged in the aftermath of the Alliance's defeat and which resolved to bring down the new government. Mara maintained a public silence which was seen to implicitly endorse their activities. And when the army intervened less than six weeks after the elections, Mara was amongst the first to join the initial administration set up by coup-leader Rabuka.

The point of the foregoing discussion has been to highlight a number of important factors which, taken together, served to undermine the legitimacy of the political institutions established by the 1970 constitution, thereby rendering them 'weak' and vulnerable to attack. This vulnerability operated at two levels. First, it is evident that any government other than the Alliance could be portrayed rhetorically as a significant threat to Fijian rights – a logical corollary to the idea that only the Alliance could guarantee the rights and interests of all Fijians. These ideas were taken much further than the original doctrine of paramountcy of interests implied, for this was basically concerned with the protection of lands and customary matters which remained constitutionally entrenched no matter which government was in power. In turn, this doctrine was invoked to deny virtually any political legitimacy to Fiji Indians and, it must be added, to those dissident Fijians who formed the backbone of the Fiji Labour Party. Put simply, the legitimacy of the new government was weakly supported, and therefore vulnerable to challenge, since it was opposed by a dominant political discourse which had succeeded in elevating a particular group of Fijians to a position of almost exclusive authority.

The second aspect of vulnerability operated at the regime level. Although the constitution was, arguably, designed to entrench a one-party dominant system, it nonetheless supported formally all those democratic constitutionalist principles associated with the notion that no one political group is entitled to lay exclusive claims to legitimacy and, through this, control of the state apparatus. It is clearly evident that neither the Alliance Party nor the military accepted the legitimacy of a regime which allowed succession of government according to democratic constitutionalist norms and principles. In other words, those 'publicly agreed procedures for the transfer of power' provided by the constitution were, when put to the test, shown to lack universal acceptance. This view has been reinforced by the promulgation of the new republican constitution, the rules of which seek to prevent the possibility of any such succession occurring again.

The new constitutional order, however, is one which undoubtedly lacks the support of a majority of the population in Fiji. Although this has not been tested by way of a referendum, one can assert fairly confidently that most Fiji Indians would regard it as illegitimate. And since the new electoral provisions for Fijians are grossly biased in favour of the eastern provinces, it is not unreasonable to assume that Fijians on the main island of Viti Levu will resent and resist eastern dominance – especially those in the west whose history of dissidence suggests more than a little reluctance to endorse eastern legitimacy. In addition, the allocation of Fijian seats is weighted most heavily against the more 'progressive' urban Fijians who make up around one third of the Fijian population but who have been awarded only five of the thirty-seven Fijian seats. Taken together, these factors suggest weak support for the new regime and, as a consequence, for any government formed under its provisions. Whether this will promote susceptibility to further military intervention, or at least a praetorian role for the military, is another question, and one best addressed now by reference to the development of Fiji's military forces and its role in contemporary politics.

The Military in Fiji

The origins and development of Fiji's military forces reflect clearly the socio-political dimensions of Fiji's pre-colonial and colonial history. When Governor Gordon took over the administration of the colony, there was already a small military force known as the Royal Army, which had been used by Fiji's leading eastern chief, Cakobau, and his British supporters in an attempt to control the central and western regions. Gordon continued to employ this unit for its original purpose of subjugation, thereby reinforcing eastern chiefly authority and interests. Following the relative success of these early pacification operations, the unit (which had meanwhile been renamed the Armed Native Constabulary) was amalgamated with the police of the Fiji Constabulary. In the early 1920s, further 'pacification' operations were conducted against striking Indian workers (Sanday 1989:3).

From the beginning, then, the armed forces in Fiji were utilised largely for coercing troublesome groups in the interests of internal political stability. This early emphasis, and the identification of 'troublesome' with dissident western Fijians and Fiji Indians, saw the already dominant position of 'loyal' easterners further reinforced through selective recruitment to the constabulary – and later to the regular armed forces. This is a very clear manifestation of Enloe's (1980: 16) conception of 'security mapping' where the ethnically-determined basis of recruitment involves convenient geographical concentrations. Further, it is evident that the early orientation of state security in Fiji was strongly biased towards 'the maintenance of congenial domestic class and ethnic patterns of order' (Enloe 1980:14).

The later development of Fiji's military as an entity distinct from the police, and as a standing army in its own right, was given its major impetus by the call of empire. Two world wars and the Malayan Emergency saw troops from Fiji serve monarch and empire in defence, presumably, of 'democracy'. Back home, however, little progress had been made with respect to democratic rights for Fiji Indians, and this had a direct effect on military recruitment for World War II. Many Fiji Indian grievances had been centred on the issue of parity of political rights and status with Europeans (not Fijians). When the war broke out, the sense of inequitable political treatment was further exacerbated by differential pay rates for Fiji Indians and Europeans in the army and most Fiji Indians declined to volunteer for service for this reason. The only Indian platoon in the army, which had been formed in 1934 despite some resistance on the part of the colonial administration and the chiefs, was disbanded (Sharma 1990:63). This not only strengthened the apparent political divide between Fiji Indians and the other communities, but served also to consolidate the army as an essentially Fijian institution.

At the time of the coup in 1987 the composition of the Royal Fiji Military Forces (RFMF) was 98 per cent Fijian. They were led by Brigadier Ratu Epeli Nailatikau, a high chief from the east and also son-in-law of Prime Minister Mara. Although many able commoners had been admitted to high-ranking positions, including the then third-ranking officer Lieutenant-Colonel Sitiveni Rabuka, those from eastern chiefly families were disproportionately represented in the officer corps. Commoners like Rabuka, who had achieved high rank, were also drawn in disproportionate numbers from the east. Saffu (1990:162) suggests that the extent of eastern dominance in the RFMF, together with the historical factors outlined earlier, was responsible for the development of a 'traditional-aristocratic' pattern of civil-military relations which operated alongside the liberal-democratic pattern throughout the independence period until May 1987. Saffu (1990:159) argues also that both patterns were compatible with civilian political supremacy until the electoral victory of the coalition when the liberal-democratic pattern was abrogated abruptly 'because it did not guarantee control of the state by chiefs and other traditionalists'. This is consistent with the arguments put forward earlier concerning the lack of legitimacy accorded both to the coalition and to the regime under which the new government was formed.

Another aspect of the analysis, and one which is vital to future developments in civil-military relations in Fiji, concerns the prospects for the traditional-aristocratic model. Saffu (1990:159) draws on Nordlinger's (1977) work in identifying the core features of the model. The most basic indicator supporting civilian supremacy is a strong identification of social and political values between civilian and military leaders in an essentially 'pre-democratic' system. Civilian leaders are regarded as legitimate insofar as they are part of the same social network of aristocratic families that provides military leaders. Sanday (1991:253) says that this pattern was reflected in a pervasive belief amongst indigenous Fijians that political power was the exclusive preserve of the chiefs. The role of the military in post-coup Fiji seemed to point to a continuation of the traditional-aristocratic pattern.

In the immediate aftermath of the coup, Rabuka established a sixteen-member Council of Ministers comprising eleven Alliance parliamentarians (including Mara) and four members of the nationalist Taukei movement. Rabuka himself, as head of this body, was the only military member. This was replaced shortly afterwards with an eighteen-member Council of Advisors which, as a necessary façade for at least qualified domestic and international acceptance, included three Fiji Indians as well as Bavadra. Rabuka, however, remained a leading member. The new arrangements, and of course the coup itself, were endorsed wholeheartedly by the Council of Chiefs who had resolved that the military should be asked to review the 1970 constitution to ensure that Fijians were guaranteed control of government at all times (Lal 1988:87). And Rabuka's ambitions for the military were expressed unambiguously in numerous statements on its future role, including an assertion that the military would remain an integral part of any kind of political system, irrespective of what form it might take (Lal 1988:113).

In the meantime, some rapprochement had been reached between the civilian actors in the play of negotiations. A degree of moderation had started to prevail as Taukeist leaders, and Rabuka himself, became increasingly marginalised in the process of negotiations which led eventually to the 'Deuba Accord' – an agreement under which both the Alliance and the deposed coalition were to participate on equal terms in a caretaker government under the governor-general, Ratu Sir Penaia Ganilau (Robertson and Tamanisau 1988:138). Although Rabuka had apparently agreed to support the new accord, it is evident that his intentions were otherwise. Two hours before the governor-general was scheduled to inform the nation of the new caretaker government, Rabuka led a second coup to enforce his original 'objectives'. Within days Rabuka announced the complete abrogation of the 1970 constitution and declared himself head of a republican govern-ment (Robertson and Tamanisau 1988:142). But Rabuka's position as head of the republic, although supported by military force, was untenable politically. Leaving international opinion aside, Rabuka could not, as a commoner, hope to legitimate himself as leader at that time. In his own rationale for both coups, Rabuka had consistently promoted the paramount importance of Fijian 'tradi-tion' and the virtually sacrosanct political position of chiefs in this context. So powerful had the rhetoric about chiefly authority become that it left Rabuka in the position of being unable to command personally the symbolic resources asso-ciated with political legitimacy in Fiji. In his own words, Rabuka had claimed that the military was 'trying to protect the chiefs and their people' and, further, that it was the 'duty of the warrior tribe to protect the chief' (quoted in Norton 1990:139).

In the wake of the second coup, then, the eastern chiefly elite returned once more to the helm of government, replacing the Taukeist council which Rabuka had installed as an interim measure. Rabuka continued for a time as a member of the ministry but was later forced to 'return to barracks' at the behest of Mara who had given him the choice of resigning either from the military, or from the government. In August 1991, however, Rabuka decided to quit the military in order to pursue a political career, and returned to the post of co-deputy prime minister and minister for Home Affairs in the interim government. Ganilau con-tinued to occupy the position of president while Mara remained prime minister until the 1992 elections. Rabuka's political ambitions, however, were well known and his decision to enter civilian politics as a leading member of the Fijian Political Party (which was formed with the backing of the leading chiefs) was a clear enough indication that he would be a contender for the prime ministership in the elections. Given the lack of suitable chiefly successors to Mara in the FPP, as well as the emergence of several rival Fijian parties, the longer-term outlook for stable government under the chiefly establishment was beginning to look more uncertain. This brings us back to the question, posed at the beginning, concerning the prospects for continuing civilian supremacy and whether the new regime is itself vulnerable to some kind of intervention.

Future Prospects

In looking at possible future directions for politics in Fiji, we must again con-sider the notion of regime vulnerability and, in this context, examine also the concepts of overt and covert regimes. In the earlier discussion of the 1970-1987 period, it was evident that although the liberal-democratic framework operated at a superficial level as an 'overt' regime, there was at the same time a stronger 'covert' regime operating through traditionalist conceptions of legitimacy. But it took a change of government under the democratic provisions of the constitution to reveal the relative strength – or weakness – of each of these. Following from this, it is logical to depict the liberal-democratic pattern of civil-military relations during the same period as an overt but weakly supported model, whereas the traditional-aristocratic pattern operated at a covert level, but was more strongly supported by the same traditionalist legitimator. The coup of May 1987, then, can be viewed not only as an act of intervention for the purpose of destroying the liberal-democratic façade, but also as an exercise in regime maintenance insofar as it restored the eastern chiefly elite to power – but this time as the overt regime.

The traditionalist regime is now supported formally (and overtly) by a constitution which does little to disguise its essentially undemocratic character. As suggested earlier, however, it lacks the support of a majority of the population, especially as it is explicitly designed to relegate the substantial population of Fiji Indians to electoral irrelevance. In addition, it discriminates heavily against urban Fijians, as well as those from the central and western regions, in favour of the eastern provinces. It is primarily for these reasons that the new regime may, in the final analysis, carry within it the seeds of its own destruction. Far from keeping the indigenous Fijians united in opposition to Fiji Indians, the new constitution is much more likely to serve as an instrument for its political fracture. How long this process may take depends on too many variables for any certain answer to be given. But on any reasonable assessment, the future stability of the chiefly regime must be in doubt – an assessment which has obvious implications for the role of the military. For whatever happens in the arena of civil politics, the military has established itself in a guardian role. In the terms expressed by Luckham (1971:27), the military now has a strong ideological disposition towards regarding itself as the 'Platonic guardian' of the national interest. This points to the continuation of a covert military regime operating beneath the level of the overt chiefly/traditionalist regime. And the praetorian character of this development does indeed suggest that the military in Fiji has become a *homus politicus* in its own right.

Conclusion

Whatever specific pattern of civil-military relations emerges in Fiji, it can be said with some certainty that democratic constitutionalist principles are unlikely to prevail in the shorter term. Despite the high-sounding title assigned to the new republic, there is no commitment on the part of either chiefly or military leaders in support of these principles. Indeed, much of their traditionalist rhetoric since the coup has been directed explicitly against the 'alien' concepts associated with democratic politics (see especially Dean and Ritova 1988). The logical foundations of the traditionalist view, and the ideology supporting it, have been dealt with critically elsewhere (see Lawson 1990a and 1990b). But whatever claims can be mounted against the logical and ethical bases of political legitimacy in contemporary Fiji, the strength of the prevailing orthodoxies lends sufficient rhetorical force to arguments countering both domestic and external pressures for 'democratisation'. The efficacy of this rhetoric is further strengthened by appeals to the slogan, increasingly popular in international discourse, of 'indigenous rights'. In addition, there is a pervasive belief that 'plural societies' are incapable of sustaining peaceful democratic politics, and can only be managed effectively through relatively authoritarian institutions (see Lawson 1990a). This means that both the military and the current civilian regime have escaped much of the international invective that might otherwise have been directed against the constitutional entrenchment of a system of political apartheid.

Most importantly, it needs to be emphasised that the *homus politicus* role of the military in Fiji is incompatible with any notion of civilian supremacy. It is especially contrary to the democratic principles embodied in the doctrine of constitutionalism. In other words, if the military becomes a de facto part of the political system insofar as it plays a covert role in determining political leadership, it can no longer be considered the apolitical institution that democratic theory demands. Finally, the effective guardianship of Fiji's 'national interest' by the military betrays an essential weakness in the political culture that has sustained the chauvinistic assertion of 'indigenous rights'. For wherever the threat of force is a necessary condition for maintaining a particular political order, it follows that the order itself lacks the degree of legitimacy required for long-term stability.

Postscript

The original version of this chapter was written before the general elections of 1992 – the first held after the 1987 coup. There has since been another round of elections in 1994, occasioned by the failure of Rabuka's government to have the budget passed. The text has been modified slightly to take account of these events, but it is worth elaborating a few further points. The 1992 elections held some surprises for those expecting that the 'party of the chiefs' would make a clean sweep of the Fijian seats. Under the leadership of Rabuka, who succeeded in replacing Mara as the effective leader of the Fijian party on the latter's retirement, the party (officially called the *Soqosoqo ni Vakavulewa ni Taukei* or SVT) failed to gain an absolute majority of seats in the House of Representatives. Seven of the Fijian seats went to opposing Fijian parties and independents. The Fiji Indian seats were fairly evenly divided between Labour and the National Federation Party, while the General Voters' Party (which is basically supportive of the SVT, although not necessarily of Rabuka himself), won all five of the General Voters' seats. Rabuka subsequently secured sufficient support from other parties and independents to gain the president's endorsement as prime minister. Rabuka's SVT government, however, lasted just over eighteen months before it fell. This was precipitated by the defection of seven SVT ministers, and followed a period of intense dissent within the government's ranks. Rabuka's party was returned at the next elections with the same majority, and again managed to put together a coalition, but the overall result confirmed that intra-Fijian disunity has become an important factor in current politics. Both elections have shown that the chiefly establishment has been sidelined to some extent in terms of electoral office, but their constitutional powers and prestige remain significant, as does the rhetoric of chiefly traditions.

10

GOVERNMENT AND THE MILITARY
IN PAPUA NEW GUINEA

R.J. May

On the eve of Papua New Guinea's independence, achieved in 1975, there was much speculation about the future prospects for democracy in this Pacific island state. As an Australian-administered territory, Papua New Guinea had been brought towards independence within a solid Westminster tradition. National elections had been conducted since 1964 (though the early parliaments tended to be dominated by members appointed by the colonial administration); a Papua New Guinean chief minister had led the government since 1972; tentative attempts had been made to foster the growth of political parties; and the traditions of an independent judiciary and a professional public service had been established. In the deliberations which culminated in the presentation of a 'home-grown' draft constitution in 1974, however, a range of institutional options was considered, the Constitutional Planning Committee drawing on a number of constitutional documents, especially those of the post-colonial states in East and West Africa.

In the light of then-recent experiences among the new states of Africa and Asia, and considering the comparatively shallow roots of national political sentiment in Papua New Guinea, particular concerns were expressed about the possibility that, in a post-independence Papua New Guinea state, democracy would yield to either a one-party state or a military takeover.

To counter any tendency towards military intervention, some commentators suggested that specific provisions be made to give the military institutional representation in government (see below). In the event, this suggestion was not taken up, and the military maintained a fairly low profile in post-independence society. But in 1987 political developments in Papua New Guinea and military coups in Fiji prompted some observers to again raise questions about the possibility of military intervention in Papua New Guinea. While a military coup seems to remain a very remote possibility, internal security problems in Papua New Guinea over recent years have brought about significant changes in the role of the military and in its relations with government.

The Colonial Heritage

The Papua New Guinea Defence Force has its origins in the formation, during World War II, of four infantry battalions in the then separate territories of Papua and New Guinea. The four battalions were brought together as the Pacific Islands Regiment (PIR), though all officers and most NCOs were Australian. The PIR fought with distinction alongside Allied troops in Papua New Guinea. It was disbanded in 1946 but was re-formed five years later.

Until well into the 1960s the PIR was essentially a component of the Australian army, and was there primarily to serve Australian defence interests. A former PIR commanding officer, Lt. Colonel Maurie Pears, later wrote, 'We saw PIR as Australia's Ghurka Unit' (Sinclair 1992:153).[1]

During the early 1960s, Indonesia's campaign against the Dutch in what was then Dutch New Guinea (now the Indonesian province of Irian Jaya) and its confrontation with Malaysia sparked fears of possible Indonesian expansionism towards Papua New Guinea, and prompted a surge of activity on Australia's part to expand the military in Papua New Guinea and to strengthen security infra-structure along the Indonesian-Papua New Guinea border. Within the space of a few years the PIR was increased from about 700 'native soldiers' with Australian officers to a force of over 3000. Indigenisation of the officer corps began, the first two officers (Ted Diro and Patterson Lowa) graduating from the Australian Officer Cadet School in Portsea in 1963. A Military Cadet School (to prepare recruits for further training at Portsea) was established in Lae. A water transport base was established in Port Moresby and the wartime naval base on Manus was resuscitated. An Army Aviation Corps was created and several Royal Australian Air Force transport aircraft were posted to Papua New Guinea.

By the mid 1960s, coincident with the perceived threat from Indonesia diminishing, the military build-up levelled off, though Papua New Guinea continued to occupy a significant place in Australian strategic planning. More significant for Papua New Guinea, however, along with the increased expenditure on the military came more serious consideration of the possible future role of a Papua New Guinea defence force. In 1966 the force's incoming commanding officer said:

---

[1]   For a detailed history of the PIR, and its involvement in World War II, see Barrett (1969), Mench (1975), and Sinclair (1990, 1992).

> The Army's role in PNG falls basically into two parts – to build an Army capable of playing a major role in the defence of the Territory against external aggression, and to provide for the future a loyal and well-disciplined indigenous force capable of supporting the Government of an independent PNG (quoted in Sinclair 1992:222-23).

In the House of Assembly, at forums at the recently-established University of Papua New Guinea (UPNG), and elsewhere, however, a number of Papua New Guineans expressed apprehension about the growth of a well-provisioned military. In a paper published in 1967, for example, a pseudonymous Papua New Guinean school teacher questioned the Australian government's expenditure on the army, suggesting 'that the army is probably the biggest single threat to the peace, security and development of our country' (Heatu 1967:33; similarly see Warubu 1968; Olewale 1972).

The issue of the military's relations with civil authorities was officially addressed in 1969 by the Australian minister for the Army, Peter Lynch. Lynch described the 'current basic roles' of the army as being to build an efficient force capable of playing a vital part in the defence of Papua New Guinea and to provide a well-disciplined, stable and reliable indigenous force completely loyal to the government (Lynch 1969:22). He went on to say:

> Emphasis is placed on loyalty to legally constituted authority. This is implicit in the Australian Government's aim of developing in the Territory a sound political structure in which the Public Service, the [Police] Constabulary and the Army have all been thoroughly trained in the concept of subordination to a legally constituted democratic government (ibid.:23).

To this end the army was involved in a 'heavy education effort', including group discussions of 'civics and christian ethics' (ibid. Also see O'Neill 1971:16-17).

Also, although civic action work had been carried out since 1951, from 1967 all major patrols and operational exercises by the PIR included civic action projects designed to 'create constructive attitudes in the minds of soldiers towards the people, and help identify the people with their Army' (Lynch 1969:23. Also see Hussey 1968).

Ironically, the success of the civic action program fuelled concerns about the future role of the military in Papua New Guinea. Vincent (Serei) Eri (who later served as defence secretary before becoming governor-general) suggested in 1969 that the army was 'replacing the Administration in the minds of the people' and 'preparing the ground for some future action', and he warned, 'it is a very dangerous situation that we are getting into' (quoted in Sinclair 1992:136). Such concerns appear to have been quite widely shared among educated Papua New

Guineans, but were countered by army commander Brigadier Hunter, who said,

> It is better to have the army out with people, learning to understand them, than to be sitting in their barracks getting big heads. What Papua-New Guinea needs is a people's army, though not in the Maoist form (*Canberra Times* 23 January 1969).

Not specifically mentioned in Lynch's 1969 statement was the army's possible future role in internal security. This issue was not long in surfacing. Following a disturbance in East New Britain in mid 1970 the Australian government placed the army in readiness to assist the administration should the situation escalate, and troops were given a hastily-arranged course in riot control. In the event the situation was resolved without the army being called in, and there was a general feeling that the administration had acted prematurely. But the events of 1970 clearly signalled a recognition of the broader role the army might be called upon to play in an independent Papua New Guinea, and, along with growing unrest on Bougainville, stimulated further debate.

Australian defence expert Robert O'Neill (1971) suggested that internal law and order was likely to become the army's major preoccupation. Australian journalist Peter Hastings endorsed this view, referring to the 'inescapable similarity between Africa and Papua New Guinea', and suggesting that after independence 'the Army will inevitably be involved in the political direction of the country' (Hastings 1971:32). The future role of the army was also the subject of a local radio program,[2] which brought together defence force personnel, politicians, and civilian commentators. Papua New Guinea's newly-elected chief minister, Michael Somare, expressed the view that 'we do probably need a defence force' – for patrolling borders and territorial waters, and 'to react in the first instance to any armed aggression' – but he suggested that it should be of a smaller size and that it should only be involved in internal security operations in 'a real national emergency'. As against this, senior Papua New Guinean officer, Major Ted Diro, saw the army as having a role to play in internal security matters, and UPNG lecturer Ulf Sundhaussen argued that given the very low level of national consciousness and 'already surfacing tendencies for separatism' the maintenance of internal security would be a task for the army in Papua New Guinea, as it was in Asia and Africa, and that the army should have 'some sort of political say'. Sundhaussen (who had studied the military's role in Indonesia) advocated the development of working relationships between officers and politicians and the integration of the military into the political and social structure. At this time there was some debate

---

[2]   'The Sword and the State'. Two-part program by Australian Broadcasting Commission, 2, 9 November 1972.

over Sundhaussen's suggestion that the military be represented in cabinet (see, for example, Sundhaussen 1973a, 1973b; Mench 1975: chapter 5, and Premdas's 1974 critique of Sundhaussen), and there were proposals, supported by Australian External Territories Minister Morrison, to combine the army and police in a paramilitary force (Morrison advocated a Malaysian-style field force). But when in 1974 the Constitutional Planning Committee (CPC) presented its report, its recommendations followed the approach outlined earlier by Somare.

The CPC began by emphasising its belief in the general principle, 'that the disciplined forces should at all times be subject to the control of the elected government' (CPC 1974:13/1). It went on to express the view that the Defence Force should be 'firmly oriented towards external defence' (ibid.:13/3):

> . . . we have very serious reservations about the possibility of a future Papua New Guinea Government using the army against its own people in any but the most extreme cases of civil disorder, and then subject also to specific conditions (ibid.*)*.

Its reservations on this issue were reinforced by concerns about what it saw as the provision of installations and equipment 'at a standard that has little relevance to the circumstances of Papua New Guinea' and about 'the elitist nature of the Defence Force' (ibid.). It consequently recommended an expansion of the police force and the appointment of a commission of inquiry to recommend on the relative size of, and allocation of resources between, the police and the military.

With minor modifications, the CPC's recommendations on the disciplined forces were accepted by parliament and were written into the constitution of the independent state (see May 1993:10-13). The supremacy of the civilian authority is laid down in Section 201, which states that the force is subject to the 'superintendence and control' of the National Executive Council (NEC) through the minister responsible for the defence force (who may not be a serving member of the force). Contrary to the CPC's recommendation, the constitution specifically excluded the office of commander-in-chief. The question of the relative size of the police and the army was not taken up, the level of military expenditure being effectively underwritten by an Australian military assistance program.

In 1973 the former PIR was redesignated Papua New Guinea Defence Force (PNGDF) and shortly before independence the formal transfer of defence powers took place. Brigadier-General Diro became the PNGDF's first Papua New Guinean commander.

The Role of the Military in Post-Independence Papua New Guinea

Papua New Guinea had an easy transition to independence in 1975. Indeed it has frequently been observed that the absence of a significant anti-colonial nationalist struggle in Papua New Guinea not only meant that Papua New Guinean soldiers had no heroic role to play in the winning of independence but that the new state was deprived of the unifying forces which such struggles were seen to have provided in many post-colonial societies.

The government which emerged from pre-self-government elections in 1972, under the leadership of Michael Somare, was a coalition government, and in the first post-independence elections in 1977 it was returned to power. Since then there have been three national elections and five changes of government. All changes of government have taken place through normal constitutional channels (three as the result of votes of no confidence and two through elections) and all have been smooth transitions. All governments have been rather fluid coalitions. The two-party Westminster-style politics envisioned by some in the 1970s has not materialised; but neither has a tendency to one-party or military regime. Papua New Guinea remains a robustly competitive political system. Separatist movements which emerged on the eve of independence, and resulted in unilateral declarations of independence in Papua and in the North Solomons (Bougainville) (Griffin 1976; May 1982) were dealt with by a combination of disregard and political negotiation. That in the North Solomons (where disputes had arisen over a large gold and copper mine) precipitated moves for political decentralisation. Following the establishment of provincial governments and the renegotiation of the Bougainville mining agreement this problem seemed to have been solved.

Preoccupied with the problems of policy making in the new state, and facing no serious external threat, Papua New Guineans were not greatly concerned about the role of the army, which maintained a fairly low profile. It was not until the 1980s, with a progressive breakdown in law and order nationally and the re-emergence of friction on Bougainville, that the role of the PNGDF again came under serious scrutiny.

At the time of the transfer of defence powers in 1975, the PNGDF had a posted strength of 3614, 14 per cent of whom were Australians, mostly officers and specialist NCOs. Less than 35 per cent of the 375 officer positions had been localised. By 1979 the number of loan personnel had fallen to 141 and by 1988 to 30, most of whom were with the Air transport Squadron. There were by 1979 almost 300 Papua New Guinean officers. Since independence, military assistance to Papua New Guinea has been provided through the Australian Defence Co-operation Program (DCP). In 1991 Australian Defence sources estimated that some 3000 PNGDF personnel had undertaken some form of training in Australia since 1975, and that about 90 per cent of the officer corps had trained or studied in Australia (JCFADT 1991:174 and JCFADT, Hearings, 22 October 1990, p.733). Additional assistance has been received from the US and New Zealand, and in 1992 Papua New Guinea signed status of forces agreements with Indonesia and Malaysia; Defence Secretary Peipul said, 'We may be able to learn from Malaysia on handling domestic security and from Indonesia on civic action'.[3]

Notwithstanding the high level of Australian assistance under the DCP, as early as 1977-78 the *Defence Report* contained complaints about deficiencies in the size and structure of the PNGDF. The *Defence Report 1980* commented that with its present budgetary allocation the PNGDF could not meaningfully achieve its primary object of defending the country from external attack. In 1983 a defence policy review recommended that the PNGDF's force strength be reduced to 3050. The proposed cut was bitterly received in defence circles, where morale was said to be low. In 1984 a Defence manpower review revealed a wastage rate among officers of 7.7 per cent and among other ranks of 15.8 per cent (*Defence Report 1984-85*:44), and the *Defence Report 1984-85* reported that the standard of discipline during 1985 was 'below the required standard' (ibid.:39). This grow-ing frustration within the PNGDF coincided with demands for increased opera-tions on the Irian Jaya border and the first call-out of the PNGDF to assist police in 1984. In 1988 the annual *Defence Report* noted that most operational units were 70 per cent below strength and that the PNGDF was having difficulty retaining specialists. That year, however, a *Defence Policy Paper* outlined proposals for a ten-year program to replace major equipment, reorganise force structure and enhance capabilities in several areas. (See also *Defence Report 1988*.) Although cabinet approval for the PNGDF's Ten-Year Development Plan did not come until late 1991, after the government had undertaken a review of internal security, several policy changes were initiated in 1988-89, against the background of the emerging conflict between the security forces and rebels on Bougainville (see below). These included decisions to increase the strength of the Force to 5200 by 1995, and to proceed with plans (approved in 1985) for the development of a reserve force.

By 1992 force strength had risen to around 4200. But in presenting the 1993 budget, the minister for Finance announced new strategies in the law and order sector, which recognised 'that there are limitations on the ability of the agencies concerned to control the current situation' (*1993 Budget Documents. Volume I. Economic and Development Policies*, p.122). With respect to the PNGDF:

> ... it is recognised that the Defence Force needs to be scaled down, become more
> involved in civic action, more involved with the village and community, more co-

---

[3]   Peipul, at a seminar at Australian National University, 19 June 1992.

ordinated with other agencies in both the law and order and other sectors, and better disciplined' (ibid.).

The 'move into Civic Action' was to be accompanied by a reduction in force strength, through attrition, from 4200 to 2500-3000, 'most of whom will perform CAP activities at the village level'; a core group of 1000 to 1500 'will receive specialised combat training to prepare them to effectively counter any major internal threat' (ibid.).

Towards the end of 1993 the PNGDF faced a financial crisis. For several years defence spending had been substantially in excess of budget allocation (in 1991 defence spending was overbudgetted by an extraordinary 81 per cent). By 1993, outstanding accounts with local suppliers and unpaid special allowances to defence force personnel amounted to several million kina, and in September it was announced that naval and air craft could not be used because of a lack of funding. In Port Moresby soldiers returning from Bougainville attacked the pay office when they failed to receive due pay and allowances. The government responded by increasing the Defence budget.

As of 1994, it remains to be seen how the conflicting pressures, on the one hand for an enlarged, better-equipped fighting force and on the other for a reduced civic-action oriented force, will be resolved.

In the period leading up to independence the possibility of ethnic fragmentation was a major concern both of the Australian administration and of the rising nationalist politicians. The emergence of a number of subnationalist or 'micro-nationalist' movements in the late 1960s and early 1970s exacerbated these fears (see May 1982). Recognising this (and bearing in mind that ethnic tensions had been a reason for the disbanding of the PIR in 1946), as early as 1951 the army's recruiting policy was carefully designed to achieve a regional balance. Initially the PIR sought to recruit equal numbers from Papua, the New Guinea islands, and the New Guinea mainland; but with the highlands closed to labour recruitment and difficulties of reaching more remote areas, in fact recruitment was biased towards the groups closest to Port Moresby, Lae and Rabaul. In 1967 an Australian officer serving with PIR, noted that 'Mutual suspicion remained high and clashes between tribal factions could, and did, flare up at any time' (Bell 1967:50).

The expansion of the PIR in 1963-65 gave the army the opportunity to achieve a better regional balance, although the fact that the army now sought higher education levels, for technical and officer training, meant that some coastal groups were still overrepresented. Thus, five of the first six officers commissioned were from the Rigo district of Central Province, and NCO ranks were said to be dominated by 'Bukas' from the North Solomons.

Initial fears of an ethnically divided army seem to have fairly quickly dissipated. In fact, Bell observed in 1967 that with the new generation of 1960s recruits came a breakdown of 'tribal loyalty' and a rise in Papua New Guinea nationalism, even though some 'inter-tribal prejudices' remained (Bell 1967:56). The achievement of integration in the PIR – the creation of what Olewale (1972:223) described as 'a sort of super-tribe' – did not go unnoticed among those apprehensive about the future role of the military, who saw the unity of the army in an emerging state characterised by fissiparous tendencies as a potential threat to democratic rule (for example, see Hastings 1971).

An official policy of recruiting 'from each region to maintain a reasonable balance within the Force vis-à-vis the population distribution throughout PNG' (*Defence Report 1977-78*:32) has been maintained since the 1960s. However the analysis of figures of force strength by rank and province (see May 1993:28) suggests that regional representation is by no means balanced. In particular, it shows a marked 'underrepresentation' of the populous highlands provinces, particularly at senior officer level, and a significant 'overrepresentation' of coastal Papuans and New Guinean islanders at senior levels.

In the latter part of the 1980s there was a hint of regionalism in rumours of collaboration between some Papuan colonels and PNGDF-commander-turned-politician Ted Diro, and regional sentiment was certainly evident in reaction outside the Force to the sacking of Nuia and three other Papuan colonels (see below); however this does not appear to have reflected any basic ethnic division with the Force.

In the early discussion of the role to be played by a defence force in independent Papua New Guinea, primary emphasis was placed on its function of defence against external threat. There was ambivalence about its possible use in maintaining internal security. As early as 1971, in the wake of increasing lawlessness in the highlands, highlands politicians called for the use of the PIR 'for security purposes' and supported proposals for the secondment of PIR officers to train police, particularly police riot squads. There was initial opposition to this but in 1973 four Australian Army officers were seconded to assist in training and administration; three of them were posted to riot squads.

As the general law and order situation in the country deteriorated, and particularly after the declaration of a state of emergency in the five highlands provinces in 1979, opposition to the use of the army for internal security purposes diminished. From 1977 there were calls for the deployment of the PNGDF to assist police in dealing with tribal fighting and criminal activity in the highlands. The first actual call-out in aid of the civilian authority, however, did not occur until 1984.

Force Strength, 31 December 1989, by Rank and Province

Province	Brig.Gen.	Col.	Lt.Col.	Major	Capt.	Lt(1, 2)	WO, Sgt	OR	OCdt	Total	%	Percent of national population 1990[c]
Southern Region[a]	**1**	**6**	**5**	**37**	**38**	**41**	**171**	**636**	**2**	**937**	**29.6**	**15.5**
Central	1	2	3	18	13	15[b]	35	173		260	8.2	3.8
Gulf		1	4	3	3		35	155		202	6.4	1.8
Western			4	3	4	10		97		118	3.0	3.0
Milne Bay		2	1	6	12	15	50	104	1	191	6.0	4.3
Oro		1	1	5	6	4	41	107	1	166	5.3	2.6
New Guinea Islands Region	**1**	**3**	**12**	**21**	**33**	**32**	**111**	**463**	**5**	**681**	**21.5**	**16.1**
East New Britain		2	1	7	3	6	38	150		207	6.5	
West New Britain		2	4	4	19	69	1			99	3.1	
New Ireland	1		6	6	8	13	17	90	1	143	4.5	2.4
North Solomons		2	2	14	4	6	51	3**		82	2.6	
Manus		3	4	4	5	31	103			150	4.7	
Highlands Region		**2**	**11**	**17**	**30**	**86**	**8**	**459**		**613**	**19.4**	**35.6**
Eastern Highlands		2	4	7	15	108	2	118		256	8.1	
Simbu		1	4	7	24	113	3			152	4.8	
Western Highlands		1	5	3	5	22	80	2		118	3.7	7.9
Enga			1	1	21	46		75		75	2.4	
Southern Highlands		3	10	4	112	1	130			12		
Momase Region		**1**	**4**	**27**	**30**	**46**	**157**	**637**	**12**	**914**	**28.9**	**27.6**
Morobe	1		3	7	12	59	184	3		272	8.6	9.9
Madang			2	9	27	138	2	185		185	5.9	
East Sepik		1	1	13	17	21	54	220	6	333	10.5	6.7
West Sepik		5	2	4	17	95	1	124		124	3.9	
National Capital District		**1**	**2**	**2**	**1**	**10**	**16**			**16**	**0.5**	**5.2**
TOTAL	**2**	**10**	**23**	**97**	**120**	**151**	**526**	**2205**	**27**	**3161**	**100.0**	**100.0**

a   Southern Highlands Province, included for most purposes in the Southern (Papuan) Region, is included here in the Highlands Region, with which it has greater cultural and developmental affinity.

b   These figures – both shown as 0 in the original data – have been interpolated from cross additions, since the table from which the figures were derived contained errors.

c   The national census could not be conducted in the North Solomons Province 'due to prevailing political situation'; an estimated figure of 160,000 has been used and the total calculated using this figure.

In 1984 the government announced a list of measures to deal with law and order problems, including call-out of PNGDF personnel to assist police. Diro, by then a member of parliament, supported the use of troops. At the end of that year the PNGDF was called out to assist police following the declaration of a state of emergency occasioned by rising urban crime and violence in Port Moresby. 'Operation Green Beret', as the exercise was called, lasted for about four months and was generally regarded as a success, though the urban crime rate quickly rose again when the state of emergency ended, and two months later the troops were called out again in the National Capital District, in an operation which lasted five months.

On several occasions in the early 1980s there were demands from national politicians to use the PNGDF to quell tribal fighting, particularly in Enga Province. In a *Post-Courier* article in 1985 former PNGDF officer Ian Glanville opposed such suggestions, arguing

> To have a disciplined, armed and trained Papua New Guinean in uniform, shooting other Papua New Guineans in a situation other than where 'the national security or the preservation of public order exists' [*sic*] will forfeit any claim we might have to being a Christian, democratic, and enlightened country, and destroy forever our fragile national unity (*Post-Courier* 10 December 1985).

However, in 1987 the PNGDF was called out to assist police in law and order operations in Morobe, Madang and Eastern Highlands provinces, and the following year was mobilised to assist in 'Operation LOMET 88' in the highlands provinces, Morobe and Madang, and later East Sepik. LOMET 88 lasted for over three months and it attracted a great deal of publicity (see below); but the PNGDF's role in it, though conspicuous, was limited – of 519 security forces personnel involved (including 308 from the Police Mobile Squad) only 33 were from the PNGDF (Draft Hansard 10 November 1988, p.28). Late in 1988 there was a further request, from the Morobe provincial law and order committee for PNGDF assistance to counter serious crime in Lae and Garaina (*Post-Courier* 20 December 1988). But by this time the Force was on standby awaiting a government decision on whether it was to be called out to assist the police on Bougainville. (The subsequent role of the PNGDF in the Bougainville crisis is discussed in more detail below.) PNGDF personnel were used again 1991 to provide additional security during the South Pacific Games in Port Moresby and to assist police in 'crime busting operations' in Morobe Province.

In 1992 it was something of a measure of the extent to which the army had come to be accepted as having a 'law and order' role that in outlining arrangements for the conduct of the national election is was said to be 'necessary to call upon the services of the Defence Force . . . to assist the Electoral Commissioner before, during and after the election' (*Post-Courier* 24 March 1992). On the eve of the elections some 1300 police and 50 soldiers paraded through Mount Hagen in a display of force.

Despite the general acceptance of the PNGDF's role in internal security situations, however, the acceptance was slow to be recognised in official statements. In 1984, shortly before the first call-out of the PNGDF to aid the civil authority, the NEC's list of priority functions put internal security last. The *Defence Report 1984-85* (p.54), however, stated that 'national security and development was foremost in our activities'. In 1987, in a statement delivered on resigning from cabinet (see below), Diro said

> Clearly a military option for the defence of Papua New Guinea is out. The Defence Force must now be tailored to give priority to training in low intensity type of operations, civil aid tasks, internal security problems, rapid deployment to assist police or in instances of hijacking and of course surveillance of both land and sea boundaries (*Times of PNG* 19-25 November 1987).

The following year Defence Secretary Mokis told an Australian seminar that his department's view was that 'there is a far greater prospect of PNG being troubled seriously by internal rather than external security problems'; he saw the main challenges coming not from tribal fighting or separatism but from increasing criminal activities:

> . . . concentrations of unemployed people, many of whom are young and smarting from unfulfilled expectations, have provided a fertile breeding ground for criminal activities. These trends have coincided with a general decline in the efficiency of PNG administration and, perhaps most notably in this context, a significant weakening of the system of justice; the police, the courts and the gaols. Other potential sources of internal security, such as tribal fighting and separatism, have caused difficulties in the past but at present seem of far less concern (Mokis 1988:2).

Yet in 1989, having noted the PNGDF's responsibility for defending the nation from 'external threats and internal uprisings', the Defence minister went on to say that 'internal uprising and internal security [was] the responsibility of the Royal Papua New Guinea Constabulary' (*Defence Report 1989*).

In 1990, facing an escalating law and order problem across the country, and with a crisis in Bougainville still unresolved, the Namaliu government set up a Security Review Task Force and, shortly after, convened a National Summit on Crime. As an outcome of these initiatives it released a report (PNG 1991) in which it was observed that 'perceived political instability...is sometimes thought to have given rise to public questioning of the durability of particular leaders, policies and even laws', and that the disciplined services had not been able to cope with 'sources of law-breaking and disorder' (ibid.:11, 17, unnumbered). It also referred to 'the growing frequency with which call-outs of the PNGDF in aid to the civil power and states of emergency have been declared' (ibid.:24). Among a number of recommendations the report proposed the establishment of a Joint Services Command Centre and the progressive integration of the disciplined forces ('subject to review and even possible reversal') (ibid.:23-30). It also suggested that 'the most serious, foreseeable threats facing Papua New Guinea are internal' and that the priorities of the PNGDF 'should be reviewed and, as may be appropriate, re-ordered' (ibid.:36). The demand for a change of focus was supported by Defence Minister Benais Sabumei, who in 1991 told a PNGDF passing out parade that 'The real future of our Defence Force is to assist the civil authorities deal effectively with these threats' (*Post-Courier* 2 July 1991).

Coincidentally with the Papua New Guinea government's security review, the Australian government undertook a review of its security assistance programs for Papua New Guinea, and in September 1991 the two governments released a statement which announced that Papua New Guinea was to give highest priority to internal security needs, and that Australian assistance would be geared to supporting Papua New Guinea's disciplined forces in maintaining internal security, including law and order. This was to be done by way of training and the provision and funding of infrastructure, equipment and other support facilities. But it is notable that, following well-publicised reports of abuses by Papua New Guinea's security forces on Bougainville, an Australian government document described Australia's military training efforts as having several components 'designed to strengthen soldiers' awareness of humanitarian law to provide guidance concerning proper treatment of civilians during security operations'. Operational training, it said, was 'based on Australian Defence Force doctrine, which in turn draws on the Geneva Convention' (Evans 1992:34-35).

Thus within sixteen years of independence the priorities of the PNGDF had been effectively reversed and the possibility of an integrated paramilitary force revived, though to date there has been no move to implement the latter proposal, which remains unpopular among both RPNGC and PNGDF personnel.

Military-Civil Relations in the Independent State

From a very early stage, the Australian officers responsible for the training of

Papua New Guinean soldiers were anxious to instil in their protégés the idea of the subservience of the military to the civil authority, and to ensure that relations between the military and politicians were cordial.

The achievement of cordial civil-military relations should have been rendered easier in post-independence Papua New Guinea by the fact that, given the nature of pre-colonial Papua New Guinean societies (for the most part small and non-hierarchical) and the recency of effective colonial administration in much of the country, defence force personnel and the emerging nationalist politicians and civil servants came from similar village backgrounds, and in the case of the better-educated had been to the same government-run schools in much the same age cohort. The PNGDF's first Papua New Guinean commander, Ted Diro, for example, came from a village in the Rigo district, where his father had been a plantation labourer and a carrier for the Allied troops during World War II. In common with the other two young men selected for early officer training, and with many of the leading politicians and civil servants of the late 1960s and 1970s, Diro had attended the government high school at Sogeri. But perhaps because of the military ethos inherited from the colonial period, and the nature of the military training, relations between senior military officers on the one hand, and politicians and public servants on the other, were not particularly close; indeed Sinclair (1992:297) describes relations in the early 1970s as 'frosty' (also see O'Neill 1971; Sundhaussen 1973b). Politicians tended to see the military as elitist and a possible threat to civilian rule, and the military had misgivings about politicians who questioned the future role of the defence force and suggested that it might be too big.

Despite this degree of separation of military and civilian circles, within the first few years of independence there were suggestions that the higher echelons of the military were being politicised.

Diro and Lowa had been rivals for the top position during their early military careers and on the eve of independence, as it became clear that Diro was the likely choice for commander, Lowa resigned and joined Prime Minister Somare's office. He subsequently contested the national elections in 1977 as a Pangu candidate, was elected to a seat in Port Moresby, and became minister for Police in the second Somare government. In the following months there were rumours that within the Somare government there were moves to oust both General Diro and the police commissioner, Pious Kerepia, both of whom were felt to be 'politically unreliable'. Lowa was said to be prominent in these moves. In November, following a series of disputes among senior police officers, Kerepia's tenure was terminated, though he protested, alleging political interference. The same month a challenge to Lowa's residential eligibility was upheld and he lost his parliamentary seat. (Lowa later became national organiser of the Melanesian Alliance party and was re-elected to parliament in 1987.)

Meanwhile, tensions in the relations between members of the government and senior PNGDF officers came to a head in what was termed 'the Diro affair'. During 1977 Diro had held discussions with a leader of the West Papuan separatist movement, Organisasi Papua Merdeka (OPM). Although Diro claimed that the Defence minister had been fully briefed on the talks, there was a feeling in cabinet that Diro had exceeded his authority and in late September it was announced that he would be officially reprimanded. The reprimand came a week later. By this time Diro had sought and received a commitment of support from senior officers, and there were rumours in Port Moresby of a possible coup (see *SMH* 6 October 1977; Hegarty 1978:402). At the time Diro told cabinet:

> ... I have now been able to assess who my friends are and who aren't ... Mr Prime Minister, I want you to know that the force is becoming sick to death of being made a political football by certain politicians and ex-politicians (quoted, *SMH* 6 October 1977).

Though one commentator described the incident at the time as 'the most serious threat to the authority of the government since independence' (Hegarty 1978:402), it appeared to blow over fairly quietly. Six years later, however, an anonymous former PNGDF officer[4] told an Australian Broadcasting Commission correspondent[5] that had Diro been sacked in 1977 PNGDF officers would have staged an already-rehearsed operation, codenamed 'Electric Shock', in which the prime minister and certain other politicians and public servants would have been taken hostage. The former officer claimed that PNGDF officers had been in contact with the Indonesian government during this period; indeed one of their major concerns had been the Papua New Guinea government's poor handling of the border situation. Diro's role in all this was unclear and the story was denied in some quarters (see *Times of Papua New Guinea* 26 August, 15 September, 7 October 1983); certainly it may have been embellished by 1983. But it served as a reminder that military intervention was not an impossibility.

Four years after the 1977 incident, Diro announced that he was resigning from the PNGDF to contest the 1982 national elections. He stood as leader of a (mostly Papuan) PNG Independent Group and was elected. In the process of coalition

---

[4]   The former officer was Tom Poang, a colonel and chief of personnel at the time, who left the PNGDF soon after and in 1983 was speaker in the Morobe provincial assembly.

[5]   Geoff Heriot, ABC 'Background Briefing' 21 August 1983.

formation the ambitious Diro was at one stage tipped as possible prime minister, but he ended up in opposition, briefly accepting leadership of the National Party, and becoming minister for Forests in 1985 when a vote of no confidence brought a change of government.

Diro was not the only former PNGDF officer to contest the 1982 elections: in Manus, James Pokasui, who had been transferred to Manus the previous year as adjutant of the Maritime Element, stood as an Independent Group candidate and was initially declared winner, though the result was subsequently overturned by the Court of Disputed Returns;[6] in Wewak, former PNGDF major Michael Malenki, who had left the PNGDF in 1977 to become electoral secretary to Prime Minister Somare but had fallen out with Somare and became national secretary of the Melanesian Alliance, stood unsuccessfully (he was later elected to the East Sepik Provincial Assembly).

With Diro's resignation from the PNGDF it was generally expected that Colonel Ken Noga, who had been the third most senior Papua New Guinean officer after Diro and Lowa, would succeed him. Instead, the position was given to Colonel Gago Mamae. In 1980 a split in the ruling Pangu-led coalition and a subsequent vote of no confidence against Prime Minister Somare had brought a new coalition government to power, headed by Somare's former deputy prime minister, People's Progress Party (PPP) leader Sir Julius Chan. In 1977 Noga had resigned from the PNGDF to contest the national elections as a pro-Pangu candidate, having rejoined the force when he failed to be elected.[7] Some suggested that Mamae had been appointed over Noga in 1981 for political reasons. The suggestion that political considerations had entered into the selection of the PNGDF command was reinforced in 1983 when, having been reelected to office in the national election of the previous year, the Somare government replaced Mamae with Noga as commander of the PNGDF. A newspaper editorial at the time asked: 'Must we continue to entertain political appointments in the public service ...?' (*Times of PNG* 26 August 1983). Mamae, after serving for a while as military attaché in Australia, resigned and became executive officer in Chan's PPP office (standing unsuccessfully as a PPP candidate in the 1987 national elections).

The politicisation of the senior PNGDF appointment was demonstrated even

---

6   Pokasui subsequently worked for Fr John Momis, parliamentary leader of the Melanesian Alliance, and was elected in 1987, becoming minister for Defence.

7   Under the provisions of the *Defence Act* 1974 it is possible for a member of the PNGDF to transfer to the reserve force, and later apply for re-admission to the regular force.

more blatantly three years later, when another vote of no confidence again removed a Somare-led coalition and brought to office a government headed by Paias Wingti and Julius Chan. Noga was himself removed and replaced by Colonel Tony Huai. Huai had been in consideration for the top position in 1982. In 1984 he resigned, criticising the government's handling of the PNGDF. He initially joined Mamae in Chan's PPP office and indicated his intention of standing for parliament in 1987. At the time of his appointment Huai was a security officer with Air Niugini and the appointment of a commander from outside the PNGDF was reportedly opposed by the Defence Department and resented by some senior officers. Opposition leader Somare described it, not without irony, as a 'dangerous precedent' (*Post-Courier* 3 December 1985).

Huai proved to be a controversial figure as PNGDF commander. Early in 1986, on his return from a visit to Indonesia, Huai told a press conference that he would closely cooperate with Indonesian army forces commander, General Benny Murdani, to stamp out the OPM. His statement attracted criticism, notably from prominent lawyer (later Justice minister) Bernard Narokobi, who said that Huai had no authority to make public statements about matters of defence policy, and called for his dismissal. Huai resigned in late 1986 but was reinstated. The following year Huai again attracted public attention when it was reported that, having been opposed to the defence provisions of the Joint Declaration of Principles then being negotiated between Papua New Guinea and Australia, on the grounds that a reference to possible 'attack from an external source' could be misread by Indonesia and create unnecessary tension, Huai had made unauthorised visits to Indonesia and had leaked details of the progress of discussions to General Murdani (see *Times of PNG* 4-10 February 1988). He was also said to have accepted gifts of uniforms and furniture from the Indonesian army chief. According to a *Times of PNG* report (24 December 1987-7 January 1988), Huai's close relations with Murdani had nearly resulted in a mutiny by senior officers and NCOs. Partly as a result of this, but also, according to Defence Minister Pokasui, because Huai had allowed infighting and political lobbying among senior officers, Huai was dismissed in late 1987. He was replaced by Colonel Rochus Lokinap. Lokinap was the first non-Papuan commander of the PNGDF, coincidentally coming from a village in Sir Julius Chan's New Ireland electorate.

By this time, too, Diro's political fortunes had begun to turn. Having been reelected in 1987 Diro managed to swing the entire bloc of members from Papuan electorates into a coalition with Paias Wingti, thus delivering government to Wingti when it looked as though a Pangu-led coalition would be returned to power. He became deputy prime minister in the new government. However, an enquiry set up by Wingti in 1987 to investigate allegations of corruption in the forestry industry had accused Diro of involvement in a number of illicit transactions and recommended prosecution. Further, in the process of investigation it was revealed that Diro had received from Indonesia's General Murdani some $US139400, ostensibly as a contribution to his 1987 election campaign expenses. This 'contribution', which had not been declared, was in defiance of a provision of the Papua New Guinea constitution which states that an organic law will be passed to prevent candidates or parties accepting contributions from foreigners (though in fact the organic law had never been passed).

Charged with perjury and facing possible prosecution, and with calls for his resignation from parliament, Diro resigned from cabinet. In subsequent statements to the press he said:

> ... the events of the past couple of months have had implications leading to rumours of disobedience in the disciplined forces ... I have been one of the experts on military coups through the world [and] ... the ingredients are here for a coup ... I do not want to be blamed when that arises. (*Post-Courier* 9, 16 November 1987; *Times of PNG* 19-25 November 1987).

In the wake of the military coups in Fiji in 1987 – the first in the island Pacific and generally unexpected – such comments were not dismissed lightly. With rumours circulating in Port Moresby about an impending coup (Saffu 1988:259-60), three senior colonels (Kwago Guria, Lima Dotaona and Robert Dademo), all of them Papuans, were removed, although the possible links between the talk of coups and the government's actions were never made clear. This action was bitterly criticised within the Papuan community, especially from within the then-recently-formed People's Action Party (PAP), a predominantly Papuan group of which Diro was parliamentary leader. Following a change of government in 1988, the three were reinstated (though Guria chose not to return).

Shortly after resigning from cabinet, Diro shifted the parliamentary allegiance of his bloc and in so doing brought about a change of government. He became minister of state in the new (Namaliu) government and having been acquitted of the perjury charges subsequently became deputy prime minister. But in 1991 he was found guilty by the Leadership Tribunal of eighty-one counts of misconduct and was forced to resign from parliament. This threatened to precipitate a constitutional crisis when the governor-general, Sir Serei Eri, formerly president of Diro's PAP, refused to sign the dismissal papers and attempted to reinstate Diro as deputy prime minister. Eventually both Diro and Eri resigned. Ironically, remembering the events of 1977, the PNGDF was placed on alert at the time 'in case of violence between ethnic groups' (*Times of PNG* 3 October 1991).

The following year, after another, Wingti-led, coalition had come to office following national elections, there was a further major reshuffle within the PNGDF. In November 1992 Lokinap's extended term as commander came to an end; criticised for his handling of the Bougainville situation, he was not reappointed. In his place Colonel Robert Dademo, one of the Force's longest-serving officers (and one of the three Papuan officers dismissed under a previous Wingti government) was appointed as Brigadier General. Dademo was generally regarded as a sound choice, though some claimed that his appointment was 'political'.

Soon after his appointment, a leaked document claimed that Dademo had recommended that five senior officers be replaced, but had been overrruled by Defence Minister Tohian. Subsequently, while Tohian was in Australia, the NEC approved the transfer of the five officers (one was posted to Indonesia, one to Australia, one to New Zealand, and two to other government departments); four officers were promoted to colonel to fill vacant positions. A *Times of Papua New Guinea* report (30 December 1992) said the moves 'strengthen the commander's position enormously and remove a number of his former rivals from key jobs in the force'.

In early 1994 Dademo reached retirement age and, in the absence of Prime Minister Wingti, Chan as acting prime minister announced the appointment, as acting commander, of Colonel Lima Dotaona. On his return a day later, however, Wingti overruled his deputy prime minister and Defence minister; the Defence Retirement Regulations were amended to raise the retirement age and Dademo's appointment was, controversially, extended.

With the politicisation of senior levels of the PNGDF and increasing pressures, budgetary and operational, upon the military, came also suggestions of declining morale and deteriorating discipline in the force.

As early as 1985 the standard of discipline in the PNGDF was said to be 'below that required' (*Defence Report 1984-85*: 39, 44) and a concentrated effort was made 'to purge the force of soldiers whose service was considered unsatisfactory'; 190 'other ranks' were discharged. The same year some forty Air Transport Squadron groundcrew were accused of 'mutiny' when they staged a strike over pay and conditions.

More serious allegations of undisciplined behaviour by the security forces arose during Operation LOMET in the highlands in 1988. Foreshadowing later developments on Bougainville, there were widespread reports of village houses, stores and community centres being burned, of pigs and cassowaries being shot, of looting, and of village people being beaten and raped (*Draft Hansard* 11 November 1988 pp.10-11, 18 November 1988 pp.16-17; *Post-Courier* 20 October 1988, 15, 17, 18 November 1988). Much of the blame was attributed to the Police Mobile Squad, which already in the mid 1970s had acquired a bad reputation in the highlands, but PNGDF personnel were also accused of offences and there were calls for its withdrawal from such operations. (Nevertheless, four years later Standish [personal communication 1992] reported similar abusive behaviour by police and PNGDF soldiers in the highlands during the 1992 elections.)

In 1988-89 problems of discipline were manifested on a larger scale in open challenges to the government's authority by elements of the military. In June 1988, the minister for Civil Aviation announced a decision to close Lae airport (it had been decided, in accordance with a recommendation of the 1983 Defence review, to relocate the airport some 40 kilometres outside Lae at an old wartime strip at Nadzab). The PNGDF, whose air element had opposed the move, responded by flying personnel from Port Moresby to Lae to 'secure the airport' against Civil Aviation authorities. Lokinap subsequently announced that all Defence Force planes would be grounded. Several days later, having been severely reprimanded by Prime Minister Wingti, Brigadier Lokinap apologised for the PNGDF's actions and assured the prime minister and the people of Papua New Guinea of the PNGDF's undivided loyalty. Nevertheless the *Defence Report 1988* (pp.5, 13) listed amongst the year's military operations: 'Operation Albatross'. This operation secured the Lae City airfield and prevented its destruction by elements of the Department of Lands and Department of Civil Aviation'.

Then in early 1989, angered at not having received expected pay increases (the first since independence), some 300-400 soldiers marched on the National Parliament, where windows were smashed, vehicles overturned, and civilians and politicians abused. There was also a smaller demonstration by PNGDF personnel in Wewak. The government promptly suspended the commander, chief of staff, and secretary for Defence, and set up a Defence General Board of Inquiry to investigate the incident. But the government quickly implemented pay increases, and while the Board of Inquiry noted a serious decline in discipline ('There is an apparent inability and or reluctance by commands at all levels to impose discipline' – *Report* p.49) and evidence of some misuse of funds and equipment, its report was largely devoted to discussing problems of morale and recommending improvements in conditions of service within the PNGDF. While the board's analysis may have been accurate, it did little to reassure the public or political leaders.

Further incidents during the early 1990s (including a strike by maritime and air element personnel in 1994) suggested that, notwithstanding action taken after the 1989 review, problems of discipline remained (see May 1993:55-56).

Overarching all these incidents, however, from 1988 was the much larger issue of the performance of the security forces on Bougainville.

In 1988, simmering discontent within the landowner group around Papua New Guinea's immense gold and copper mine on Bougainville erupted into a major confrontation.[8] Mine installations were subjected to a series of arson and sabotage attacks, during which pylons carrying power lines to the mine and town at Panguna were blown up, and workers attempting to repair lines were threatened by armed men. (Among the leadership of the militant landowner group was a former PNGDF officer trained in the use of explosives.) Late in 1988 the mine operator, Bougainville Copper Ltd (BCL), temporarily closed the mine and a government committee attempted to negotiate a settlement with the dissident group. But following further acts of sabotage against BCL installations and government property, police reinforcements were called in and a curfew was imposed in the mine area. Shortly after this riots broke out in the nearby town of Arawa after a series of incidents, not directly related to the mine dispute, in which three people were killed. With tension rising and longstanding separatist sentiments regaining strength, the curfew was reimposed and PNGDF troops (whose call-out had been authorised in December 1988) were brought in to assist police restore law and order. By March 1989 there were approximately 600 police and military personnel on Bougainville, under the direction of a joint planning committee headed by the provincial administrative secretary. Within weeks of its arrival the PNGDF had suffered its first casualties when a PNGDF patrol was ambushed, and it was reported that the PNGDF had launched a 'full-scale military operation' against 'the rebels'. Shortly after, dissident leader Francis Ona announced a revised set of demands against the mining company and the government, which, apart from massive financial compensation, included a call for the withdrawal of all security forces. 'We are not part of your country any more,' he told the government, 'We belong to the Republic of Bougainville' (*Niugini Nius* 12 April 1989). Premier Joseph Kabui described the situation as serious: the issue was no longer merely about land, he said, but also involved the question of secession (*Post-Courier* 23 May 1989).

After further attacks on the mine had forced its closure, the government announced tighter security measures, including wider powers for the police and army under an amended *Defence (Aid to Civil Power) Regulation*. However, the government wanted to avoid at all costs a military operation, Prime Minister

---

8   For a more detailed account of the background to the 'Bougainville crisis', the ongoing events, and their broader implications, see May (1990), May and Spriggs (1990), Oliver (1991), Spriggs and Denoon (1992), Liria (1993) and *The Contemporary Pacific* 4(2), 1992, special issue, 'A legacy of development: three years of crisis in Bougainville'.

Namaliu said, and was not entertaining the possibility of military action 'at this point' (*Canberra Times* 26, 27 May 1989). But when talks failed, Namaliu ordered an all-out attack on the rebels, who were now calling themselves the Bougainville Revolutionary Army (BRA).

The government's repeated attempts to negotiate with Ona were seen by some, both within and outside the security forces, as a sign of weakness on the part of the government. Police Commissioner Paul Tohian was reported to have complained of 'political interference with essential police work and political indecision', and to have threatened to defy government directives in his attempts to capture Francis Ona. When, in response, prominent Bougainvillean politician and minister for Provincial Affairs, Fr John Momis, criticised Tohian and threatened to move for his dismissal, a group of about one hundred angry policemen marched on Momis's home and warned him against sacking the commissioner. Shortly after this, the acting PNGDF chief of staff, Colonel Leo Nuia, publicly rebuked the Defence minister, saying he 'should refrain from making wild statements on matters affecting the operations of the soldiers and police' on Bougainville (*Niugini Nius* 12 April 1989). The acting commander and the chief of PNGDF operations on Bougainville also publicly criticised the government's handling of the crisis. Within the PNGDF and RPNGC there were many who felt that they could 'clean up' the situation on Bougainville if only they were not held back by politicians. As against this, there is little doubt that heavy-handed actions by the security forces – primarily, it seems, the police mobile squad, but also the PNGDF – did much to alienate villages and catalyse demands for secession.

In June 1989 the government declared a state of emergency on Bougainville. Police Commissioner Tohian was made controller of the state of emergency with the PNGDF commander on Bougainville his deputy. Diro, whose decision to cross the floor of parliament had resulted in a change of government, became minister of state and chairman of the parliamentary National Emergency Committee, and later, for a while, deputy prime minister. Diro's comparatively 'hard line' approach to the Bougainville situation was indicated in a statement he made in parliament in proposing the extension of the state of emergency – that 'It is a military problem. It is no longer a police law and order problem' – and in instructions passed on to the Bougainville commander, Colonel Dotaona, which were leaked to the press (see *Post-Courier* 12, 27 July 1989).

At the end of 1989 the Bougainville mine, which had provided Papua New Guinea with around 40 per cent of its exports and about 17 per cent of its government revenue, was 'mothballed'. The following month cabinet approved an 'all out war' against the rebels; the military option, Prime Minister Namaliu declared, is now the only option.

Yet shortly after this intensification of the conflict a ceasefire was negotiated and the government agreed to the withdrawal of troops. This decision was not well received within the security forces, and although it was apparently intended by the government that the provincial police establishment remain to provide some semblance of law, Tohian ordered the early removal of all police, as well as the army, leaving the province virtually in the hands of the BRA. In submissions to an Australian parliamentary committee the action was described as 'a fairly serious breakdown in the control by the Papua New Guinean Government of its force' and bound to lead to chaos (JCFADT, Hearings, 22 October 1990, pp.752, 783-84).

Subsequently, on his way from a party in Port Moresby, Tohian called over his car radio for police and army personnel to arm themselves, arrest the prime minister, and take over the government. He and the officer in charge of the police riot squads were arrested and initially charged with treason, but the incident was not taken very seriously (being commonly referred to as 'the barbecoup') and the charges were subsequently dropped. (In 1992 Tohian was elected to the National Parliament and became minister for Defence.)

Two months after the withdrawal of the security forces, with negotiations for a settlement of the conflict failing to materialise, the national government cut off communications with Bougainville and imposed 'selective economic sanctions'. This action, announced by the acting prime minister, Diro, shortly after Prime Minister Namaliu left on an overseas trip, was seen by some as a deliberate attempt to undermine proposed peace talks (see *Australian* 3 May 1990; May and Spriggs 1990:113). Two days later the BRA made a unilateral declaration of independence for the 'Republic of Meekamui'. Among those named in the interim government of the republic, the 'minister for defence and police', Joe Pais, and the commander of the BRA, Sam Kauona, were both former PNGDF officers.

In September 1990 PNGDF troops landed on Buka Island in the north, following a request from local leaders, and the BRA was reported to have surrendered control of Buka soon after. The PNGDF was supported by a locally-organised Buka Liberation Front (BLF); (the BLF chairman described the front as an 'authorised unauthorised security force' sanctioned by the PNGDF and the government) though according to one account many on Buka 'feared the BLF more than the BRA and Defence Force soldiers' (Spriggs 1992:12; also see *Post-Courier* 19 December 1990). However, the arrival of troops on Buka did little to resolve the situation, which Spriggs (1992:12) described as 'a state of civil war, with fighting between the BRA and the BLF all over the island and the PNGDF seemingly taking little part in proceedings'. On Buka there were mounting accusations of human rights violations and military action against civilian targets; an

Amnesty International report in November 1990 listed nineteen cases of 'extrajudicial execution' and over fifty cases of torture and ill-treatment by the security forces, as well as abuses by the BRA (Amnesty International 1990b. Also see Spriggs and Denoon 1992). After a boat carrying supplies, authorised by the prime minister, had been prevented from sailing by the PNGDF commander on Buka, who threatened to fire on it, the *Times of Papua New Guinea* (13 December 1990) commented: 'Confusion reigns . . . There does not seem to be any clear directives [*sic*] as to who is in authority . . .'

In early 1991 a second round of peace talks was held, resulting in the Honiara Declaration, which recorded the two parties' commitment to a peaceful resolution of the conflict. Among other things the Honiara Declaration agreed to the establishment of a civilian Task Force, appointed by the minister for Provincial Affairs in consultation with a Bougainville Interim Legal Authority, to co-ordinate the restoration of services, and to accept a Multinational Supervisory Team (MST) to oversee the process of reconciliation and rehabilitation. While negotiations over the implementation of the Honiara Declaration were still proceeding, however, and with Diro again acting prime minister, some 300 PNGDF soldiers, under the command of Colonel Nuia, landed on north Bougainville and launched an operation against the BRA. Nuia claimed that the troops had been requested by local chiefs, but his action violated the terms of the Honiara Declaration and had not been authorised by the government. He came under strong criticism, especially from Momis, who described the incursion as 'totally illegal . . . totally irresponsible' and likely to jeopardise peace initiatives. Momis called for the sacking of officers involved. In the event, Nuia received a reprimand, but the operation was retrospectively endorsed by cabinet.

In the following months the extent of the growing tension between civil and military authorities in relation to Bougainville became evident on a number of occasions. In May, responding to Momis's attacks on Nuia's 'invasion' of Bougainville the previous month, an army major publicly accused the minister of promoting secession and being a BRA collaborator (*Post-Courier* 17 May 1991). And on Buka, Nuia physically attacked a leading member of the civilian Task Force and had another arrested and charged with sedition. Not surprisingly the civilian administrator on Buka expressed himself as not happy with the working relationship between the military and the Task Force. PNGDF opposition to the idea of a MST was also a reason for its failure to materialise.

Nuia's somewhat erratic behaviour had already caused some concern among the Defence establishment and in June 1991 his unauthorised disclosure, to an Australian television reporter, concerning the use of Australian-supplied helicopters on Bougainville (see May 1993:22, 65), embarrassed the government and finally led to his dismissal. Momis said: 'If we don't put a stop to it, we cannot stop a coup' (*Post-Courier* 25 June 1991). (Subsequently Nuia challenged the legality of the action and in 1992 was reinstated and put in charge of Special Projects.).

Resentment in military and defence circles of what was seen as indecision and political interference in the handling of the Bougainville situation was sharpened by Nuia's sacking and was expressed in calls for clear directions on the specific role of PNGDF commander on Bougainville and his relation to the Task Force, and in reports that the PNGDF strength on Bougainville was 'being scaled down drastically' (*Post-Courier* 11 July 1991).

But the removal of Nuia and the briefing of the new PNGDF commander on Bougainville did not resolve the tensions between military and civilian officials. In July 1991, on the eve of further peace talks, it was announced that the Bougainville civilian administrator had imposed a curfew on parts of Buka and requested the government to withdraw the security forces from north Bougainville back to Buka. Subsequently it was reported that the security forces had imposed a new blockade on Bougainville, 'as a protest over what they claimed to be lack of consultation with them about the national Government's restoration program particularly over the co-ordination of ship and aircraft undertaking the restoration exercise' (*Post-Courier* 24 December 1991). Ships and aircraft were being prevented from travelling regardless of whether they had authorisation from civilian officials. One of the casualties of this action was a chartered aircraft which was to have taken Bougainville leaders to Honiara for talks with a national government delegation. The following year an international delegation of church leaders, whose visit to Bougainville had been authorised by the national government, was turned away by the security forces, causing the *Post-Courier's* editorial writer to ask, 'Who controls Bougainville? . . . What authority does the national Government have over the military if its decisions about visits are going to be overturned?' (21 October 1992).

In 1992-93 the Bougainville conflict spilled over the international border between Papua New Guinea and the Solomon Islands, when PNGDF troops launched several unauthorised raids into the Solomon Islands in pursuit of BRA supporters. On one occasion shots were exchanged between Papua New Guinea security forces and Solomon Islands police, and on another the Solomon Islands island of Oema was 'annexed' by PNGDF troops. Echoing the earlier *Post-Courier* editorial, a *Sydney Morning Herald* editorial (16 April 1993) asked:

> What is going here? Who is calling the shots? . . . Increasingly [the PNGDF] will equate its own worth, its very identity and honour with achieving a victory, whatever the cost. In so doing it will grow less responsible to central control.

Conclusion

On the eve of independence, many, especially among Papua New Guinea's emerging political leaders, looked with some apprehension to the future role of the PNGDF. Well funded by the colonial government, well trained and possessing a degree of cohesion unusual in the fragmented society of the emerging state, and actively involved in village-level civic action, the military was seen by some as a potential challenge to the authority of an independent government and a threat to the continuation of a democratic political system. Not all of those who foresaw a political role for the military, however, anticipated a coup-style take-over. Hastings, for example, suggested that 'Australian democracy' was unlikely to take root and that 'we might be sensible to look towards 'guided democracy', to a presidential system, to a strong army loyal to a strong central executive' (1969:191-92. Also see Nelson 1972:208).

Concern about the future role of the Defence Force was reflected in the independence constitution, which rejected the idea of the military's participation in government and defined the Defence Force's primary function as that of defending the country against external threat, placing restrictions on its use for internal security purposes.

Contrary to pessimistic predictions, after independence Papua New Guinea's democratic system prospered, and in the absence of external threat the military languished, notwithstanding substantial financial assistance through Australia's Defence Co-operation Program. But within a decade of independence, growing problems of lawlessness and disorder began to threaten the position of national political leaders, and even some who had earlier looked apprehensively at the PNGDF, began to call for an expanded role of the Defence Force in assisting police to maintain internal security.

The first rift between civil and military leaders – the so-called Diro Affair of 1977 – was not long in coming; but though it generated rumours of an impending coup it proved to be inconsequential. On the other hand, the resignation of several senior officers, including the deputy commander and the commander, to pursue careers in civil politics, established an early precedent and suggested a possible safety-valve against the build-up of military antagonism towards the civilian government. There was also, from the early 1980s, clear evidence of a politicisation of at least the senior levels of the PNGDF.

With a resurgence of tribal fighting and a growing problem of criminality, more and more politicians looked to the military to support the increasingly inadequate attempts of the police to contain lawlessness and maintain the authority of the state. From 1984 the army was regularly involved in 'law and order' operations and there was growing acceptance that the PNGDF's role in internal security was likely to be more significant than its function of safeguarding the country against external threat.

In this respect, the emergence of the Bougainville crisis was a watershed in changing perceptions of the PNGDF. What began as a police action against disgruntled landowners developed into a full-blown insurrection in which the PNGDF was called upon to maintain the integrity of the Papua New Guinea state. In the process, severe doubts have been cast upon the capacity of the Defence Force to act in internal security situations. A belief within the security forces that they have been deprived of adequate funding and have been subjected to 'political' interference predates the Bougainville crisis but has been exacerbated by events on Bougainville since 1988. The effects of such feelings have been a growing tension in relations between military personnel and civil authorities, factionalism within the PNGDF's senior command structure, and a general lowering of morale and discipline. Notwithstanding this, by the early 1990s, with the Bougainville conflict still not resolved and growing threats to the authority of the state from urban and rural lawlessness, a series of reviews and summit meetings resulted in a significant shift in perceptions of the role of the PNGDF, placing primary emphasis on its role in maintaining internal security.

Such developments have coincided with an apparent tendency towards tighter social control in Papua New Guinea and an expressed admiration of Indonesian, Singaporean and Malaysian models (see May 1993:74). In 1992 this prompted a group of NGO and church organisations to warn against an 'increasing and dangerous trend towards the militarisation of [Papua New Guinea] society'; 'We need not have a military coup', their statement said, 'to militarise society' (*Post-Courier* 7 August 1992).

The spectre of a military coup has been raised on several occasions. Indeed, in many respects Papua New Guinea presents the classic preconditions for military intervention (see chapter 1). Most observers, however, continue to see a coup as a remote possibility. This is not least because of the logistic difficulties which an attempted coup would pose for a relatively small army with limited transport capabilities in a physically and socially fragmented society in which even popularly elected national and provincial governments have difficulty maintaining their authority. Beyond this, even in relation to Bougainville the military's corporate interests do not appear to have been well defined in political terms, and electoral politics has provided a well-trodden exit route for soldiers with personal political ambitions. But while the military's subordination to civilian authority seems to be fairly well assured in the foreseeable future, the PNGDF has become politicised at senior levels and appears increasingly prone to challenge government decisions. If the integrity of the Papua New Guinea state becomes more dependent on the support of the security forces in the face of growing law and order problems, these tendencies may increase. Such a development would involve a slight shift along the 'civilocracy'/'militocracy' continuum (Bebler 1990), but, at least in terms of participation and competition, within a continuing essentially democratic political framework.

REFERENCES

Abueva, J.V., 1971. *Ramon Magsaysay: A Political Biography.* Manila: Solidaridad Publishing House.

Ahamed, E., 1980. *Bureaucratic Elites in Segmented Economic Growth: Bangladesh and Pakistan.* Dhaka: The University Press.

———, 1988. *Military Rule and Myth of Democracy.* Dhaka: The University Press.

———, 1989. 'The Six-Point Programme: its class basis', in E. Ahamed (ed.), *Society and Politics in Bangladesh.* Dhaka: Academic Publishers.

———, 1990. 'Coup of 1975 against Sheikh Mujib', *Journal of South Asian and Middle Eastern Studies* XIII(3):63-80.

Ahmed, M., 1991. *Bangladesh: Constitutional Quest for Autonomy.* Dhaka: The University Press.

Alavi, H., 1966. 'The army and bureaucracy in Pakistan', *International Socialist Journal* 3(14):140-181.

———, 1979. 'The state in post-colonial societies: Pakistan and Bangladesh', in H. Goulbourn (ed.), *Politics and State in the Third World.* London: MacMillan, pp. 38-69.

Albright, D.E., 1980. 'A comparative conceptualization of civil-military relations', *World Politics* 32(4):553-76.

Amnesty International, 1990a. *Myanmar. 'In the National Interest'. Prisoners of Conscience, Torture, Summary Trials under Martial Law.* ASA 16/10/90. London: Amnesty International.

———, 1990b. *Papua New Guinea. Human Rights Violations on Bougainville, 1989-1990.* ASA 34/05/90. London Amnesty International.

Apter, D., 1962. 'Some reflections on the role of political opposition in new nations', *Comparative Studies in Society and History* 4(2):154-168.

Army General Headquarters, 1990. *Pakistan Army Green Book.* Rawalpindi.

Ashkenazy, D. (ed.), 1994. *The Military in the Service of Society and Democracy. The Challenge of the Dual-Role Military.* Westport: Greenwood Press.

Ba Than, 1962. *The Roots of the Revolution.* Rangoon: Director of Information.

Ball, N., 1981. *The Military in the Development Process: A Guide to Issues.* Claremont: Regina Books.

Barrett, D., 1969. 'The Pacific Islands Regiment' in K.S. Inglis (ed.), *The History of*

Melanesia. Canberra: The University of Papua and New Guinea and the Research School of Pacific Studies, The Australian National University, pp. 493-502.

Baxter, C. and Rahman, S., 1991. 'Bangladesh military: political institutionalisation and economic development', *Journal of Asian Studies* 26.

Bebler, A., 1990. 'Typologies based on civilian-dominated versus military-dominated political systems', in A. Bebler and J. Seroka (eds), *Contemporary Political Systems. Classifications and Typologies*. Boulder: Lynne Rienner, pp. 261-274.

Bell, H., 1967. 'Integrating the P.I.R.', *New Guinea* 2(2):49-58.

Berghahn, V. R., 1981. *Militarism: The History of an International Debate: 1861-1979*. London: Cambridge University Press.

Bienen, H., 1971. *The Military and Modernization*. Chicago: Aldine Atherton.

———, 1983. 'Armed forces and national modernization', *Comparative Politics* 16(1): 1-16.

Bienen, H. and Morell, D., 1974. 'Transition from military rule: Thailand's experience', in C. McA. Kelleher (ed.), *Political-Military Systems. Comparative Perspectives*. Beerly Hills: Sage, pp. 3-26.

Boonprasert, C., 1990. 'Personal concepts and experiences on the military role in democratic and security development', *Journal of Social Sciences* 27:201-2.

Bunbongkarn, S., 1987a. 'Political institutions and processes', in S. Xuto (ed), *Government and Politics in Thailand*. Singapore: Oxford University Press, pp. 41-74.

———, 1987b. *The Military in Thai Politics 1981-1986*. Singapore: Institute of Southeast Asian Studies.

———, 1992. 'Thailand in 1991, coping with military guardianship', *Asian Survey* 32(2): 132-3.

Burk, J. (ed.), 1993. *The Military in New Times. Adapting Armed Forces to a Turbulent World*. Boulder: Westview.

Cady, J., 1958. *A History of Modern Burma*. Ithaca: Cornell University Press.

Chaleamtiarana, Thak, 1975. *Thailand: The Politics of Despotic Paternalism*. Bangkok: Social Science Association of Thailand.

Chazan, N., Mortimer, R., Ravenhill, J. and Rothchild, D., 1988. *Politics and Society in Contemporary Africa*. Boulder: Lynne Rienner.

Chomsky, N., 1991. *Deterring Democracy*. London: Verso.

Christian, J., 1945. *Burma and the Japanese Invader*. Bombay: Thacher and Company Ltd.

Clapham, C. and Philip, G. (eds), 1985. *The Political Dilemma of Military Regimes*. London: Croom Helm.

Cohen, S.P. 1986. 'State building in Pakistan', in A. Banuazizi and M. Weiner (eds), *The State, Religion and Ethnic Politics*. Lahore: Vanguard Books, pp. 299-332.

———, 1984. *The Pakistan Army*. Berkeley: University of California Press.

Constitutional Planning committee (CPC), Papua New Guinea, 1974. *Final Report*. Port Moresby.

Crouch, H., 1978. *The Army and Politics in Indonesia*. Ithaca: Cornell University Press.

———, 1979. 'Patrimonialism and military rule in Indonesia', *World Politics* 31(4): 571-87.

———, 1985. 'The military and politics in South-East Asia', in H.A. Zakaria and H. Crouch (eds), *Military-Civilian Relations in South-East Asia*, Singapore: Oxford University Press, pp. 287-317.

————, 1988. 'The military mind and economic development', in Soedjati Djiwandono J. and Yong Mun Cheong (eds), *Soldiers and Stability in Southeast Asia*, Singapore: Institute of Southeast Asian Studies, pp. 49-72.

Daalder, H., 1969. *The Role of the Military in the Emerging Countries.* 'S-Gravenhaage: Mouton.

Dahl, R.A., 1989. *Democracy and its Critics.* New Haven: Yale University Press.

Danopoulos, C.P. (ed.), 1988. *Military Disengagement from Politics.* New York: Routledge.

De Pauw, J.W. and Luz, G.A. (eds), 1992. *Winning the Peace. The Strategic Implications of Military Civic Action.* New York: Praeger.

Dean, E. and Ritova, S., 1988. *Rabuka: No Other Way.* Sydney: Doubleday.

Decalo, S., 1976. *Coups and Army Rule in Africa: Studies in Military Style.* New Haven: Yale University Press.

Defence General Board of Inquiry, Papua New Guinea, 1989. *Report of the Defence General Board of Inquiry into Administration and Management of the Papua New Guinea Defence Force and the Defence Department.* Boroko: Department of Defence.

Diamond, L., 1992. 'Promoting democracy', *Foreign Policy* 87:25-46.

Diamond, L., Linz, J.J. and Lipset, S.M. (eds), 1988. *Democracy in Developing Countries.* Boulder: Lynne Rienner.

————, 1990. *Politics in Developing Countries. Comparing Experiences with Democracy.* Boulder: Lynne Rienner.

Director of Information, 1960. *Is Trust Vindicated?* Rangoon: Government of the Union of Burma.

Dowse, R.E., 1969. 'The military and political development', in C. Leys (ed.), *Politics and Change in Developing Countries*, Cambridge: Cambridge University Press, pp. 213-46.

Eide, A. and Thee, M. (eds), 1980. *Problems of Contemporary Militarism.* London: Croom Helm.

Enloe, C., 1980. *Ethnic Soldiers: State Security in Divided Societies.* Harmondsworth: Penguin Books.

Ershad, H.M., 1981. 'Role of Military in Underdeveloped Countries', *Bangladesh Army Journal* (January 1981).

Evans, G., 1992. *Government Response to the Report of the Joint Committee on Foreign Affairs, Defence and Trade on Australia's Relations with Papua New Guinea.* Mimeo.

Ewins, R., 1992. *Colour, Class and Custom: the Literature of the 1987 Fiji Coup.* Regime Change and Regime Maintenance in Asia and the Pacific Discussion Paper 9, Department of Political and Social Change, Research School of Pacific Studies, Australian National University.

Feith, H., 1962. *The Decline of Constitutional Democracy in Indonesia.* Ithaca: Modern Indonesia Project, Southeast Asia Program, Cornell University.

Finer, S.E., 1962. *The Man on Horseback: The Role of the Military in Politics.* London: Pall Mall.

————, 1974. *Comparative Government.* Harmondsworth: Penguin Books.

————, 1978. 'The military and politics in the Third World', in W.S. Thompson (ed.), *The Third World: Premises of U.S. Policy.* San Francisco: Institute of Contemporary Studies, pp. 75-114.

————, 1982. 'The morphology of military regimes', in R. Kolkowicz and A. Korbonski (eds), *Soldiers, Peasants and Bureaucrats. Civil-Military Relations in Communist and Modernizing Societies*, London: George Allen & Unwin, pp. 281-309.

———, 1985. 'The retreat to the barracks: notes on the practice and the theory of military withdrawal from the seats of power', *Third World Quarterly* 7(1):16-30.

———, 1991. 'Military regimes', in V. Bogdanor (ed.), *The Blackwell Encyclopaedia of Political Science*. Oxford: Blackwell, pp. 366-7.

First, R., 1970. *The Barrel of a Gun: Political Power in Africa and the Coup d'Etat*. London: Allen Lane.

Fitch, I.S., 1989. 'Military professionalism, national security and democracy: lessons from the Latin American experience', *Pacific Focus* 4(2):99-147.

Gallie, W.B., 1956. 'IX. Essentially contested concepts', *Proceedings of the Aristotelian Society* 56:167-98.

Gastil, R.D., 1985. 'The past, pesent, and future of democracy', *Journal of International Affairs* 38(2):161-179.

Goodman, L.W., 1990. 'The military and democracy: an introduction', in L.W. Goodman, J.S.R. Mendelson and J. Rial (eds), *The Military and Democracy. The Future of Civil-Military Relations in Latin America*, Lexington: Lexington Books, pp. xiii-xx.

Goodman, L.W., Mendelson, J.S.R. and Rial J. (eds), 1990. *The Military and Democracy. The Future of Civil-Military Relations in Latin America*. Lexington: Lexington Books.

Gow, J., 1991. *Legitimacy and the Military: The Yugoslav Crisis*. London: Pinter.

Griffin, J., 1976. 'Secessionist movements and their future in Papua New Guinea', *World Review* 15(1):23-36.

Grundy, K.W., 1968. *Conflicting Images of the Military in Africa*. Short Studies and Reprint Series, No. 3. Department of Political Science and Public Administration, Makerere University College.

Guyot, J.F., 1974. 'Ethnic segmentation in military organizations: Burma and Malaysia', in C.McA. Kelleher (ed.), *Political-Military Systems. Comparative Perspectives*. Beverly Hills: Sage, pp. 27-37.

Guyot, J.F. and Willner, R.A. (eds), 1970. *Journal of Comparative Administration* 2 (special issue).

Hadenius, A., 1992. *Democracy and Development*. Cambridge: Cambridge University Press.

Hakes, J.E., 1973. *Weak Parliaments and Military Coups in Africa: A Study in Regime Instability*. Sage Research Papers in the Social Sciences. Comparative Legislative Studies Series 90-004 Vol. 1.

Halpern, M., 1963. *The Politics of Social Change in the Middle East and North Africa*. Princeton: Princeton University Press.

Hansen, H.B., 1977. *Ethnicity and Military Rule in Uganda. A Study of Ethnicity as a Political Factor in Uganda*. Uppsala: Scandinavian Institute of African Studies.

Harries-Jenkins, G. and van Doorn, J. (eds), 1976. *The Military and the Problem of Legitimacy*. London: Sage.

Hastings, P., 1969. *New Guinea. Problems and Prospects*. Melbourne: Cheshire.

———, 1971. 'Thoughts on Taurama. The myth of a "non-political army"', *New Guinea* 6(1):28-32.

Hawes, G., 1989. 'Aquino and her administration: a view from the countryside', *Pacific Affairs* 62(1):9-28.

Heatu, Basita, 1967. 'New Guinea's coming army', *New Guinea* 2(3):32-33.

Heeger, G.A., 1977. 'Politics in the post-military state: some reflections on the Pakistani experience', *World Politics* 29(2):242-62.

Hegarty, D., 1978. 'Political chronicle: Papua New Guinea', *Australian Journal of Politics and History* 24(3):401-08.

Heinz, W.S., Pfennig, W. and King, V.T., 1990. *The Military in Politics: Southeast Asian Experiences*. Centre for South-East Asian Studies, The University of Hull.

Hernandez, C.G., 1985. 'Constitutional authoritarianism and the prospects of democracy in the Philippines', *Journal of International Affairs* 38(2):243-258.

Herspring, D.R. and Volgyes, I. (eds), 1978. *Civil-Military Relations in Communist Systems*. Boulder: Westview Press.

Hewison, K., Robison, R. and Rodan, G. (eds), 1993. *Southeast Asia in the 1990s: Authoritarianism, Democracy and Capitalism*. Sydney: Allen & Unwin.

Hoadley, J.S., 1975. *Soldiers and Politics: Civil-Military Relations in Comparative Perspective*. Cambridge: Schenkman Publishing Company.

Hong, D.S., 1990. 'Min'gun kwan'gye-ui pyonhwa-wa chonmang', *Sasang* 2(3): 105-142.

Horowitz, D.L., 1980. *Coup Theories and Officers Motives. Sri Lanka in Comparative Perspective*. Princeton: Princeton University Press.

———, 1985. *Ethnic Groups in Conflict*. Berkeley: University of California Press.

Huntington, S.P., 1957. *The Soldier and the State. The Theory and Politics of Civil-Military Relations*. Cambridge, Mass.: The Belknap Press.

———, 1968 *Political Order in Changing Societies*. New Haven: Yale University Press.

———, 1991. 'How countries democratize', *Political Science Quarterly* 106(4): 597-616.

Hussey, G., 1968. 'Army civic action', *Australian External Territories* 8(6):31-34.

Im, H.B., 1987. 'The rise of bureaucratic-authoritarianism in South Korea', *World Politics* 39(2):231-257.

International Human Rights Law Group, 1990. *Post-Election Myanmar: A Popular Mandate Withheld*. Washington: International Human Rights Law Group.

Jackman, R.W., 1976. 'Politicians in uniform: military governments and social change in the Third World', *American Political Science Review* 70(4):1078-96.

Jahan, R., 1972. *Pakistan: Failure in National Integration*. Dhaka: University Press.

Janowitz, M., 1964. *The Military in the Political Development of New Nations: An Essay in Comparative Analysis*. Chicago: University of Chicago Press.

———, 1971. 'The comparative analysis of Middle Eastern military institutions', in M. Janowitz and J. van Doorn (eds), *On Military Intervention*, Rotterdam: Rotterdam University Press, pp. 301-333.

———, 1977. *Military Institutions and Coercion in the Developing Nations*. Chicago: University of Chicago Press.

Jenkins, D., 1984. *Suharto and his Generals: Indonesian Military Politics 1975-1983*. Ithaca: Cornell University Press.

Johansen, R.C., 1992. 'Military policies and the state system as impediments to democracy', *Political Studies* 40 (special issue):99-115.

Johnson, J.J., (ed.), 1962. *The Role of the Military in Underdeveloped Countries*. Princeton: Princeton University Press.

Joint Committee on Foreign Affairs, Defence and Trade ((JCFADT), The Parliament of the Commonwealth of Australia, 1989-91. Hearings. Canberra: Official Hansard Reports.

———, 1991. *Australia's Relations with Papua New Guinea*. Canberra: Senate Publishing and Printing Unit.

Kabwegyere, T.B., 1974. *The Politics of State Formation: The Nature and Effects of Colonialism in Uganda*. Nairobi: East African Literature Bureau.

Kahin, G. McT., 1952. *Nationalism and Revolution in Indonesia*. Ithaca: Cornell University Press.

Kang, M., 1983. 'Kwallyojok kwonwi chui-ui han'gukjok saengsong', *Han'guk Chongch'i Hakoebo* 17.

Kelleher, C.McA. (ed.), 1974. *Political-Military Systems. Comparative Perspectives*. Beverly Hills: Sage.

Kennedy, C.H. and Louscher, D.J. (eds), 1991. *Civil Military Interaction in Asia and Africa*. Leiden: E.J. Brill.

Khan, F.M., 1963. *The Story of the Pakistan Army*. Lahore: Oxford University Press.

Khin Yi, 1988. *The Dobama Movement in Burma (1930-1938)*. Ithaca: Southeast Asia Program, Cornell University.

Kim, J.H., 1978. *The Garrison State in Pre-War Japan and Post-War Korea: A Comparative Analysis of Military Politics*. Washington: University Press of America.

Kim, S.I., 1992. 'Yukigu ch'onya-ui kobaek', *Wolkan Ch'oson* (1): 292-396.

Kim, S.J., 1971. *The Politics of Military Revolution in Korea*. Chapel Hill: University of North Carolina Press.

Kim, Y.M., 1985. 'The political economy of military rule: a comparative study of Brazil, South Korea, Peru, and Egypt', unpublished doctoral dissertation, State University of New York at Buffalo.

———, 1986. 'Han'guk-ui chongch'i pyondong-kwa Yusin ch'eje', in Korean Political Science Association (ed.), *Hyondae Han'guk Chongch'i-wa Kukka*. Seoul: Popmunsa.

Koenig, W., 1990. *The Burmese Polity, 1752-1819*. Ann Arbor: Michigan Papers on South and Southeast Asia, Center for South and Southeast Asian Studies. University of Michigan, Number 34.

Kolkowicz, R. and Korbonski, A. (eds), 1982. *Soldiers, Peasants and Bureaucrats. Civil-Military Relations in Communist and Modernising Societies*. London: George Allen & Unwin.

Lal, B., 1988. *Power and Prejudice: The Making of the Fiji Crisis*. Wellington: New Zealand Institute of International Affairs.

Lapitan, A.E., 1989. 'The re-democratisation of the Philippines: old wine in a new bottle', *Asian Profile* 17(3):235-242.

Lawson, S., 1990a. *Constitutional Change in Contemporary Fiji: The Apparatus of Ideological Justification*. Peace Research Centre, Research School of Pacific Studies, Australian National University, Working Paper No. 93.

———, 1990b. 'The myth of cultural homogeneity and its implications for chiefly power and politics in Fiji', *Comparative Studies in Society and* History 32 (4): 795-821.

———, 1991. *The Failure of Democratic Politics in Fiji*. Oxford: Clarendon Press.

————, 1993. 'Conceptual issues in the comparative study of regime change and democratization', *Comparative Politics* 25(2):183-205.

Lee, H.B., 1968. *Korea: Time, Change, and Administration*. Honolulu: East-West Center Press.

Lee, J.M., 1969. *African Armies and Civil Order*. London: Chatto and Windus.

Lefever, E., 1970. *Spear and Scepter: Army Police and Politics in Tropical Africa*. Washington: The Brookings Institution.

Legge, J.D., 1972. *Sukarno: A Political Biography*. London: Allen Lane.

Lifschulz, L., 1979. *Bangladesh: The Unfinished Revolution*. London: Zed Books.

Lintner, B., 1989. *Outrage: Burma's Struggle for Democracy*. Hong Kong: Review Publishing.

Linz, J.J. and Stepan, A. (eds), 1978. *The Breakdown of Democratic Regimes*. Baltimore: Johns Hopkins University Press.

Liria, Y.A., 1993. *Bougainville Diary*. Melbourne: Indra Publishing.

Lissak, M., 1976. *Military Roles in Modernisation: Civil-Military Relations in Thailand and Burma*. Beverly Hills: Sage.

Lloyd, P.C., 1973. *Classes, Crises and Coups*. London: Paladin.

Lovell, J.P., 1975. 'The military and politics in postwar Korea', in E.R. Wright (ed.), *Korean Politics in Transition*. Seattle: University of Washington Press.

Lowenthal, A.F., 1974. 'Armies and politics in Latin America', *World Politics* 27(1): 107-30.

Luckham, A.R., 1971. 'A comparative typology of civil-military relations', *Government and Opposition* 6(1):5-35.

————, 1979. 'Militarism and international dependence: a framework for analysis', in J.J.Villamil (ed.), *Transnational Capitalism and National Development. New Perspectives on Dependence*, Hassocks: Harvester Press, pp. 145-82.

————, 1991. 'Introduction: the military, the developmental state and social forces in Asia and the Pacific: issues for comparative analysis', in V. Selochan (ed.), *The Military, the State, and Development in Asia and the Pacific*, Boulder: Westview Press, pp. 1-49.

Lynch, P.R., 1969. 'The coming army', *New Guinea* 4(1):21-23.

Maniruzzaman, T., 1976. 'Bangladesh in 1975: the fall of the Mujib regime and its aftermath', *Asian Survey* 16(2):119-29.

Maung, M., 1959. *Burma's Constitution*. The Hague: Martinus Nijhoff.

May, R.J., 1990. 'Papua New Guinea's Bougainville crisis', *The Pacific Review* 3(2): 174-77.

————, 1992. *Vigilantes in the Philippines: from Fanatical Cults to Citizens' Organisations*. Philippine Studies Occasional Paper No. 12. Centre for Philippine Studies, University of Hawai'i at Manoa.

————, 1993. *The Changing Role of the Military in Papua New Guinea*. Canberra Papers on Strategy and Defence No. 101. Strategic and Defence Studies Centre, Research School of Pacific Studies, Australian National University.

————, 1994. 'The study of regime change and regime maintenance in Asia and the Pacific: a tentative agenda', *Regime Change and Regime Maintenance in Asia and the Pacific. Discussion Paper 1*. Department of Political and Social Change, Research School of Pacific and Asian Studies, Australian National University.

———— (ed.), 1982. *Micronationalist Movements in Papua New Guinea*. Political and

Social Change Monograph 1. Canberra: Department of Political and Social Change, Research School of Pacific Studies, Australian National University.

May, R.J. and Spriggs, M. (eds), 1990. *The Bougainville Crisis*. Bathurst: Crawford House Press.

Mazrui, A.A., 1976. 'Soldiers as traditionalizers: military rule and the re-Africanization of Africa', *World Politics* (2):246-72.

McKinlay, R.D. and Cohan, A.S., 1975. 'A comparative analysis of the political and economic performance of military and civilian regimes: a cross-national aggregate study', *Comparative Politics* 8(1):1-30.

————, 1976. 'Performance and instability in military and non-military regime systems', *American Political Science Review* 70(3):850-864.

Mench, P., 1975. *The Role of the Papua New Guinea Defence Force*. Development Studies Centre Monograph No. 2. Canberra: The Australian National University.

Mendelson, E.M., 1975. *Sangha and State in Burma*. Ithaca: Cornell Unversity Press.

Mohamad, G., 1989. 'The 'Manikebu Affair': literature and politics in the 1960s', *Prisma* 46:70-88.

Mokis, S.P., 1988. 'A Papua New Guinea security viewpoint and its implications on PNG/ Australia relations'. Paper presented to Bicentennial Conference, 'Australia and the World: Prologue and Prospects', Strategic and Defence Studies Centre, Research School of Pacific Studies, Australian National University, Canberra.

Morrison, I., 1947. *Grandfather Longlegs*. London: Faber and Faber.

Mountbatten, L., 1960. *Report to the Combined Chiefs of Staff by the Supreme Allied Commander, Southeast Asia 1943-1945*. New Delhi: English Book Store.

Needler, M.C., 1980. 'The military withdrawal from power in South America', *Armed Forces and Society* 6(4):614-24.

Nelson, H., 1972. *Papua New Guinea. Black Unity or Black Chaos?* Ringwood Vic.: Penguin Books.

Nordlinger, E.A., 1970. 'Soldiers in mufti: the impact of military rule upon economic and social change in the non-Western states', *American Political Science Review* 64(4):431-48.

————, 1977. *Soldiers in Politics: Military Coups and Governments*. Englewood Cliffs: Prentice-Hall.

Norton, R., 1990. *Race and Politics in Fiji*. Second edition. St. Lucia: University of Queensland Press.

Nugroho, Notosusanto, 1980. *The National Struggle and the Armed Forces in Indonesia*. Jakarta: Centre for Armed Forces History, Department of Defence.

Nun, J., 1967. 'The middle-class military coup', in C. Véliz (ed.), *The Politics of Conformity in Latin America*. Oxford: Oxford University Press, pp. 66-118.

————, 1986. 'The middle class military coup revisited', in A.F. Lowenthal and J.S. Fitch (eds), *Armies and Politics in Latin America*, New York: Holmes and Meier, pp. 59-95.

O'Donnell, G.A., 1973. *Modernization and Bureaucratic Authoritarianism. Studies in South American Politics*. Berkeley: University of California Press.

————, 1979. 'Tensions in the bureaucratic-authoritarian state and the question of democracy', in D. Collier (ed.), *The New Authoritarianism in Latin America*. Princeton: Princeton University Press, pp. 285-318.

O'Donnell, G.A., Schmitter, P.C. and Whitehead, L. (eds), 1986. *Transitions from Autho-*

ritarian Rule. Baltimore: Johns Hopkins University Press.

O'Neill, R.J., 1971. 'The army in Papua-New Guinea', *New Guinea* 6(1):6-27.

Olewale, E., 1972. 'The impact of national institutions on village communities', in M.W. Ward (ed.), *Change and Development in Rural Melanesia.* Canberra: The University of Papua and New Guinea and the Research School of Pacific Studies, The Australian National University, pp. 219-24.

Oliver, D., 1991. *Black Islanders. A Personal Perspective of Bougainville 1937-1991.* Melbourne: Hyland House.

Olsen, E.A. and Jurika, S., 1986. *The Armed Forces in Contemporary Asian Societies.* Boulder: Westview Press.

Overholt, W.H., 1986. 'The rise and fall of Ferdinand Marcos', *Asian Survey* 26(11): 1137-63.

Papua New Guinea, Independent State of, 1991. *Government Paper. Security for Development. Integrating the Government's Response to the National Summit on Crime into a Comprehensive and Planned Approach to Law and Order.* Port Moresby: Acting Government Printer.

Park, C.H., 1978. *Korea Reborn: A Model for Development.* Englewood Cliffs: Prentice-Hall.

Perlmutter, A., 1977. *The Military and Politics in Modern Times* New Haven: Yale University Press.

————, 1980. 'The comparative analysis of military regimes: formations, aspirations, and achievements', *World Politics* 33(1):96-120.

————, 1981. *Political Roles and Military Rulers.* London: Frank Cass.

————, 1982. 'Civil-military relations in socialist authoritarian and praetorian states: prospects and restrospects', in R. Kolkowicz and A. Korbonski (eds), *Soldiers, Peasants and Bureaucrats. Civil-Military Relations in Communist and Modernizing Societies,* London: George Allen & Unwin, pp. 310-31.

Philip, C.H., 1962. *The Evolution of India and Pakistan.* London: Oxford University Press.

Premdas, R.R., 1974. 'A non-political army', *New Guinea* 9(1):29-37.

Pye, L., 1962. 'Armies in the process of political modernisation', in J.J. Johnson (ed.), *The Role of the Military in Underdeveloped Countries,* Princeton: Princeton University Press, pp. 80-89.

————, 1966. *Aspects of Political Development.* Boston: Little, Brown and Company.

Rapoport, D. C., 1982. 'The praetorian army: insecurity, venality, and impotence', in R. Kolkowicz and A. Korbonski (eds), *Soldiers, Peasants, and Bureaucrats. Civil-Military Relations in Communist and Modernizing Societies,* London: George Allen & Unwin, pp. 252-80.

Reyes, L., 1988. 'The Philippines constitutional system', in J.Barton Starr (ed.), *The United States Constitution: Its Birth, Growth and Influence in Asia.* Hong Kong: University of Hong Kong Press, 259-73.

Rial, J., 1990a. 'The armed forces and the question of democracy in Latin America', in L.W. Goodman, J.S.R. Mendelson and J. Rial (eds), *The Military and Democracy. The Future of Civil-Military Relations in Latin America,* Lexington: Lexington Books, pp. 3-21.

————, 1990b. 'The armed forces and democracy: the interests of Latin American military corporations in sustaining democratic regimes', in L.W. Goodman, J.S.R. Mendelson and J. Rial (eds), *The Military and Democracy. The Future of Civil-Military Relations in Latin America*, Lexington: Lexington Books, pp. 277-95.

Riggs, F., 1964. *Administration in Developing Countries: the Theory of Prismatic Society.* Boston: Houghton-Mifflin.

Rizvi, H.A. 1986. *The Military and Politics in Pakistan*. Lahore: Progressive Publishers.

———, 1989. 'The legacy of military rule in Pakistan', *Survival* 31(3):255-68.

Robertson, R. and Tamanisau, A., 1988. *Fiji: Shattered Coups.* Leichardt: Pluto Press.

Rouquié, A., 1987. *The Military and the State in Latin America*. Berkeley: University of California Press.

Rudolph, L., and Rudolph, S. H., 1964. 'Generals and politicians in India', *Pacific Affairs* 37:1:5-19.

Saffu, Y., 1988. 'Political chronicle: Papua New Guinea', *Australian Journal of Politics and History* 34(2):250-62.

———, 1990. 'Changing civil-military relations in Fiji', *Australian Journal of International Affairs* 44(2):159-170.

Salim, Said, 1991. *Genesis of Power: General Sudiman and the Indonesian Military in Politics 1945-9*. Singapore: Institute of Southeast Asian Studies.

Samudavanija Chai-Anan and Bunbongkarn, S., 1985. 'Thailand', in H.A. Zakaria and H. Crouch, eds, *Military-Civilian Relations in South-East Asia*. Singapore: Oxford University Press, pp. 78-117.

Sanday, J., 1989. *The Military in Fiji: Historical Development and Future Role.* Strategic and Defence Studies Centre, Research School of Pacific Studies, Australian National University, Working Paper No. 201.

———, 1991. 'The politicisation of military professionalism in Fiji', in V. Selochan (ed.), *The Military, the State and Development in Asia and the Pacific.* Boulder: Westview Press.

Sarkesian, S., 1981. *Beyond the Battlefield: The New Military Professionalism.* New York: Pergamon.

Scarr, D., 1988. *Fiji: The Politics of Illusion: The Military Coups in Fiji.* Kensington: New South Wales University Press.

Schmitter, P.C., 1971. 'Military intervention, political competitiveness and public policy in Latin America: 1950-1967', in M. Janowitz and J. van Doorn (eds), *On Military Intervention*, Rotterdam: Rotterdam University Press, pp. 425-506.

——— (ed.), 1973. *Military Rule in Latin America: Function, Consequences, and Perspectives.* Beverly Hills: Sage.

Seitz, S.T., 1991. 'The military in Black African politics', in C.H. Kennedy and D.J. Louscher (eds), *Civil Military Interaction in Asia and Africa*, Leiden, E.J. Brill, pp. 61-75.

Selochan, V., 1989. *Could the Military Govern the Philippines?* Quezon City: New Day Publishers.

———, 1990. 'Professionalization and politicization of the armed forces of the Philippines'. Unpublished PhD thesis, Australian National University.

———, 1991a. 'The armed forces of the Philippines and political instability', in V. Selochan (ed)., *The Military, the State, and Development in Asia and the Pacific.* Boulder: Westview Press.

——— (ed.), 1991b. *The Military, the State, and Development in Asia and the Pacific.* Boulder: Westview Press.

Selth, A., 1989. *Death of a Hero: The U Thant Disturbances in Burma, December 1974.* Griffith University, Centre for the Study of Australia-Asia Relations, Australia-Asia Paper 49.

Sharma, D., 1990. 'The making of a Fijian military man', *Islands Business*, November.

Shils, E., 1962. 'The military in the political development of new states', in J.J. Johnson (ed.), *The Role of the Military in Underdeveloped Countries*, Princeton: Princeton University Press, pp. 7-68.

Silverstein, J., 1956. 'Politics, parties and the national election in Burma', *Far Eastern Survey* 25:177-184.

————, 1964. 'First steps on the Burmese way to socialism', *Asian Survey* 4(2):716-722.

————, 1972. *The Political Legacy of Aung San.* Ithaca: Southeast Asia Program, Department of Asian Studies, Cornell University.

————, 1977. *Burma: Military Rule and the Politics of Stagnation.* Ithaca: Cornell University Press.

————, 1980. *Burmese Politics: The Dilemma of National Unity.* New Brunswick: Rutgers University Press.

————, 1982. 'Burma in 1981: The changing of the guardians begins', *Asian Survey* 22(2):180-90.

————, 1992. 'Burma in an international perspective', *Asian Survey* 32(10):951-63.

Simutupang, T.B., 1989. 'Indonesia: leadership and national security', in M. Ayoob and Chai-Anan Samudavanija (eds), *Leadership Perceptions and National Security*, Singapore: Institute of Southeast Asian Studies, pp. 110-141.

Sinclair, J. 1990. *To Find a Path. The Life and Times of the Royal Pacific Islands Regiment. Volume I - Yesterday's Heroes 1885-1950.* Brisbane: Boolarong Publications.

————, 1992. *To Find a Path. The Papua New Guinea Defence Force and the Australians to Independence. Volume II - Keeping the Peace 1950-1975.* Bathurst: Crawford House Press.

Snitwongse, K., 1990. 'From armed suppression to political offensive: attitudinal transformation of Thai military officers since 1976', *Conflict* 10: 91, 93-4, 103.

Soedjati, Djiwandono J. and Yong, Mun Cheong (eds), 1988. *Soldiers and Stability in Southeast Asia.* Singapore: Institute of Southeast Asian Studies.

Sohn, H.K., 1989. *Authoritarianism and Opposition in South Korea.* London: Routledge.

Spriggs, M., 1992. 'Bougainville update: August 1990 to May 1991', in M. Spriggs and D. Denoon (eds), *The Bougainville Crisis. 1991 Update.* Political and Social Change Monograph 16. Canberra: Department of Political and Social Change, Research School of Pacific Studies, Australian National University, in association with Crawford House Press, Bathurst, pp. 8-41.

Spriggs, M. and Denoon, D. (eds), 1992. *The Bougainville Crisis. 1991 Update.* Political and Social Change Monograph 16. Canberra: Department of Political and Social Change, Research School of Pacific Studies, Australian National University, in association with Crawford House Press, Bathurst.

Stepan, A., 1973. 'The new professionalism of internal warfare and military role expansion', in A. Stepan (ed.), *Authoritarian Brazil: Origins, Policies, Future*, New Haven: Yale University Press, pp. 47-68.

Stepan, A., 1978. *The State and Society: Peru in Comparative Perspective.* Princeton: Princeton University Press.

Stepan, A., 1988. *Rethinking Military Politics. Brazil and the Southern Cone.* Princeton:

Princeton University Press.

Suharto, 1989. *Soeharto: Pikiran, Ucapan, dan Tindakan Saya: Otobiografi* (seperti dipaparkan kepada G. Dwipayana dan Ramadhan K.H.). Jakarta: Citra Lamtoro Gung Persada.

Sundhaussen, U., 1973a. 'New Guinea's army. A political role?', *New Guinea* 8(2):29-39.

————, 1973b. 'Australia's future defence relations with Papua New Guinea: a second look', *Australia's Neighbours* February-March 6-7.

————, 1982. *The Road to Power: Indonesian Military Politics 1945-1967*. Kuala Lumpur: Oxford University Press.

————, 1984. 'Military withdrawal from government responsibility', *Armed Forces and Society* 10(4):543-62.

————, 1985. 'The durability of military regimes in South-East Asia', in H.A. Zakaria and H. Crouch (eds), *Military-Civilian Relations in South-East Asia*, Singapore: Oxford University Press, pp. 269-86.

Sørensen, G., 1993. *Democracy and Democratization. Processes and Prospects in a Changing World*. Boulder: Westview Press.

Thee, M., 1980. 'Militarism and militarisation in contemporary international relations', in A. Eide and M. Thee (eds), *Problems of Contemporary Militarism*. London: Croom Helm.

Thompson, W.R., 1973 *The Grievances of Military Coup Makers*. Beverley Hills: Sage Professional Papers.

————, 1975. 'Regime vulnerability and the military coup', *Comparative Politics* 7(4):459-488.

Tinker, H., 1961. *The Union of Burma*. Third edition. London: Oxford University Press.

Valenzuela, A., 1985. 'A note on the military and social science theory', *Third World Quarterly* 7(1):132-43.

Van Gils, M.R. (ed.), 1971. *The Perceived Role of the Military*. Rotterdam: Rotterdam University Press.

Varas, A., 1990. 'Civil-military relations in a democratic framework', in L.W. Goodman, J.S.R. Mendelson and J. Rial (eds), *The Military and Democracy. The Future of Civil-Military Relations in Latin America*, Lexington: Lexington Books, pp. 199-218.

Vatikiotis, M., 1987. 'Marching to a new drummer', *Far Eastern Economic Review* 26 November 1987: 35.

Von Clausewitz, C. (ed. A. Rapoport), 1832/1968. *On War*. Harmondsworth: Penguin.

Von der Mehden, F.R., 1964. *Politics of the Developing Nations*. Englewood Cliffs: Prentice-Hall.

Warubu, Kokou, 1968. 'That army again!', *New Guinea* 3(2):8-10.

Welch, C.E., 1971. 'Cincinnatus in Africa: the possibility of military withdrawal from politics', in M. Lofchie (ed.), *The State of Nations: Constraints on Development in Independent Africa*, Berkeley: University of California Press, pp. 215-238.

————, 1974a. 'Personalism and corporatism in African armies', in C.McA. Kelleher (ed.), *Political-Military Systems. Comparative Perspectives*. Beverley Hills: Sage, pp. 125-145.

————, 1974b. 'The dilemma of military withdrawal from politics: some considerations from tropical Africa', *African Studies Review* 17(1):213-28.

Wurfel, D., 1989. 'The Philippines' precarious democracy: coping with foreign and domestic pressures', *International Journal* 14(3): 676-697.

Yoon, W.Z., 1973. *Japan's Scheme for the Liberation of Burma: The Role of the Minami Kikan and the 'Thirty Comrades.'* Athens: Ohio University Center for International Studies, Southeast Asia Program, Papers in International Studies, Southeast Asia Series, No. 27.

Zagorski, P.W., 1992. *Democracy vs. National Security: Civil-Military Relations in Latin America.* Boulder: Lynne Rienner.

Zakaria, H.A. and Crouch, H. (eds), 1985. *Military-Civilian Relations in South-East Asia.* Singapore: Oxford University Press.

Zolberg, A., 1968. 'The structure of political conflict in the new states of tropical Africa', *American Political Science Review* 62:70-87.

Zuk, G. and Thompson, W.R., 1982. 'The post-coup military spending question', *American Political Science Review* 76(1):60-74.

INDEX